Books in the *MIT Sloan Management Review* Series

INNOVATION

DRIVING PRODUCT, PROCESS, and MARKET CHANGE

INNOVATION

DRIVING PRODUCT, PROCESS, and MARKET CHANGE

Edward B. Roberts

Editor

JOSSEY-BASS
A Wiley Company
www.josseybass.com

Published by

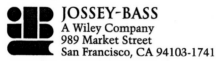

JOSSEY-BASS
A Wiley Company
989 Market Street
San Francisco, CA 94103-1741

www.josseybass.com

Copyright © 2002 by Massachusetts Institute of Technology, 77 Massachusetts Avenue, Cambridge, MA 02139.

Jossey-Bass is a registered trademark of John Wiley & Sons, Inc.

Jossey-Bass books and products are available through most bookstores. To contact Jossey-Bass directly, call (888) 378-2537, fax to (800) 605-2665, or visit our website at www.josseybass.com.

Substantial discounts on bulk quantities of Jossey-Bass books are available to corporations, professional associations, and other organizations. For details and discount information, contact the special sales department at Jossey-Bass.

We at Jossey-Bass strive to use the most environmentally sensitive paper stocks available to us. Our publications are printed on acid-free recycled stock whenever possible, and our paper always meets or exceeds minimum GPO and EPA requirements.

Library of Congress Cataloging-in-Publication Data
Innovation : driving product, process, and market change / Edward B. Roberts, editor.
        p. cm.
A collection of 12 articles previously published in MIT's Sloan management review.
Includes bibliographical references and index.
  ISBN 978-0-7879-6213-5
  1. Technological innovations—Economic aspects. I. Roberts, Edward Baer.
  HC79.T4 15463 2002
  658.5'14—dc21   2002001832

CONTENTS

building the expertise needed to achieve competitive advantage.

INNOVATION

DRIVING PRODUCT, PROCESS, and MARKET CHANGE

EDWARD B. ROBERTS
EDITOR

Innovations, whether of product, process, or market, always move through two quite different stages. First, someone has to come up with the new idea. Then someone (often someone *other than* the idea originator) has to refine, focus, and implement that idea. And most of the resources are applied during this latter implementation period. Furthermore, my own studies indicate that in the majority of cases, the initiating idea comes from outside the implementing organization. In many cases, the innovator is simply adapting someone else's invention to a different set of circumstances.

Most often, the original ideas that lead to these innovations emerge from a perceived market or production need rather than from the push of underlying technology.[1] Science is far less frequently the direct organizational root of an innovation, and then usually in a field like biotechnology, advanced materials, or optics, where the lab is close to the market implementation of change.

Thus, for an organization to innovate effectively, it must construct strong channels to those outside worlds that are sources of ideas for change. At the same time, strong internal connections must exist between the market-facing parts of the company (sales and marketing, distribution, and field service) and the technology-creating parts (engineering, scientific research, manufacturing, and operations).

The *MIT Sloan Management Review (SMR)* has always presented its readers with leading ideas about managing the innovation process. Years ago I edited a collection of *SMR* articles on the same subject, *Generating Technological Innovation.*[2] Now, after more than a decade in which the topic of managing innovation, especially technology-based innovation, has been the dominant issue in maintaining worldwide competitiveness, I revisit it in this new anthology of *SMR*'s best thinking on the subject.

In three sections, this book explores the key managerial issues of the innovation process. Part One focuses on the critical behaviors that must occur *within a firm* to conceive and eventually implement technological and market changes. Part Two discusses the radical shift from innovating almost entirely with a firm's own resources to *collaborating with external partners* who provide technological, marketing, distribution, and manufacturing capabilities. And Part Three explores perspectives on how *software, user communities,* and *innovation families* can be applied to driving the innovative process.

In Chapter One Constantinos Markides highlights internal innovative processes from a strategic perspective, emphasizing especially those approaches that at the overall business level cause a new game to be played in the marketplace. "Companies," Markides writes, "do new or even crazy things, like using a new distribution method in the industry (Hanes), a new selling approach (Bank One), a new manufacturing method (Toyota), or totally bypassing distribution intermediaries (Dell Computer)." Markides concentrates on ways to attack established industry leaders without the help of radical technological innovation. In Chapter Two John Seely Brown and Paul Duguid, drawing on life experience in organizations with a reputation for being innovative (such as BBN Technologies and the Xerox Palo Alto Research Center), affirm the need for organizations to maintain the "explore-exploit" conflict. Overly emphasizing creativity may produce a series of brilliant inventions, such as those that emanated from the Xerox Palo Alto Research Center, only to have them commercialized by new start-up companies with no economic ties to Xerox. In contrast, overly emphasizing the push to commercialize may quickly drain whatever creative juices once existed in a firm. Anil Khurana and Stephen R. Rosenthal, in Chapter Three, examine in depth the creative front end of product development processes. They do not want to leave to chance the "cross-functional front-end strategic, conceptual, and planning activities that typically precede the detailed design and development of a new product." In seeking to achieve Markides's market-oriented change goals, Khurana and Rosenthal provide a well-engineered front-end process to try to satisfy customers who buy not only the tangible product but also a package that includes "the company, the brand image, the sales interaction, the delivery process, the after-sales service, and the follow-up relationship."

A major shift that has occurred in many firms' innovation efforts has been the recognition that a company must step back from just creating individual products, however attractive, if it is to ensure a continuing flow of new products that transform markets. Instead, it needs to build strong platforms that rest on its core capabilities, from which individual products can then be rolled out time and time again, with dramatically decreased lead time. In Chapter Four Marc H. Meyer and James M. Utterback detail the insights and practices needed to initiate a product platform process and to go from platforms to product families. They use as examples such prolific flows as the Sony Walkman's 160 variations over a decade and Black & Decker's overall transformation of its power tools business. Through mapping product families and assessing core competencies, the authors seek to eliminate "two essential problems: redundancy of both technical and marketing effort and lack of long-term consistency and focus." Chapter Five, by David Robertson and Karl

Ulrich, follows this theme. It provides a detailed presentation of platform tools that permit planning for both product commonality, which saves costs and time, and product differentiation, which maximizes attractiveness to customers.

Part Two discusses a revolution that has occurred in product-market innovation. As my recent global benchmarking study of the world's top four hundred R&D-spending companies found, 85 percent of these giants are now relying heavily on external sources of technology as part of their overall innovation process.[3] These moves to the outside create both dependency constraints and risks while leveraging flexibility and other benefits. Fortunately, the data show that most of the firms have gained in their performance effectiveness from accessing these external resources. Chapter Six, by Edward B. Roberts and Wenyun Kathy Liu, adds an external-resourcing perspective to the work of my MIT colleague, James M. Utterback, in addressing the changing nature of innovation requirements over the long life cycle of a new technology. The authors show "that a company should use, in a timely and appropriate way, every form of business development—alliances, joint ventures, licensing, equity investments, mergers, and acquisitions—in order to perform optimally over its underlying technology life cycle." They point out that "doing so requires integrated technology and market and financial planning that may be beyond most companies." James Brian Quinn goes even further, arguing in Chapter Seven that, beyond partnering, the actual outsourcing of various stages of the innovation process has become necessary because of the specialist knowledge required in fields such as pharmaceuticals, networking equipment, and even corporate services. Quinn contends that "the supplier side of the process has become the major source of new high-tech jobs, new companies, and economic growth worldwide." In Chapter Eight Jeffrey H. Dyer, Prashant Kale, and Harbir Singh examine the strategic-alliance practices of two hundred companies, reporting that almost half of all alliances fail. But the authors' analyses demonstrate great benefits for carrying out these partnerships.

With regard to alliances, they explain that "the ability to form and manage them more effectively than competitors can become an important source of competitive advantage." In Chapter Nine, using data from seventeen member countries of the Organization for Economic Cooperation and Development over the past quarter century, Michael E. Porter and Scott Stern offer a different twist on the concept of innovating in combination with outside resources. "Innovation," the authors find, "is strongly affected by location: the *external* environment for innovation. . . . Choosing R&D locations . . . should not be driven by input costs, taxes, subsidies, or even the wage rates for scientists and engineers. . . . Instead, R&D investments should flow preferentially to the most fertile locations for innovation."

Part Three explores three very new perspectives on the overall innovative process. In Chapter Ten James Brian Quinn, Jordan J. Baruch, and Karen Anne Zien examine the potential of software to improve the innovation process. Unlike Michael A. Cusumano and Richard W. Selby in *Microsoft Secrets*,[4] Quinn, Baruch, and Zien do not focus on innovating in software products or in software development per se. Instead, they are intrigued by the possibility of overall acceleration of technology-based innovation by employing software as a critical tool. "Software," they suggest, "is especially helpful in allowing workers, technologists, and managers to visualize solutions and work together on complex systems." They propose that the right software can enhance a company's innovative potential by allowing fewer people to do more: "Properly designed software systems allow smaller, more flexible teams to perform at greater levels of sophistication than larger teams can without them." Eric A. von Hippel is also interested in software, but more as a current prominent example of what he sees as a fundamental change in innovation. In Chapter Eleven von Hippel goes far beyond his earlier findings that users, not manufacturers, are the sources of key innovations in a number of different fields, such as scientific instruments and software tools. He now shows that in a diverse range of fields communities of users are coming together to account for evolution of innovations and the building of innovation families. In Chapter Twelve Robert I. Sutton returns in a vital way to the themes discussed by Markides in Chapter One. Both Sutton and Markides are seeking to learn how companies can achieve dramatic innovation inside the firm as well as in its markets, without concentrating on deep technological change. Sutton's last words are wise, not weird: "Ultimately, anything that brings in new knowledge, helps people see old things in new ways, or helps a company break from the past will do the trick."

NOTES

1. J. M. Utterback, "Innovation and the Diffusion of Technology," *Science,* February 15, 1974.
2. E. B. Roberts, ed., *Generating Technological Innovation* (New York: Oxford University Press, 1987).
3. E. B. Roberts, "Benchmarking Global Strategic Management of Technology," *Research-Technology Management,* March-April 2001, *24,* 25–36.
4. M. A. Cusumano and R. W. Selby, *Microsoft Secrets* (New York: Free Press, 1995).

PART ONE

Innovating from the Inside

CHAPTER ONE

Strategic Innovation

CONSTANTINOS MARKIDES

n spring 1902 Jim Penney opened his first dry-goods store in Kemmerer, Wyoming, and began his attack on the big retail chains of the time, including Sears and Woolworth, which date back to 1886 and 1879, respectively. By 1940 J. C. Penney had grown to 1,586 stores and annual sales of $302 million.

▼ In January 1936 Lever Bros., a subsidiary of Unilever, introduced a new food product in the U.S. market, a vegetable shortening called "Spry." The new product went up against Procter & Gamble's established market leader, Crisco, which had been introduced in 1912. Spry's impact was phenomenal: in a single year, it had reached half the market share of Crisco.

▼ In the early 1960s Canon, a camera manufacturer, entered the photocopier market—a field totally dominated by Xerox. By the early 1980s, having seen such formidable competitors as IBM and Kodak attack this same market without much success, Canon

First published in the Spring 1997 issue of *MIT Sloan Management Review*.

emerged as the market leader in unit sales. Today it is a close second to Xerox.

▼ In 1972 Texas Instruments (TI), a semiconductor chip supplier, entered the calculator business—a field already occupied by Hewlett-Packard, Casio, Commodore, Sanyo, Toshiba, and Rockwell. Within five years TI was the market leader.

▼ In 1976 Apple introduced the Apple II, in direct competition with IBM, Wang, and Hewlett-Packard in the professional and small-business segment, and Atari, Commodore, and Tandy in the home segment. Within five years Apple had become the market leader.

▼ In 1982 Gannett Company Inc. introduced a new newspaper into a crowded field of seventeen hundred dailies. By 1993 *USA Today* had become a top-selling newspaper with an estimated 5 million daily readers.

▼ In 1987 Howard Schultz bought Starbucks Coffee from the original owners. In the next five years he transformed the company from a chain of 11 stores to some 280 stores in 1993. Sale revenues grew from $1.3 million in 1987 to $163.5 million in 1993.

▼ In the late 1980s Yamaha tried to revitalize its declining piano business by developing digital technology so customers could either record live performances by the pianists they'd chosen or buy such recordings on diskettes and play the same composition on their pianos. Sales in Japan have been explosive.

These are certainly nice success stories, but there is more to them than that. The common theme underpinning all these accounts is simple: the companies succeeded dramatically in attacking an established industry leader *without* the help of a radical technological innovation. This feat is not easy. Existing academic evidence shows that attacks on established leaders usually end up in failure—notwithstanding well-publicized cases of market leaders, such as IBM and General Motors, losing big to new competitors.[1] A series of studies show that the probability of a first-ranked firm in a particular industry surviving in first place is about 96 percent—almost a certainty.[2] For the second-ranked firm, the probability of survival is 91 percent, and for the third-ranked firm, 80 percent. In fact, most of the turnover that occurs among the top five in an industry is due to mergers rather than to new entrants that outcompete market leaders.

Thus, despite some well-documented cases of dramatic success in competing with an industry leader (for example, Xerox versus Canon, or Caterpillar versus Komatsu), the vast majority of attackers fail quite miserably, while established leaders hang on to their market shares for long periods. This is exactly the reason why the success stories I first mentioned are so interesting. Not only have the companies not failed in attacking the established leaders; they have actually succeeded in dramatically increasing their market share and sometimes even emerged as the new industry leader. And they did all this without riding the wave of technological discontinuity. How did they do it?

THE COMMON ELEMENT

After studying more than thirty successful attackers, I believe that the simple answer is that they broke the rules of the game in their industry. The common element in all the successful attacks is *strategic innovation*. Significant shifts in market share and fortunes occur not because companies try to play the game better than the competition but because they change the rules of the game.

Consider, for example, the case of Canon. Back in the 1960s Xerox had a lock on the copier market by following a well-defined, successful strategy. The main elements of Xerox's strategy were segmenting the market by copier volume and consciously deciding to go after the high-speed copier market to tap the corporate reproduction market. This inevitably defined its customers as the big corporations, which by itself determined the distribution method that

Xerox adopted—a direct sales force. At the same time, Xerox decided to lease rather than sell its machines, a strategic choice that had worked well for the company in its earlier battles with 3M.

This strategy proved to be so successful that several new competitors, such as IBM and Kodak, tried to enter this huge market by adopting the same or similar strategies. Canon, on the other hand, decided to play the game differently. It segmented the market by end user and targeted small and medium-sized businesses, while also producing personal copiers for individuals. Canon also decided to sell its machines outright through a dealer network, and, while Xerox emphasized the speed of its machines, it concentrated on quality and price as its differentiating features. As a result, whereas IBM and Kodak failed to make any significant inroads in the market, Canon emerged as the leader, in unit sales, within twenty years of attacking Xerox.

Another classic example of a company breaking the rules of the game in its industry is Apple Computer. In the mid-1970s the established leader in the computer business was IBM. The main elements of the successful IBM strategy were to target corporations as customers; to manufacture the heart of the IBM computer, the microprocessor; to write its own software programs; and to sell the computers through a direct sales force. Apple totally changed these norms: it targeted individuals and small businesses as its customers, purchased its microprocessors from an outside source, and distributed its machines through retail stores across the country. Apple quickly emerged as the new market leader.

There are many other examples of companies that broke the rules. Dell Computer bypassed intermediaries and sold directly to the end consumer. Hanes Corporation created a totally new distribution outlet for women's panty hose—supermarkets and drugstores. Nucor Steel completely rethought the steel fabricating process and formed minimills. Toyota developed a new inventory and manufacturing philosophy in the car industry. Medco Containment Services provided companies with prescription drugs through the mail rather than through retail drugstores. Perdue differentiated what was widely considered a commodity, chickens. Timex sold cheap watches through drugstores. Southwest Airlines flew point to point rather than using the hub-and-spoke system.

These examples highlight my thesis: without the benefit of a new technological innovation, it is extremely difficult for any firm to successfully attack the established industry leaders or to successfully enter a new market where established players exist. The strategy that seems to improve the probability of success in those situations is the strategy of breaking the rules—strategic innovation.

However, it is *not* enough to proclaim the virtues of breaking the rules and to prompt companies to "just do it." It is easy to argue for innovation and to dissect strategic successes afterward. Over and above deciding *when* it makes sense to break the rules and when it is better to play the existing game (an extremely difficult question in itself), the real question is, How do innovative strategists hit on their strategic masterstrokes? In other words, how do strategists think of new ways of competing in a market when everybody else seems to miss them? Is there a systematic way of thinking about the issues that allows a company to come up with ideas that break the rules?

Companies do new or even crazy things, like using a new distribution method in the industry (Hanes), a new selling approach (Bank One), a new manufacturing method (Toyota), or totally bypassing distribution intermediaries (Dell Computer). Their actions, however, are nothing more than the manifestation of innovation.[3] The real question is, What allowed these companies to think of all these possibilities? What are the sources of their innovation?

Before tackling the issue of how to come up with new strategic ideas, I will make five crucial points:

1. The strategy of breaking the rules is not new. Nor is it something that has suddenly become important because of a more

demanding competitive environment. As any military historian would tell us, this old concept is something that military strategists (from Alexander the Great to Hannibal to the South Vietnamese generals in the 1960s) have used to their advantage. Any guerrilla army's tactics—adopted when the odds are stacked against it—are nothing more than breaking the rules. As the company examples suggest, the strategy has been used throughout business history as well.

2. Breaking the rules is *one* way to play the game. All firms should not adopt it, and they should not adopt it all the time. Whether a company should break the rules depends on factors such as the nature of the industry, the nature of the game, the industry payoffs, the firm's competitive position, and so on. Firms have to consider, evaluate, and make decisions on these factors individually.

3. How to break the rules depends on the business that the firm is in as well as the firm's strengths and weaknesses. Whether a company should bypass intermediaries (like Dell) or reposition its product (like Perdue) depends on market realities. The basic criteria for deciding whether to adopt a particular tactic are customer needs or wants and company strengths and weaknesses.

4. The strategy is, by definition, risky. Yet a company can manage the risk, primarily by experimenting in a limited way or limited area before fully adopting the new strategy.

5. Coming up with new ideas does not guarantee success. It's one thing to think of a new idea but another to make it work. The whole organization must be managed appropriately to give the new strategy a chance.

SOURCES OF STRATEGIC INNOVATION

How can a manager systematically think about breaking the rules? Suppose you are determined to go out and break the rules. How do you do it? How do innovative companies hit on their strategic masterstrokes? As any manager knows, there is nothing more difficult than coming up with really new ideas.

Based on my research, I believe strategic innovation happens like this: As already proposed by Abell, all companies in an industry have to decide three basic issues at the strategic level: *Who* is going to be our customer? *What* products or services should we offer the chosen customer? *How* should we offer these products or services cost-efficiently?[4] The answers to the *who-what-how* questions form the strategy of any company. Some will argue that the answers to these questions *are* the strategy of a company (see Figure 1.1).

The answers that a company gives to the *who-what-how* questions are conditioned by what that company thinks its business is. Who you see as your customers depends on what business you believe you are in. If, for example, you think you are in the electricity business, the customers you see will be different from those of the company that believes it is in the energy business. I return to this crucial point later.

Every company makes choices with respect to the *who-what-how* questions. Thus some companies may choose to focus on specific customer segments and offer specific products or services. Others may choose to be global players offering one or many products or services. Yet others may choose to focus on a specific technology or distribution method and offer specific products or services to one or many customer segments. Once they've made a choice,

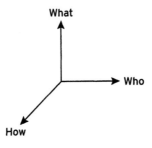

Figure 1.1. Strategic Positioning Map.

companies are not stuck with these choices forever. A company can always change its customer orientation or product offering, which may be difficult but not impossible. However, over time, a given industry positioning map becomes filled—that is, most of the possible customer segments are taken care of, most products and services are offered in one form or another, and most possible distribution or manufacturing methods or technologies are utilized.

Strategic innovation occurs when a company identifies gaps in the industry positioning map, decides to fill them, and the gaps grow to become the new mass market. By *gaps* I mean (1) new, emerging customer segments or existing customer segments that other competitors have neglected; (2) new, emerging customer needs or existing customer needs not served well by other competitors; and (3) new ways of producing, delivering, or distributing existing or new products or services to existing or new customer segments. Gaps appear for a number of reasons, such as changing consumer tastes and preferences, changing technologies, changing governmental policies, and so on. Gaps can be created by external changes or proactively by the company.

Obviously, the first requirement for becoming a strategic innovator is to identify gaps before everybody else does. However, being the first to identify the right gaps does not guarantee success; a company has to competitively exploit the gap. Based on my research, I believe that companies can identify positioning gaps and thus hit on their strategic masterstrokes in various ways: by accident or luck, by experimenting, through a series of seemingly unrelated steps or actions, or through a proactive thinking process. I now focus on the last option—the thinking approach.

FIVE WAYS TO KICK-START STRATEGIC INNOVATION

How can a company proactively and systematically think about and develop a new game plan? Five generic approaches of the successful strategic innovators can provide clues:

1. Redefine the business.
2. Redefine the *who*. Who is our customer? A company should think of new customers or new customer segments and develop a game plan that serves them better.
3. Redefine the *what*. What products or services are we offering these customers? A company should think of new customer needs or wants and develop a game plan that better satisfies these needs.
4. Redefine the *how*. Companies should leverage existing core competencies to build new products or a better way of doing business and then find the right customers.
5. Start the thinking process at different points. For example, instead of thinking, This is our customer, this is what he or she wants, and this is how we can offer it, start by asking, What are our unique capabilities? What specific needs can we satisfy? Who will be the right customer to approach?

Next I explore each method in turn.

Redefine the Business

Every individual's behavior is conditioned by his or her mental model of the world. Similarly, the behavior of every organization is conditioned by its dominant mental models (see box, What Are Mental Models?). Perhaps a company's most dominant mental model is its perception of what business it is in. The definition that a company gave to its business long ago, either explicitly or implicitly, conditions how that company sees its business, which, in turn, determines how it is going to play the game, that is, its strategy. Perhaps the most effective way for a company to start playing the game differently is by questioning the existing definition of its business.

My research suggests that successful strategic innovators all follow very different tactics from those of every other competitor in the industry. Behind these tactics is the thinking process that managers went through and the questions they asked to come up with the tactics. In most cases, the source of strategic innovation is

▼

What Are Mental Models?

A prerequisite to strategic innovation is an honest, fundamental question-ing of the mental models, or industry recipes, that seem to govern the behavior of any individual or organization.[1] A mental model is nothing more than our beliefs about an issue—our family or our business or the world as a whole. Thus, for example, when a person says, "I think everybody should go to church on Sunday," he or she is simply expressing his or her mental model. Other words for the same thing are *rules and regulations, habits, managerial frames, assumptions, mindsets, paradigms, conventional wis-dom, industry recipes, customs, institutional memory,* and so on.[2]

Research has shown that every human being has a mental model, which develops over time primarily through education and experience. Similarly, organizations develop mental models, manifested in the culture, routines, and unwritten rules of behavior. Thus we hear statements such as, "This is how we do business in this industry," which are the expression of that orga-nization's mental model. Like those of individuals, organizational mental models develop over time through education and experience.

Mental models can be good because they allow us to process information and make decisions quickly. However, very strong mental models can hinder active thinking and the adoption of new ideas because they act as filters that screen incoming information. As a result, if we have very strong mental models, we tend to hear what already supports our existing beliefs and ways of operating, while any new information that does not support what we believe we discard as wrong or not applicable. It is therefore essential

---

[1] A very good discussion of mental models and how to escape them is found in J. C. Spender, *Industry Recipes* (Oxford, England: Blackwell, 1990); and P. Grinyer and P. McKier-nan, "Triggering Major and Sustained Changes in Stagnating Companies," in *Strategic Groups, Strategic Moves, and Performance,* H. Daems and H. Thomas, eds. (New York: Else-vier, 1994), pp. 173–195. A very practical discussion is found in J. A. Barker, *Paradigms: The Business of Discovering the Future* (New York: HarperCollins, 1992).

[2] A survey of the academic literature has identified eighty-one words that have been used to describe the same thing. See J. Walsh, "Managerial and Organizational Cognition: Notes from a Trip down Memory Lane," *Organization Science,* May-June 1995, *6,* 280-321.

that we routinely question our mental models. Questioning does not necessarily mean abandoning. We can question our mental models and decide
that nothing's wrong with them. But the questioning should allow us to
think actively about assumptions we make about our business and about
our behavior in that business.

Usually, human beings and organizations escape their mental models only
after a crisis. Many firms discover new ways of competing only when their
backs are against the wall. Outsiders who have different mental models
from prevailing ones can also be catalysts in prompting an organization to
rethink its business. Thus a new CEO, especially one from a totally different
industry, can kick-start the strategic innovation process.

Benchmarking can also encourage active questioning of existing mental
models and open minds to other possibilities. Or the company can develop
an attitude that continually asks why—for example, Why are we selling our
products like this? When this question is legitimized by, for example, stories
of organizations that are profitably selling their products in a different way,
the *why* question can produce powerful results. Another tactic is to create a
crisis by giving the organization a new objective to aim for—a strategic
intent.[3] If people think it is a worthwhile, challenging objective, they will soon
realize that it cannot be achieved by doing the same old things better. They'll
recognize that they have to think and behave differently to achieve the goal.

There are many tactics that a company can use to escape its mental models.[4] Strategic innovation will not occur unless a company first questions
those models.

---

[3] See G. Hamel and C. K. Prahalad, "Strategic Intent," *Harvard Business Review,* May-June
1989, *67,* 63-76.

[4] Other tactics to use to question mental models include the following: monitor the company's *strategic* health as opposed to its *financial* health; experiment with new ideas; benchmark; ask the *what if* question; monitor maverick competitors and new entrants; talk with
noncustomers; bring in outsiders; institutionalize a questioning culture; develop the right
incentives.

an honest questioning of the answer that managers gave long ago, either explicitly or implicitly, to the question, What business are we in?

What business a company believes it is in determines who it sees as its customers, its competitors, its competitive advantage, and so on. It also determines what the company thinks are the success factors in the market and thus ultimately determines how it plays the game. If a company starts playing the game in a totally different way from everyone else, the reason may be that it is playing a different game altogether.

For example, Hal Rosenbluth, president and CEO of Rosenbluth Travel, described how he transformed his company from a $20 million business in 1978 to a $1.3 billion global travel management company by 1990: "Our biggest competitive advantage was to understand that as deregulation changed the rules of travel, we were *no longer in the travel business so much as we were in the information business*" [emphasis added].[5] This fundamental rethinking of its business led Rosenbluth to take a series of actions (such as acquiring computers and airline reservation systems, developing a private reservation data system and relational databases, and so on) that, to an outsider, may have seemed very strange. However, all these actions made perfect sense. If you are in the travel information business, this is what you need to do to be successful. Rosenbluth claimed that the company had undergone a similar transformation one hundred years before, when his great-grandfather had an insight about the business. He realized that "he wasn't just in travel, selling tickets to people who wanted to cross the Atlantic. He was in family immigration, getting whole clans of people successfully settled in America."

Such redefinition of the business is at the heart of strategic innovation. Many of today's strategic innovators started on their revolutionary journey by first redefining their business. Thus Howard Schultz, president of Starbucks, does not believe he is in the coffee business; instead, he is in the business of creating a consumption experience, of which coffee is a part. A visit to one of his stores is "romance, theatrics, community—the totality of the coffee experience."[6] If you think you are in the experience business rather than the coffee business, you will behave very differently from any competitor that thinks it is in the coffee business—not better, just differently.

In another example, Apple Computer's Steve Jobs and Stephen Wozniak did not think they were in the computer business. To them, computers were supposed to be fun. This mindset led to Macintosh's user-friendliness and to the physical interaction with the computer via a mouse. And Leclerc in France does not see itself as being in the supermarket business but as a crusader out to change retail distribution in France. Once we understand its conception of who it is, many of its strategic tactics (such as undertaking more than fourteen hundred legal cases against distributors in France) begin to make sense.

Such redefinition of the business can come only if companies ask, What business are we really in? While asking the question does not ensure a new or even better definition, discovering something new will *never* happen if companies never ask the question.

How to Define the Business. There is no right or wrong way to define the business. You can never know beforehand whether a certain definition will be a winner.[7] The important thing is to ask the question, to think of the implications of a possible redefinition, to assess what new tactics to adopt if you were to redefine, to think whether your core competencies will allow you to carry out these tactics efficiently, and so on. Thus, asking the question is only a trigger to thinking actively.

If we look historically at the issue of how to define the business, we can identify three schools of thought. Traditionally, companies defined their business by the *product* they were selling. Thus there were companies in the car business (Ford), the airplane business (Boeing), or the cigarette business (Philip Morris). However, after Levitt's article in the early 1960s, this way of defining the business came under severe attack.[8] Levitt argued that defining the business by product is too narrow and can lead a company astray. He championed the notion that a company should define its business by the *customer function* it is trying to fulfill. Thus "the railroads are in trouble today . . . because they let others take customers away from them because they assumed themselves to be in the railroad business rather than in the transportation business. The reason they defined their industry wrong was because they were railroad-oriented instead of transportation-oriented; they were product-oriented instead of customer-oriented."

This way of looking at the business emphasized the importance of customers and encouraged companies to identify the underlying functionality of their products. By asking what benefits the customer derives from a product, a company can identify its true value added and define its business. Thus, instead of thinking of your business as the car business, it is better to think of it as the transport or entertainment business or whatever other function your product is fulfilling. A third perspective has emerged that argues that companies must think of their business as a portfolio of *core competencies.*[9] For example, Sony might say it is in the business of selling pocketability, or Apple might say that it is in the business of supplying user-friendliness.

Not one of these three approaches to defining the business is the right one; each has its merits and its limitations. What is a good definition for one company may be bad for another. It all depends on each company's unique capabilities and which definition allows the company to employ its capabilities in the best possible way and thus gain competitive advantage. What usually kick-starts strategic innovation is not the adoption of any one of the three approaches. Rather it is continual switching from one definition to another and continual thinking about the business implications for the company as it switches from one definition to another. The breakthrough usually comes when a company has a dominant way of defining its business, say, customer driven, and suddenly begins thinking of its business in a different way, say, product driven.

A company should go through a four-step exercise to define its business:

1. *List all possible definitions of the business.* (For example, BMW is in the car business, the prestige car business, the transport business, the ego business, the business of satisfying the transport needs of yuppies, the driving business, the engineering business, the up-market global car business, and so on.) Make the list as long as possible.

2. *Evaluate each definition according to a series of criteria.* If we define our business as x, who are the customers and what do they need? Who are our competitors? Can we satisfy these customer needs in a unique or better way relative to our competitors? Is our definition of the market attractive (that is, growing in the future, protected by barriers, and so on)? What will be the key success factors in this business? Can we deliver? How do our competitors behave, and what does that imply about how they have defined the business? Does this definition allow us to satisfy our personal objectives for this company? The same questions should be used to evaluate every possible definition. The goal is to identify the definition that gives your company maximum leverage relative to competitors.

3. *Choose one definition.* This is a crucial step. Making a choice implies certain follow-up decisions (for example, that the company will invest in certain products or certain country subsidiaries and not in others). It also implies that certain managers will lose out in the next budget round and others will win. As a result of the serious implications that this decision entails, most companies fail to choose a definition.

4. *Ask these questions:* If our competitor redefined the business, what strategy would it be following? How can we prepare for it?

This is the process that a company should go through to decide how to define its business. Imagine the power of revisiting these questions every year or two—including a follow-up question: Have any changes occurred that make another definition of the business more attractive to our company? This is the source of strategic innovation. Just when everybody else has settled into a certain accepted definition and behaves accordingly, you "discover" a new definition that allows you to start playing the game differently and catch everybody off guard. But, again, to discover a new definition, you must continually explore.

Very few companies decide explicitly what business they are in, let alone think about how to redefine the business. Yet this is the most important element of any strategy. Even the few companies that go through this exercise explicitly either fail to make a specific decision or, having decided what business they are in, fail to revisit the decision, believing that it is cast in concrete, never to be revisited.

Redefine the *Who*

The second source of strategic innovation is a fundamental rethinking of the question, Who is my customer? Implicit in this is the notion that the choice of customer is a strategic decision: companies should choose their customers strategically rather than accept as a customer anyone who wants to buy. The criterion for choosing who will be a customer should be an assessment of whether a customer is "good." The trick, therefore, is to identify which customers are good for the company (and keep them or go after them) and which are not (and avoid or get rid of them). A good customer for one company may be a bad customer for another, depending not only on the customer's intrinsic characteristics (willing to pay on time, able to pay, profitable) but also on whether the company is able to serve that customer better or more efficiently than its competitors as a result of its unique bundle of assets and capabilities. How many companies think about this question explicitly and proactively? How many have explicit criteria by which they judge every customer? More important, how many companies get rid of existing customers that they have identified as bad customers?

In terms of strategic innovation, the purpose of thinking strategically about this question is either to identify new customers or to resegment the existing customer base more creatively and thus form new customer segments. Many companies seem to believe that new customer segments emerge only when new customer *needs* emerge. New customer needs are certainly an important source of new customer segments (and something that I discuss in more length later) but are not the only one. Often, customer needs remain the same, but customer *priorities* change; for example, customers still need warmth and style in their overcoats, but, compared with thirty years ago, style has risen, for whatever reason, on the list of customer priorities. Thus a company that identifies such changing priorities, not needs, can carve out a specific niche of customers who value style highly.

Similarly, a company can identify a specific customer segment that competitors are not currently serving. The reason this segment is not served is not because companies do not know about the needs of those customers. They may know the needs but have decided that the customer segment is not big enough to go after or that they cannot serve this segment profitably. If a new company can serve this niche efficiently, it has a new customer segment at its disposal, not because any new customer needs have emerged but because the company has found a more efficient way to fill existing needs.

Another way to identify new customer segments is by more creatively segmenting the existing customer base to put different segments together according to a new logic. Recombination of customer segments may also allow a company to create a new need and grow a particular segment.

My goal is not to make an exhaustive list of all possible ways a company can identify new segments. Rather, I suggest that new customer segments can be developed not only from new customer needs but in various ways. However, a company cannot identify new segments unless it proactively thinks about who its customer really is.

Inevitably, if a company identifies a new customer base, it will start behaving in a way that best satisfies the specific needs of those customers. This behavior will most likely be different from that of established competitors who are serving different customers. Thus the company will be breaking the rules.

Consider, for example, the Canon case: whereas Xerox leases big photocopiers to corporations through a direct sales force, Canon sells its personal photocopiers to end users through a dealer network. Thus Canon has adopted a different product, along with different selling and distribution strategies. It is breaking the rules. But how did Canon think of these new rules? Could Canon have started by identifying individuals as a potential customer segment and then asked what these individuals wanted? To Canon, the answer was small personal copiers. It then asked, How can we get these copiers to them? Through dealers. Thus the innovative Canon strategy is nothing more than doing exactly what is needed to satisfy the needs of its chosen customer segment.

Many companies that are strategic innovators began this way. They identified a customer segment (usually but not always the low end of the market) or a niche that was not currently served by existing competitors. Then they designed their products and delivery systems to fit the requirements of this customer segment. This source of strategic innovation underpins the success of companies such as Wal-Mart, Canon, Apple, Southwest Airlines, the Body Shop, Texas Instruments (in personal calculators), Lan & Spar Bank, J. C. Penney (in the early 1900s), *USA Today*, Komatsu, Honda (in motorcycles and cars), and so on.

For example, at a time when other airlines were using hub-and-spoke systems, Herb Kelleher, CEO of Southwest Airlines, decided to break the rules: "We wound up with a unique market niche: we are the world's only short-haul, high-frequency, low-fare, point-to-point carrier. . . . We wound up with a market segment that is peculiarly ours, and everything about the airline has been adapted to serving that market segment in the most efficient and economical way possible."[10] Little-known Enterprise Rent-A-Car, America's biggest rental firm, has a strategy that focuses not on the traditional customer segment, people who rent cars at airports, but on people who rent cars not only at airports but wherever they need them. As a result, the company has positioned its 2,400 offices within fifteen minutes of 70 percent of the U.S. population and picks up customers from their homes at no extra cost.[11]

Merely choosing a niche is not strategic innovation. For the choice of niche to qualify as strategic innovation, it must grow to eventually become the mass market, and the company's way of playing the game must become the new game in town. Thus the choice of the *right* niche qualifies as strategic innovation. Therefore strategic innovators emerge in this manner: at a given time the mass market is served by a number of competitors. A new company spots a segment or a new niche and goes after it. The existing competitors do not bother because the company is not really taking customers away from them (that is, they still control the mass market). Given the way the new company plays the game in its little niche, they may not even see it as a competitor. Then, suddenly, the niche grows, and the niche company emerges as the new market leader. All other competitors take notice and search frantically for a response. In the meantime, academics the world over label the new company a maverick competitor that won by breaking the rules. This scenario seems to fit perfectly the success stories of companies like Canon, Apple, Southwest Airlines, Wal-Mart, Dell, Snapple, CNN, MTV, Nucor, and so on.

What eventually led to these companies' success was the choice of a specific market niche that grew phenomenally. But what does it mean when the niche grows to become the new mass market? That what was important to only a few people is now important to almost everybody. For example, concern for the environment grew in the 1980s and along with it the fortunes of the Body Shop. How did this happen? Either the need was already there, and a company was lucky or quick enough to climb on the rising wave just in time, or the company helped grow this need so as to exploit it. Thus the important thing is to pick the right niche.[12]

How do strategic innovators pick the right niche? There is really no magic formula. Picking the right niche requires a deep understanding of customer needs and priorities and how they will change. It also requires the courage (most vividly evident in entrepreneurs) to risk pursuing what appears to be a promising customer segment but which may turn out to be a fatal mistake.

Redefine the *What*

The third source of strategic innovation is an honest rethinking of the question, What products or services should we be selling to our customers? Implicit is the notion that the choice of products or services is a strategic decision: companies should decide strategically what to offer their customers. Many companies seem to believe that the choice of customers automatically leads to the choice of products and services to offer. This may be true, but from a strategic-innovation perspective it also helps to think of the *what* first and then think of *whom* to target. Thus instead of saying, These are our customers, so let's think what they want so we can offer it to them, it may help to start like this: These are the products and services that we want to offer, so let's think about who would want to buy them.

Thinking strategically about what to offer the customer should be part of any strategy process. However, for strategic innovation to occur, a company would have to be the first to identify new or changing customer needs, wants, or priorities and therefore be the first to develop new products, services, or better ways to satisfy these needs. For example, at Canon strategic innovation may have happened in this way: Canon somehow identified (through customer surveys or observation or whatever) that customers did not like waiting in line to use the central photocopier. As a result, Canon came up with the idea of developing personal copiers to serve this need. But if that were the Canon product, the customer would automatically emerge as the individual to whom Canon would have to sell through dealers. Thus Canon ends up with a strategy that is totally different from Xerox's. How then did Canon identify customers' changing needs or priorities? More important, how did Canon go from hearing people say, "I don't like standing in line" to developing the personal copier? In other words, how do strategic innovators identify new customer needs and the products to satisfy those needs?

The first and obvious way to identify new customer needs is, of course, to ask the customer. However, although absolutely necessary, simply asking the customer or monitoring customer changes in most cases does not lead to strategic innovation, because the customer can only tell you of needs or wants.[13] What must be done to satisfy them requires a creative leap by the company. And this is extremely difficult.

Consider, for example, the case of a German company that manufactures coffee percolators.[14] When it asked customers what they wanted from their percolators, they answered, "Good-quality coffee." The problem was that what the company needed to do to achieve this customer need was not immediately obvious. It required a lot of creativity to come up with concrete ideas to satisfy this need. Usually, customer needs or changing customer behaviors are obvious. The real innovation is to go beyond the obvious—to truly understand what is behind what the customer is saying and what products or services the company can develop to satisfy the customer's needs.

Asking customers is only one way to identify new products or services. Equally important is to develop a deep understanding of the customer's business and how the customer is satisfying its own customers' needs. In this way, a company can think ahead and identify new services to offer before the customer even thinks of them.

How can you better understand your customers' business? There are several tactics: talk to the customers' customers, talk to their competitors, talk to their suppliers, talk to their employees, understand their value chain, become partners with customers, monitor noncustomers, monitor new entrants, and so on.

To truly understand the customer, a company needs to become customer oriented rather than supply oriented. A company that aspires to be more customer oriented must, at the very least, change its underlying culture, structure, systems, and incentives to allow its people to achieve this goal. Simply pronouncing the virtues of customer orientation without fundamentally changing the underlying organizational environment will not deliver any results.

Outside benchmarking can be a useful source of new trends and new products. For example, Hanes had its innovative idea to distribute women's panty hose through supermarkets when, in 1968, the president of Hanes's hosiery division, Robert Elberson, noticed that a West German panty hose manufacturer had introduced its line to supermarkets in several metropolitan areas in the eastern United States. Similarly, Kresge Co. transformed itself into Kmart in the late 1950s, after its president, Harry Cunningham, had spent two years studying discount stores, especially Korvette.

Another useful tactic is to experiment continually with new products until you hit on a latent, not obvious need. For example, more than one thousand new soft drinks appear annually in Japan; only 1 percent survive.[15] A company cannot create a new niche or discover a latent consumer need unless it tries.

Redefine the *How*

Asking customers, thoroughly understanding the customers' business, or becoming a truly customer-oriented company can all be important drivers of strategic innovation. But is that enough? For example, did Sony come up with the Walkman by focusing on the customer? Did Yamaha develop its electronic pianos as a result of deeper customer understanding? Although the answer to both questions may be yes, this line of questioning points to another possible source of strategic innovation: building on the organization's existing core competencies to create a new product or a new way of doing business that is totally different from the way competitors currently do business.

Consider the following scenario: Canon begins by considering its already established dealer network that sells cameras to end consumers. In thinking about diversifying into the photocopier business, it therefore recognizes the need to leverage this dealership asset along with its knowledge of marketing to the end consumer. This line of thinking lets Canon identify end consumers as potential customers and so develop the personal copier that it then distributes through dealers.

This plausible scenario suggests that a company can create a new game by leveraging its existing competencies. The classic case, as the Canon example suggests, is to take the knowledge of doing business in one market and utilize it in another market. Thus Canon has developed a deep knowledge of the end consumer as a result of its camera operations and also has an established dealer network. What better solution than to take these two valuable assets and utilize them in the photocopier business by developing personal copiers and targeting the end consumer. To an outsider or to Xerox this may be breaking the rules, but to Canon this is simply leveraging its existing strengths.

3M provides another example of the same principle. In 1995, 3M sold nearly $1 billion in microreplication products, ranging from smart adhesives to liquid crystal display film. All these products stem from a single technology, which was first applied in the overhead projector lens thirty years ago. According to the inventor of the first microreplication product, Roger Appeldorn, nobody planned these products: "We didn't sit down and say, 'Microreplication is the next thing to do; let's go do it.' It doesn't work this way. It evolved. It reached a critical mass. And it suddenly proliferated."[16]

Leveraging existing core competencies is certainly one way to create new products or new ways to compete. However, most major breakthroughs occur not so much from amortizing existing competencies but from exploiting them to create and accumulate new strategic assets more quickly and cheaply than competitors. Companies can dynamically exploit existing core competencies in three ways:[17]

1. *Share core competencies.* A company can use a core competence amassed during the building or maintaining of a strategic asset in one small-business unit (SBU) to help improve the quality of a strategic asset in another SBU. For example, what Honda learns as it gains experience in managing its dealer network for small cars may help it improve the management of its largely separate network for motorbikes. Similarly, when Canon had successfully established itself in both the camera and photocopier businesses, many of the strategic assets that underpinned the respective SBUs could not be shared directly. The dealer networks and component manufacturing plants were largely specific to each SBU. But in the course of producing and marketing cameras, the camera division extended this initial asset by a mix of learning by doing and further purchases of assets in the market. As a by-product of this asset accumulation, the camera business also developed a series of competencies, such as how to increase the effectiveness of a dealer network, how to develop new products combining optics and electronics, and how to squeeze better productivity from high-volume assembly lines.

Because Canon is in two businesses, cameras and photocopiers, in which the processes of improving dealer effectiveness, speeding up product development, or improving assembly line productivity are similar, it can improve the quality of the strategic assets in its photocopier business by transferring competencies learned in its camera business and vice versa. This relatedness—similarities in the processes required to improve the effectiveness and efficiency of separate, market-specific stocks of strategic assets in two businesses—opens up opportunities for asset improvement advantages that allow a company to play a different game in a different market.

2. *Reuse competencies.* A company can use a competence developed during the building of strategic assets in existing businesses to create a *new* strategic asset in a *new* business faster or more cheaply. For example, Honda can use the experience of building motorbike distribution to form a new, parallel distribution system for lawn mowers, which are generally sold through different outlets. Similarly, by operating in the photocopier market and building the asset base required to outcompete rivals, the Canon SBU accumulated its own, additional competencies that the camera SBU had not developed. These included building a marketing organization targeted to business rather than personal buyers and developing and manufacturing a reliable electrostatic printing engine.

When Canon diversified into laser printers, the new SBU started with an endowment of assets, additional assets acquired in the market, and arrangements to share facilities and core components. But even more important for its long-term competitiveness, the new laser printer SBU was able to draw on the competencies of its sister businesses in cameras and photocopiers to create new market-specific strategic assets faster and more efficiently than its competitors. This kind of relatedness, in which companies can deploy the competencies amassed by existing SBUs to speed up and to reduce the cost of forming new market-specific strategic assets for a new SBU, is the asset creation advantage that companies can use to break the rules.

3. *Expand competencies.* A company can expand its existing pool of competencies because, as it builds strategic assets in a new business, it learns new skills. For example, in the course of building a new distribution system for lawn mowers, Honda may learn new skills so it can improve its distribution system for motorbikes. Similarly, in creating the assets required to support the design, manufacture, and service of the more sophisticated electronics demanded in the laser printer business, Canon may have developed

new competencies to improve its photocopier business. Alternatively, combining the competencies developed in its photocopier and laser printer businesses may have helped it to quickly and cheaply build the strategic assets required to succeed in a fourth market—plain-paper facsimile machines.

Strategic innovation takes place when a company tries to satisfy customer needs based on new strategic assets that are unfamiliar to existing competitors. In the process the assets of established players become obsolete. Maverick competitors create such new assets by utilizing their core competencies to either develop new assets or bundle existing strategic assets in unique combinations. Successful innovators need therefore to identify and deploy the right core competencies. A better understanding of changing customer needs can lead to a better understanding of which core competencies to emphasize and develop. Similarly, a better understanding of a company's core competencies can lead to better segmentation, choice of customers, and a more productive development of new strategic assets that allow the company to break the rules.

Start the Thinking Process at Different Points

The final source of strategic innovation is the thinking process for developing new ideas. New ideas emerge more easily if managers can escape their mechanistic way of thinking and look at an issue from different perspectives or angles. The goal, therefore, is to start the thinking process at different points. For example, instead of thinking, This is our customer, this is what he or she wants, and this is how we can offer it, start by asking, What are our unique capabilities, what specific needs can we satisfy, and who will be the right customer to approach?

At the strategic level a company has to decide the *who*, the *what*, and the *how*: Who are our customers? What do they want? How can we satisfy these wants? The thinking process could therefore go through three stages. Start by defining who the selected customers are and then decide on the what and the how. Or start by deciding first what products and services to offer and then decide the who and the how. Or start with the how and then decide the who and the what.

Another useful thinking process is to take the accepted definition of the business as given and then try to think of (1) new customers or new customer segments, (2) new customer needs, or (3) new applications of core competencies. After coming up with a number of ideas, a company can revisit the question, What is our business? and, for every possible new definition, repeat the three steps. Again, the objective is to see the business from as many different perspectives as possible so managers can find new ways to play the game.

CONCLUSION

I began by identifying Canon as a strategic innovator that beat the industry leader, Xerox, by breaking the rules. While there is no question that Canon broke the rules in the copier business, consider the different ways Canon *may* have come up with its innovative strategy:

1. While Xerox plays the game, believing that it is in the photocopier business, Canon begins by seeing itself in the consumer electronics business—perhaps a legacy of its success in the camera business. By thinking of itself as a consumer electronics company, Canon immediately recognizes that the way to play this game is through low price and high quality. It therefore puts all its energy toward developing a reliable copier at an affordable price. When it introduces such a copier, the first users report how good and cheap this wonderful new machine is, and millions of people suddenly discover that they too need a personal copier at home. The personal copier market explodes, and Canon emerges as the market leader.

2. Based on its experiences in the camera business, Canon starts by identifying individuals as a promising customer segment. Its answer to the question, What do individuals want? is small personal copiers. And to, How can we get these copiers to them? their answer is through dealers. Thus the innovative Canon strategy, when compared with Xerox's strategy, is nothing more than doing exactly what is needed to satisfy the needs of the chosen customer segment.

3. Canon somehow (through customer surveys or observation or whatever) discovers that customers do not like to wait in line for the central photocopier. As a result, Canon comes up with the idea of personal copiers. But if that is the Canon product, the Canon customer automatically emerges as the individual to whom Canon has to sell through dealers. Thus, again, the strategy ends up being totally different from Xerox's.

4. Canon begins by considering its already established dealer network that sells cameras to end consumers. By thinking about diversifying into the photocopier business, it therefore recognizes the need to leverage the dealership asset along with its technology and its knowledge of marketing to the end consumer. This line of thinking lets Canon identify end consumers as the potential customer and develop the personal copier, which it then distributes through dealers.

Each scenario or a combination may have taken place. Perhaps all did. A company can use any one or a combination of the above tactics to strategically innovate.

Two Caveats

It is worth reemphasizing that coming up with new ideas is one thing; succeeding in the market is another. Many readers may rush to identify numerous companies that appear to have strategically innovated in the manner described, only to go bankrupt in a few years. Osborne Computer is one example. Very much like the founders of Apple Computer, Adam Osborne founded Osborne

Computer in 1981 to sell portable PCs. He went after a new customer niche, one of the sources of strategic innovation. Osborne remarked, "I saw a truck-size hole in the industry, and I plugged it."[18] Osborne Computer grew to $100 million in sales within eighteen months, only to go bankrupt in 1983.

There are many stories of companies that strategically innovated but failed. People Express's failed strategy has similarities to the successful strategy of Southwest Airlines. The demise of the retail chain Next in the United Kingdom contrasts sharply with the success of the Body Shop, even though both companies strategically innovated in the same way, by identifying new customer needs.

Similarly, there are numerous examples of companies that tried to strategically innovate by redefining their business, only to discover that it did not guarantee success. Xerox's attempts to go from the copier business to the office-of-the-future business to the documents business is one case. The failed diversification attempts of the 1960s and 1970s on the shaky ground of a broader business definition should be a warning. Nor is initial success through strategic innovation a guarantee for long-term success—witness the declining fortunes of Apple Computer and Kmart.

All these examples of strategic innovations that failed make the point that any idea, however good, is bound to fail if it is not implemented effectively. Even worse, any idea, however good and however well implemented, will eventually fail if it is not supported by continual innovation. This, however, should not detract from the value of generating new ideas that break the rules. Just because good ideas are only *one* element that determines corporate success and do not guarantee success does not mean that companies should not bother coming up with new ideas.

Finally, I have presented my ideas as if one individual or a group somehow comes up with all these ways to break the rules in a rational manner. This is certainly one way for strategic innovation to take place, but not the only way. A company must also strive to institutionalize innovation by establishing the appropriate culture, structure, incentives, systems, and processes that somehow allow innovation to happen as part of daily business. How 3M has institutionalized innovation can be a model for other companies that aspire to the same goal. Similarly, a company may want to identify specific obstacles or constraints that prevent it from being entrepreneurial and find ways to remove or bypass them. These are important issues but not my major concern here. I have been concerned only with the rational approach to strategic innovation. By not discussing institutionalized innovation, I do not suggest that it is unimportant. It is a topic that deserves a separate analysis.

Acknowledgments

The author thanks Sumantra Ghoshal, Dominic Houlder, Jane Carmichael, Charles Lucier, and Paul Geroski for many useful comments on earlier drafts.

NOTES

1. There is only one major exception to this generalization: in cases when the attacker utilizes a dramatic technological innovation to attack the leader, seven of ten market leaders lose out. See J. M. Utterback, *Mastering the Dynamics of Innovation* (Boston: Harvard Business School Press, 1994).

2. S. Davies, P. Geroski, M. Lund, and A. Vlassopoulos, "The Dynamics of Market Leadership in U.K. Manufacturing Industry, 1979–1986," working paper 93 (London: Centre for Business Strategy, London Business School, 1991); and P. Geroski and S. Toker, "The Turnover of Market Leaders in U.K. Manufacturing: 1979–1986," mimeograph (London: London Business School, 1993).

3. Whether these new approaches make sense for a particular firm (that is, whether they will lead to success or failure) depends primarily on the economic merits of these ideas and the company's ability to deliver them competitively. For example, do these new moves allow the company to offer something new to the customer (that he or she

wants)? Do they allow the company to offer something better or more efficiently? Are the new offerings something that the customer values? Thus the success of the new ideas will depend on customer needs and on the core competencies of the innovating company.

4. D. Abell, *Defining the Business: The Starting Point of Strategic Planning* (Upper Saddle River, New Jersey: Prentice Hall, 1980).

5. H. Rosenbluth, "Tales from a Nonconformist Company," *Harvard Business Review,* July-August 1991, *69,* 32.

6. C. McCoy, "Entrepreneur Smells Aroma of Success in Coffee Bars," *Wall Street Journal,* January 8, 1993, sec. B, p. 2.

7. The whole purpose of redefining the business is to identify a specific definition that allows you to maximize the impact of your unique capabilities relative to your competitors. Thus what is a good definition for your company may be totally inappropriate for another company; and what is a good definition for your competitor—given its particular strengths—may be totally inappropriate for you. Thus what is a "good" definition is in the eyes of the beholder. However, even if you can find a "good" definition for your company, you just enhance your chances of success, but this does not mean that you are guaranteed success.

8. T. Levitt, "Marketing Myopia," *Harvard Business Review,* July-August 1960, *38,* 24–47.

9. See, in particular, G. Hamel and C. K. Prahalad, *Competing for the Future* (Boston: Harvard Business School Press, 1994), p. 83.

10. C. A. Jaffe, "Moving Fast by Standing Still," *Nation's Business,* October 1991, p. 58.

11. "America's Car Rental Business: Driven into the Ground," *Economist,* January 20, 1996, pp. 76–79.

12. This point is also raised by Gerard Tellis and Peter Golder. Their argument is that "strategic innovators" have a vision of the mass market and actively try to produce quality products at low prices to make them appealing to the mass market. Thus the secret of their success is the fact that they target the mass market and succeed in serving it. Although I agree with the point, my research suggests that the importance of luck, good timing, and external events should not be underestimated as ingredients in the success of the

strategic innovators to "pick" the right niche at the right time. See G. Tellis and P. Golder, "First to Market, First to Fail? Real Causes of Enduring Market Leadership," *Sloan Management Review,* Winter 1996, *37,* 65–75.

13. There is a vast literature on the usefulness and the limits of "getting close to the customer." See, in particular, S. Macdonald, "Too Close for Comfort? The Strategic Implications of Getting Close to the Customer," *California Management Review,* Summer 1995, *37,* 8–27; and I. Simonson, "Get Closer to Your Customers by Understanding How They Make Choices," *California Management Review,* Summer 1993, *35,* 68–84.

14. K. Ohmae, "Getting Back to Strategy," *Harvard Business Review,* November-December 1988, *66,* 149–156.

15. "What Makes Yoshio Invent," *Economist,* January 12, 1991, p. 61.

16. T. Steward, "3M Fights Back," *Fortune,* February 5, 1996, p. 44.

17. For a fuller discussion of this point, see C. Markides and P. Williamson, "Related Diversification, Core Competences, and Corporate Performance," *Strategic Management Journal,* 1994, *15,* 149–165; and C. Markides and P. Williamson, "Corporate Diversification and Organizational Structure: A Resource-Based View," *Academy of Management Journal,* 1996, *39*(2), 340–367.

18. "Osborne: From Brags to Riches," *BusinessWeek,* February 22, 1982, p. 86.

CHAPTER TWO

Creativity Versus Structure: A Useful Tension

JOHN SEELY BROWN
PAUL DUGUID

M anagement training rightly stresses the resolution of tensions and conflicts. But there are some organizational tensions and conflicts that managers shouldn't try to resolve. For example, a necessary tug-of-war exists between how companies generate knowledge in practice versus how they implement it through process. The tension reflects the countervailing forces that, on the one hand, spark invention and, on the other, introduce the structure that transforms those inventions into marketable products. In isolation these forces can destroy a company, but conjointly they produce creativity and growth.

New knowledge, vital for growth, frequently emerges from small communities of practice. In other words, research groups often develop a common set of habits, customs, priorities, and approaches that both produce new insights and enable them to flow with little attention to how they might be transferred to outsiders.

First published in the Summer 2001 issue of *MIT Sloan Management Review*.

During the early days of Fairchild Semiconductor (the company that spawned Intel and just about every major Silicon Valley chip developer), the founders worked in overlapping groups on a variety of tasks, all of which came together to produce successful semiconductors. According to Christophe Lecuyer's history of Fairchild in *The Silicon Valley Edge: A Habitat for Innovation and Entrepreneurship*, Jay Last worked with Gene Kleiner on a step-and-repeat camera and with Robert Noyce on photographic emulsions. Meanwhile, Gordon Moore developed the aluminum process and joined Jean Hoerni and Noyce in their silicon oxide experimentation, and Hoerni and Noyce teamed up on the integrated circuit. Shared knowledge, inherent coordination, and collective understanding were necessary to make that collaborative inventiveness possible. The same challenge, approached by five separate labs within a corporation, would be more difficult (if not impossible), in part because of debilitating discussions over who does what and when.

Creative shared practice also was evident in the group that invented the computers at the heart of the original Internet. In a 1998 interview with *PreText Magazine,* Frank Heart recalled that "everyone knew everything that was going on, and there was very little structure. There were people who specifically saw their role as software, and they knew a lot about hardware anyway; and the hardware people all could program."

Alan Kay, reflecting on the more homogeneous group that developed the graphical user interface (GUI) at Xerox Palo Alto Research Center (PARC), describes the dynamics in similar terms. In Michael Hiltzik's *Dealers of Lightning: Xerox PARC and the Dawn of the Computer Age,* Kay observes, "Everybody has to be able to play the whole game. Each person should have certain things they're better at than the others, but everyone should be pretty good at anything."

Such tight-knit, innovative communities can thrive within established companies. For example, Heart's group formed within Bolt, Beranek and Newman (BBN Technologies) and Kay's within Xerox.

Alternatively, they can *be* the company, as in the case of Fairchild's early days.

Knowledge creation and wealth creation, however, do not necessarily move hand in hand. Knowledge may emerge in closely knit groups. Wealth comes from growth. And growth will often unravel such groups. Companies develop into distinct communities: design, engineering, software, hardware, marketing, sales, and so forth. At this stage the coordination that had been implicit becomes an explicit headache.

Once separated, groups develop their own vocabularies; organizational discourse sounds like the Tower of Babel. At Xerox, for example, when managers tried to extend the knowledge created at PARC to the rest of the company, what had been intuitive among scientists working on the GUI proved almost unintelligible to the engineers who had to turn the ideas into marketable products. Insurmountable barriers of misunderstanding and then distrust developed between the communities. The scientists dismissed the engineers as copier-obsessed "toner heads," whereas the engineers found the scientists arrogant and unrealistic. Thus one of the greatest challenges that innovative companies face is the step from initial innovation to sustainable growth.

When an organization reaches a certain stage in its development, instead of developing like a self-organizing string quartet, it becomes more like an orchestra whose disparate sections now need a conductor. At that point, establishing business processes becomes important. Process helps coordinate different communities so that their practices, while allowed to flourish, don't grow out of touch with one another. Ideally, processes must permit rigor without rigidity.

That balance is not easy to achieve. Process emphasizes the hierarchical, explicit command-and-control side of organization—the structure that gets things done. By contrast, practice emphasizes the implicit coordination and exploration that produces things to do. Practice without process tends to become unmanageable; process without practice results in the loss of creativity needed for sustained innovation.

Timing is equally important. Netscape serves as an example of a company that introduced formal processes too late. The company was by most accounts brimful of bright ideas and creative groups, but it lacked the discipline necessary to take on its top rival, Microsoft. As CEO Jim Barksdale noted in *Competing on Internet Time: Lessons from Netscape and Its Battle with Microsoft,* by Michael Cusumano and David Yoffie, "There's a stage in a company's life where it's fine to be loosely controlled. There's another stage where you have to get more and more serious. What you don't want is to get too serious too soon. That stifles things." But because Netscape assumed for too long that its apparently greater creativity alone would defeat Microsoft, it was slow to develop business strategies to channel that creativity.

The early history of Xerox indicates how, conversely, introducing process too early may restrict inventiveness. Hoping to harness a profusion of ideas and an explosion of growth that accompanied the development of the 914 copier (well before the creation of Xerox PARC), the board of directors brought in new management from Ford Motor Co. But, as later Xerox president David Kearns recalls in Erica Schoenberger's book *The Cultural Crisis of the Firm,* the managers screwed down the clamps of process so tight that, for a time, they stifled a highly creative company.

Aware that process can be suffocating—and seeking to foster creativity outside a process-driven structure—corporations often try to loosen the ties that bind them. AT&T's Bell Labs, Lockheed's Skunkworks, General Motors' Saturn plant, and Xerox PARC all reflect attempts at such loosening. These experimental "sandboxes" try to provide a safe environment for knowledge creation. But they too easily isolate new practices from essential process. Consequently, reintegrating ideas back into the organization can be remarkably difficult. So, for example, the knowledge that had flowed easily within PARC did not flow across its borders to the rest of the corporation.

Of course, many of the ideas created at PARC ultimately did align themselves with productive processes: the precursors to the PC, the mouse, and Windows interface, to name a few. But because profoundly different practices separated the research groups within Xerox, the ideas flowed outside to Apple Computer, Adobe Systems, and Microsoft—companies that had better processes in place for turning such embryonic concepts into products. Similarly, the ideas created at Bell Labs made the trek to Shockley Semiconductor, while the Shockley-developed semiconductor trekked first to Fairchild and then to various "Fairchildren," such as Intel, Advanced Micro Devices, and National Semiconductor. In those examples, existing companies were unable to create the processes needed to take advantage of new ideas, so new companies formed.

Companies that fail to control the conflicting forces of practice and process at best alternate between attempts to foster creativity and attempts to exert control. At worst, they pull apart or atrophy. Practice shuns process and vice versa. In contrast, productive companies yoke the two forces together, seeking—to borrow a phrase explored by knowledge and innovation specialist Dorothy Leonard—"creative abrasion." In our examples, however, the abrasion comes not between different cognitive styles, as Leonard suggests, but between practice (which tends to follow the path of least resistance) and process (which tries to map a route). In trying to harness the two forces, managers resemble Plato's famous charioteer struggling to control an unruly pair of horses while each tries to pull in the direction it favors—one forever soaring up, the other plunging down. We have all seen the wild swings that come as each horse gets its head in turn: from quality to reengineering, from reengineering to knowledge management, and so on. The best-managed companies are those that can maintain forward progress, favoring neither practice nor process, but managing both.

CHAPTER THREE

Integrating the Fuzzy Front End of New Product Development

ANIL KHURANA
STEPHEN R. ROSENTHAL

M any companies formulate product strategies, routinely choose among new product concepts, and plan new product development projects. Yet when asked where the greatest weakness in product innovation is, the managers at these companies indicate the fuzzy front end.[1] They recite some familiar symptoms of front-end failure:

▼ New products are abruptly canceled in midstream because they don't "match the company strategy."
▼ "Top priority" new product projects suffer because key people are "too busy" to spend the required time on them.
▼ New products are frequently introduced later than announced because the product concept has become a moving target.

Times have changed since 1983, when Donald Schön described product development as a "game" in which "general

---

First published in the Winter 1997 issue of *MIT Sloan Management Review.*

managers distance themselves from the uncertainties inherent in product development and . . . technical personnel protect themselves against the loss of corporate commitment."[2] Since then, new product development has become a core business activity that needs to be closely tied to the business strategy and a process that must be managed through analysis and decision making.[3] Now general managers cannot distance themselves from the uncertainties of product development, nor can technical personnel protect themselves against corporate commitment.

As enhanced capabilities for concurrent engineering, rapid prototyping, and smoothly functioning supplier partnerships have helped reduce product design and development times, management attention has begun to shift to the cross-functional front-end strategic, conceptual, and planning activities that typically precede the detailed design and development of a new product.[4] Here new product ideas gain the shape, justification, plans, and support leading to their approval and subsequent execution. Yet despite widespread recognition of the front end's importance, there has been limited systematic examination directed at improving its effectiveness.

Our exploratory study of front-end activity in eleven companies highlights best practice based on our assessment of seven critical activities. We begin by taking a systems view of the front-end process based on existing academic and practitioner literature. After discussing how companies should manage the front end as part of a normative model of the process, we use data from case studies to identify challenges and solutions.[5] Next we describe an approach for creating a successful process and present a checklist and diagnostic for front-end practice.

WHAT IS THE "FRONT END"?

Prior research has focused on the success factors for new product development (NPD). While many of these factors relate to design execution and project management issues, some pertain to the front end.[6] Consistent with Roberts's model, we classified the front-end-related success factors identified in prior research into *foundation* and *project-specific* elements.[7] The distinction is important because the two require different skills and levels of effort. Also, without adequate foundation elements, product and project success becomes a matter of luck. Project-specific activities focus on the individual project and require the project team's effort to ensure a useful product definition and project plan. These include a product concept statement and evaluation, product definition, and project planning. Foundation elements, on the other hand, cut *across* projects and form the basis for project-specific activities. Thus they typically require enterprisewide support, senior-management participation, and a cross-functional effort.

Foundation Elements

Without a clear product strategy, a well-planned portfolio of new products, and an organization structure that facilitates product development via ongoing communications and cross-functional sharing of responsibilities, front-end decisions become ineffective.[8] Achieving these preconditions provides a foundation for streams of successful new products.

Key product strategy elements include the formulation and communication of a strategic vision, a product platform strategy, and a product line strategy to support the go/no-go decision for a new product.[9] Previous research suggests that familiarity with the product strategy enables appropriate decisions on NPD timing and target markets and also an assessment of the fit between the product and the core competence of the business unit.[10]

In addition to a product vision, business units need to plan their portfolio of NPD activities, which goes beyond the traditional marketing view of having a product for every segment, market, and price point. Portfolio planning should map all new product initiatives across the business to balance risk and potential return, short and long time horizons, or mature and emerging markets. At the same time, the portfolio plan should ensure consistency with the product and business strategy.[11] If well done, it facilitates the allocation of scarce resources to NPD projects.

An essential precondition is establishing the organization structure for NPD. Decisions on structure, communication networks, and roles are made at a business-unit level. Research has highlighted several requirements for the product development organization and its functioning,[12] such as using a matrix or project form, organizing NPD around core business/product teams rather than traditional functions, using design and communication tools including information systems, and establishing controls and incentives as rewards.[13]

Project-Specific Elements

Product-specific front-end activities help clarify the product concept, define product and market requirements, and develop plans, schedules, and estimates of the project's resource requirements. However, they stop far short of creating detailed designs and specifications for the product and its components.

The product concept is a preliminary identification of customer needs, market segments, competitive situations, business prospects, and alignment with existing business and technology plans. Research suggests that the product concept should be clear so that managers can sense whether the newly defined opportunity seems worth exploring.[14] Managers need to understand customer needs and identify the potential technologies and applications to satisfy them.[15] For tangible products the product concept is usually illustrated with a sketch or three-dimensional model. Because such concepts are relatively inexpensive to produce, managers often create several before selecting one to fully design and develop. Early targets—measured in product cost, product performance, project cost, and time to market—set the stage for generating various product concepts.

The product definition, an elaboration of the product concept,[16] incorporates judgments about the target market, competitive offerings, and the time and resources for bringing the new product to market. The definition activity includes identification of customer and user needs, technologies, and regulatory requirements. These lead to a choice of product features and functions, target market segments, and design priorities. Research on the implementation of the front end indicates that an explicit, stable product definition and an understanding of the trade-offs among customer requirements, technology, and resource/cost constraints are important factors for success.[17]

Project planning includes project priorities and tasks, a master schedule, projected resource requirements, and other supporting information. Here it is critical to communicate the project priorities, provide adequate resources, and anticipate contingencies. And despite progress in NPD practices, typical systems do not adequately address these critical issues.[18]

The Front-End Process

We take a process view of the front end because earlier studies and our preliminary research suggested that the individual activities, while logically interrelated, often are treated independently.[19] Accordingly, we present a systems view of the front end (see Figure 3.1). This process description is consistent with growing empirical evidence of the need to simultaneously consider overall product strategy (foundation elements) with project-relevant input, such as product ideas, market analysis, and technology options.[20] *Thus understanding the interrelationships between the activities is as important as the activities themselves.*

Product strategy and portfolio plans should drive the complete NPD effort, in conjunction with the capabilities and competencies of the product development organization, with its inherent assumptions about roles, communications, and culture. These elements are thus preconditions or foundations for the explicit activities in NPD. Many companies implement a formal phase-review management system to define and guide the explicit project-specific activities;

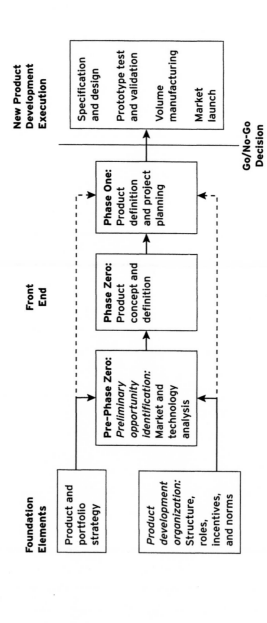

Figure 3.1. A Model of the New Product Development Front End.

this review process involves the process itself, roles that make it work, and primary deliverables.[21]

Phases of the Front-End Process. Companies generally begin work on new product opportunities (often called "pre–phase zero") when they first recognize, in a semiformal way, an opportunity.[22] If the newly defined opportunity is worth exploring, the company assigns a small group, sometimes including suppliers, to work together on the product concept and definition (phase zero).

In phase one the company assesses the business and technical feasibility of the new product, confirms the product definition, and plans the NPD project. Thus the development team identifies the new product, its development, and the business rationale for proceeding. The front end is complete at the end of this phase when the team presents the business case and the business unit either commits to funding, staffing, and launch of the project or kills the project.

Front-End Roles. A core team (including the project leader) and an executive review committee of senior functional managers responsible for making the go/no-go decision typically conducts the process we've described. During phase one, if not sooner, companies assign individuals from all functional areas as members of the core team for the product development project. Normally, if a company approves the project at the end of phase one, a full complement of people to design, develop, test, manufacture, and launch the new product supplements the core team. Previous studies have indicated that team structure varies in composition, size, and leadership.[23] Often the core team includes selected suppliers as partners; their knowledge of technology, costs, and design and manufacturing lead times can contribute to product definition and project planning.

Primary Front-End Deliverables. The front-end activities result in the product concept (clear and aligned with customer needs), the product definition (explicit and stable), and the project plan (priorities, resource plans, and project schedules).[24]

FRONT-END CHALLENGES AND SOLUTIONS

To understand the front-end processes and practices at fifteen business units in eleven U.S., Japanese, and European companies, we interviewed more than seventy-five managers (for our research approach see the Appendix at the end of this chapter). Our study focused on incremental innovations—the majority of NPD efforts. Accordingly, our findings deal with improving the performance of existing products or extending them to new applications, rather than with developing radically new products.

We have grouped the typical practices that characterize the foundation elements and project-specific activities into three implementation clusters—high, medium, and low (see Table 3.1). This analysis of our data also supports our earlier literature-based classification of the three foundation elements and the three project-specific activities. Our analysis does recognize an additional activity: adding value-chain considerations to the front-end process.

We found significant gaps in how the case study companies implemented the seven front-end elements, even for those companies that claimed to have the front-end product generation processes we described earlier (see Table 3.1). Even the companies that prepared their own detailed process descriptions generally didn't avoid problems that they could have resolved at the front end. In fact, only companies F and, possibly, G and J. could claim to have most of the capabilities for an effective front end.

Foundation Elements at the Case Study Companies

Next we discuss in detail how the case study sites managed the foundation elements in order to provide insights for companies trying to improve their NPD efforts.

Table 3.1. Front-End Activities.

▼

| | **Typical Practices** | **Degree of Implementation** | | |
		High	**Medium**	**Low**
Foundation elements	Product strategy formulation and articulation	Clear and well communicated by a responsible individual or group	Partly exists, but no individual or group is consistently responsible	Unclear or nonexistent
	Product portfolio planning	Explicit and thorough	Implicit at best	Not done or considered
	Product development organization structure	Clear and well communicated	Clear in theory but not always in practice	Ambiguous
Project-specific elements	Product concept	Detailed customer and technology choices and features with clear priorities	Detailed customer and technology choices and features; unclear priorities	Haphazardly done
	Product definition	Complete and generally unchanging	Complete but unstable	Incomplete at go/no-go decision
	Value-chain considerations in product definition	Upstream and downstream issues considered; part of routine core team responsibilities	Many issues considered; project manager responsible for ensuring all such issues are covered	Product development means product only; supply chain issues rarely brought up
	Front-end project definition and planning	Explicit and thorough	Done but not rigorous	Casual

(continued)

Table 3.1. Continued.

▼

Implementation	Degree of Implementation in Companies Studied		
	High	Medium	Low
Product strategy	D, F, G, J	B, E, H, I, K	A, C
Product vision			
Technology planning			
Product portfolio planning	F, J	A, D, E, G, K	B, C, H, I
Evaluation of risk and diversification			
Cross-project understanding			
Link to resource planning			
Product development organization structure	F, G, J	A, C, D, H, I, K	B, E
Cross-functional project organization			
Clear roles			
Established communication structures			
Leadership by executive reviews			
Product concept	C, D, F, G	A, B, I, J	E, H, K
Clear concept			
Understand management vision for product			
Identify customer needs			
Product definition	C, F	A, D, G, I, J	B, H, K
Complete and explicit definition			
Stable; avoid unnecessary change			
Anticipate market and technology evolution			
Value-chain considerations	A, F, J	C, D, G, H	B, E, I, K
Early supplier involvement			
Downstream issues–logistics, service			
Service and logistics representative on team			
Front-end project definition and planning	F, J	A, C, D, G, H, K	B, E, I
Clear project priorities			
Aggregate NPD project planning			
Contingency planning			

Note: Letters refer to the eleven companies in the research.

Product Strategy. Our research suggests that despite their intentions, very few companies have clear product strategies to guide their decisions on new product opportunities. In our sample of eleven companies, we rated only two as outstanding (F and G) and two as satisfactory (D and J), while the remaining seven were seriously lacking. We identified several deficiencies in formulating and articulating a product strategy and the connections between product strategy and the core NPD activities (see Figure 3.1):

▼ There were product development teams and product managers, but no one was in charge of formulating a product strategy, even at the senior-management level.
▼ Several of the companies made NPD decisions based on project-specific criteria rather than considerations of strategic fit.
▼ Business strategy was not specific to markets and products.
▼ R&D, largely insulated from the product development group, funded projects based on superior technology rather than on their potential to satisfy particular product requirements.

The outstanding companies in our sample had countered these deficiencies. The power of a clear product strategy was evident at company F, where we studied the fourth in a series of eight planned sequential product launches based on a common platform.[25] The company had designed this platform to meet explicit customer, market, and technology guidelines, with which each successive release was consistent. The vision of the business, product, project, and technology enabled successive product development teams for this platform to consistently deliver a product that met every target.

Product Portfolio Planning. More than a third of the companies studied did not plan a product development portfolio. Even when they did, planning at all but two of the research sites, F and J, was sporadic and incomplete. This neglect can be traced to a combination of vague product strategy, measurement difficulties in establishing risk/return profiles, and ambiguous overall responsibility.

While company H traditionally lacked a clear product strategy, senior managers had begun to realize that they were in a mature, threatened business. In response, they made their functional managers aware of basic portfolio planning, with encouraging results. Their portfolio now includes a combination of different products with both established and new technologies, instead of traditional projects with incremental improvements to the familiar product line. The company also enhanced the role of the executive review committee, known as the "product approval committee," to include assessment of the match between a new product concept and the existing product portfolio in risk, time horizons, and markets.

In contrast, company F—which is very successful in its business—constantly monitored the parameters of its product development portfolio, such as time horizon, risk, expected returns, required investments, and needed capabilities. Senior managers and project and product managers continually discussed the nature of the development portfolio and additions to make.

Regardless of the methods a company uses for new product portfolio planning, it needs to be part of an integrated front-end process. Our research suggests that there is often a discontinuity between portfolio planning and the front end of the traditional process. For example, if a project is killed at the front end because of technological infeasibility, the resulting gap in the development portfolio will become apparent only if front-end activities and portfolio planning are linked.

Product Development Organization Structure. We focus here on three roles at the front end—the project leader, the core team, and the executive review group—and on related communication structures.[26] At the companies that measured best along this dimension (F, G, and J), the project leader was responsible for promoting the interests of the project and the core team right from the start. This role included lobbying for support and resources (being an "ambassador") and coordinating technical or design issues.[27] These project leaders initiated such communication early during the product/project definition and planning stages. At company F project managers established communication channels, role definitions, and cross-functional mechanisms for the development team, as part of the product and project definition.

All the companies in our sample, except for companies B and E, had a cross-functional core team do the analytical work of product definition and project planning. However, the role of the team varied among the companies and development projects. Company A's first autonomous product development team was successful because four ambitious, creative team members communicated well. However, subsequent teams were not as successful because the core team members were unclear about their responsibility in creating the product concept and definition. In contrast, teams at company F operated more systematically and successfully. A small core team including the idea champion, a senior manager, and a potential project leader met early on and negotiated key roles and responsibilities. This nucleus group then recruited the full team and ensured that all members agreed on the definition of roles and responsibilities. This structure of team roles and responsibilities was part of the product concept statement and was formally acknowledged in the product definition and project-planning documents. Establishing the core team early, clearly defining roles and responsibilities for the team, and facilitating supporting communications played a major role in company F's success both in NPD process and the market itself.

Product success appears to be strongly associated with establishment of a cross-functional executive review committee. Only companies F and J had such a review. Company A's review committee focused on technical issues, with the result that executives failed to have a holistic perspective. In contrast, the committee at company F used each phase review to develop strategic and operational skills and establish norms for communication and consensus building. It also guided the core team while making critical choices and trade-offs or making decisions that might have an impact on the business unit's strategy beyond that particular product. At both companies F and J, the executive group worked like a business team rather than functional representatives, consistently developed product strategy and engaged in new product portfolio planning, and formulated explicit project priorities (time, cost, and quality).

For an effective front-end process, the roles of the project leader, the core team, and the executive review committee must complement each other. Explicitly defining these roles by answering the following questions will make the front end less "fuzzy":

▼ Should the core team resolve product definition and project-planning issues or refer them to an executive committee?

▼ Who is responsible for ensuring that product definition and concept testing are balanced between thoroughness and speed?

▼ Who should ensure that resources are allocated to a project as specified in the project plan?

▼ Who should identify emerging technologies for inclusion in future product platforms?

▼ Who has the authority to ensure that products developed by several business units or a unit and one or more "partners" are aligned along product/component interfaces, development schedules, market focus, and technology commitments?

Project-Specific Activities at Case Study Companies

Now we concentrate on project-specific activities at the front end: clarifying the product concept, stabilizing the product definition, considering the value chain in the product definition, and defining and planning the front-end project.

Product Concept. Our research revealed that clarifying the product concept at the front end was surprisingly difficult. Only four companies (C, D, F, and G) had succeeded in consistently developing clear, explicit, and precise descriptions of the product concept. At several companies the concept was unclear because senior managers did not communicate their expectation of the product's core benefits, choice of market segments, and pricing to the development team.

One company resolved this gap between management's vision of the product concept and the team's understanding of it by setting specific criteria for the features appropriate to the product. It created a database for new product features—based on various inputs from field service, special customers, R&D, marketing, and customer feedback. It then assessed these inputs in phases zero and one, based on senior management's vision of the product, engineering feasibility, market needs, resource requirements, price targets, and schedule—and classified them into "red," "green," and "yellow" items. The company would never pursue red items in the current program (but could consider them for the next-generation product). Green items were necessary for the current product; the company chose them based on need, feasibility, and other constraints. Yellow items needed more evaluation, so the company postponed them for subsequent release.

At several case study sites, the product concept was unclear because the companies did not clearly understand customer needs. When such problems recur, as we found at companies H and K, products lack what Clark and Fujimoto call "external integrity."[28] To make customer expectations and product features more consistent, sophisticated companies (such as companies C and F) try to look beyond the customer's "voice" to "action," by using techniques such as videotapes of customers' use of existing products.

Product Definition. All the companies in our study realized the pivotal importance of the early product definition. Yet most had failed to generate clear, stable definitions. While rapid shifts in technology and markets make it impossible for some companies to freeze the product definition, most of the companies studied acknowledged the difficulties this caused in the execution stages of product development projects and the high associated costs. In fact, only managers at companies C and F felt that they had developed approaches for dealing with instability and change.

For technology-driven companies (especially company H), delays in product definition entailed the risk of an unstable, expanding definition in which design engineers continued to add unneeded complexity. Managers at companies C and F made a concerted effort to freeze the product definition early on. For them the challenge was to balance the requisite flexibility with the avoidable uncertainty.

Company F discovered a creative solution for keeping up with and capturing market information while minimizing changes in the product definition—what we call the "missed elevator" approach. The program manager realized that technological or feature enhancements for any product would never end. He required the product definition to include new features and feasible solutions to customer needs, as long as they could definitely be achieved by the planned milestone for that product release. If a customer need or technology-driven feature "missed the elevator," it would go into the next product release, or "elevator." This approach to managing product development by having multirelease platform planning may become the next form of product development and management. Not only does it help achieve a balance between stability and flexibility, but it also leverages technological strengths and organizational resources.[29] Thus more companies now include in their front-end deliberations the definition of multiple-release products, in which each release intentionally involves only a moderate level of new technology development.

Value-Chain Considerations. While NPD research has highlighted the suppliers' role in NPD, we found that some companies have a broader value-chain perspective at the product concept and definition stages.[30] This becomes necessary as product designs and market delivery systems are more competitive and complex. And customers do not buy only the tangible product but a package that includes the product itself, the company, the brand image, the sales interaction, the delivery process, the after-sales service, and the follow-up relationship. The development team should envision and plan for this package at the front end; otherwise it may ignore downstream requirements and not design products for ease of distribution, installation, or repairs.

We found that these practices, while familiar at the execution stage, are less aggressively and creatively pursued at the front end. Of the eleven companies in the study, only four (A, D, F, and J) were adequate along this dimension. We observed several failures and some creative solutions. Company A, a special industrial products manufacturer, faced new maintenance problems and poor telecommunications support in providing field service. As a result, field service engineers became regular members of the core development team at the front end. At company D the NPD team consulted with so-called customer supply specialists.

As another example, Hewlett-Packard's (HP's) printer division had thousands of stock-keeping units (SKUs) for its products being shipped to different parts of the world. HP resolved this problem of excess variety with "design for postponement"; it redesigned the product so that only the core printer SKU was stocked in regional distribution warehouses. It stocked attachments, such as power packs, power cables, connectors, and even instruction manuals in different languages, at the distribution points and assembled the final package for shipment only after it received a firm shipment order. In fact, it designed the packaging itself so that it could easily insert and assemble all the attachments. The result was enhanced flexibility and reduced inventory costs, along with the needed product variety.[31] For all subsequent product development efforts, HP has routinely included downstream considerations at the front end.

Front-End Project Definition and Planning. At this part of the front end, we observed confusion about project priorities, incomplete resource planning, and inadequate contingency planning. Our discussions with core team members and project leaders led us to believe that fuzzy project priorities were the single most important reason for NPD delays, product overengineering, and product-strategy mismatches. For example, company A initiated its midrange product as a cheap-technology, low-performance version of its high-end product. Yet management had always visualized a cheap-technology, high-performance product. Finally, when the product came on the market several months behind schedule, it exceeded its performance targets but no longer met its unit-cost goals. At another company managers solved this common problem by comparing—at the front end—three kinds of project priorities for any NPD project: scope (product functionality), schedule (timing), and resources (cost). Senior management, the core team, and the (as yet unappointed) project leader at the pre–phase zero stage decided the relative ranking of the three priorities for the project's duration and communicated it to all project participants.

Companies must anticipate resource requirements, train people to acquire the necessary capabilities, and then ensure needs-availability matching based on project priorities. Executives repeatedly told us that they had too few people to staff their many NPD projects. At company J managers used a capacity matrix to assess and assign staff. Senior managers selected the best projects, set goals, and reserved resources. Company F, which also used a form of capacity matrix, faced a complicated challenge of resource planning. Like every organization, it had a core group of irreplaceable people who were in great demand for every project. When planning a next-generation product, the managers realized that the team member they wanted was heading a current project. To avoid such problems in the future, management resolved to both train more people for such assignments and also plan early for staffing and skills requirements.

Companies can manage the risks of NPD with thorough contingency planning—generating multiple product concepts, developing alternative technologies in parallel, and, in some instances, even creating competing designs for products or subsystems.[32] Yet, surprisingly, we found that most companies (including company F) focused contingency plans mostly on regulatory issues, such as safety or environmental requirements. Apparently, project planners assumed that they would find technology solutions without considering cost and quality. When the timing of a new product introduction is important, reasonable backup plans are needed to avoid delayed market launch. One approach is to build in contingent product features in case the planned ones do not work. Taking risk management seriously and linking product definition activities with project planning can lead to appropriate contingency plans.

Recognizing Interrelationships

Next we discuss several critical interrelationships among individual success factors and approaches for managing them.[33] Our examples are from company F, which had the most effective front end of the cases studied.

▼ Companies should consider product strategy and the product development portfolio at the start of the project-specific front end. Company F held a kickoff meeting even before it had refined the concept and assembled the full core team. Attendees included senior managers, the idea champion, and some core team members. While much discussion focused on the basic product concept, it also included how the concept filled a gap in the business strategy and how it related to and compared with other products and ongoing projects. As a result, subsequent problems of mismatches between the product and the product strategy or shortage of project staffing were rare.

▼ Companies should have a clear product strategy to enable a stable product definition. Everyone at company F accepted the notion that product strategy should guide technology choices and selected product features. Thus the company used its multirelease product strategy to simplify the definition: its adoption of the "missed elevator" approach simultaneously encouraged stable technology and feature choices that were governed by a long-term vision over several product releases while facilitating new releases on time.

▼ Companies should integrate portfolio planning and NPD project planning. Company F had established two distinct but formally linked planning processes. The strategic planning process involved managers from various functions and considered product strategy, product development portfolios, and overall resources. Thus portfolio planning yielded long-term commitments that the managers could invoke when planning staff requirements and project priorities for a specific new product concept. They implemented two important practices when planning individual projects: (1) establishment of schedules and allocation of staff and budgets, and (2) specification of inputs, such as technology from other business groups. First, they made the strategic business plan available to all core team members and considered the product definition in the context of the strategic business plan. Second, senior managers oversaw the core team's decisions and actions. For example, the project manager may be a part of the strategic business planning process or may report to someone who is.

A WELL-ENGINEERED FRONT-END PROCESS

How can a company improve its front-end practices to achieve success in NPD? Is it enough to improve the activities we have described? We suggest that best practice in NPD goes beyond simply adopting these activities. Success depends on how companies integrate dimensions and elements of product development.[34]

Our research highlighted certain challenges in integration of the front end beyond the obvious need for cross-functional effort.

First, because project-specific activities build on foundation activities, companies should ensure that the foundation elements are aligned with the product development process and project-specific activities. Second, they should ensure consistency between strategic and operational activities. The challenge is to make strategy explicit enough to guide day-to-day choices for NPD. We found the integration of these two factors was rare but extremely potent. At the companies studied, we observed several kinds of integration problems:

▼ Senior managers sometimes delegated the formulation of a product strategy to product and R&D managers.

▼ The product development staff often made decisions that affected other products and business-unit strategy. (While the core team faces technical uncertainty about the product and manufacturing and distribution processes, resolving cross-project issues or providing guidelines should be senior-management responsibilities.)

▼ Managers in various functions and organizational levels rarely ensured consistency and links among R&D activities, product strategy, and current product development. (Huge R&D investments can be wasted by pursuing superior technology capability unnecessary to the organization's espoused business strategy.)

▼ Managers frequently took on product development projects without committing adequate resources. (Often there is a misconception that product development staff working on multiple projects improves efficiency. The result is long delays in product launch and lost revenues. With ongoing downsizing in many companies, this kind of neglect is becoming chronic.[35] Senior managers need to help product and R&D managers understand a project's relative importance.)

▼ Senior managers did little to measure and reward cross-functional teamwork. (Front-end participants need to know that management values their contributions.)

Balancing Front-End Explicitness and Flexibility

Management of the front end also requires a balance between getting things right and being flexible during NPD execution. Other front-end elements and activities should also be balanced. There is a natural tension between planning to reduce risk and responding to inherent uncertainties. For example, we suggest that product strategy and portfolio planning be explicit, yet we recognize that some subsequent shifts in the product definition are inevitable, forcing contingent actions. Furthermore, postponing the final decisions at the front end by continuing the development of parallel concepts or solutions may reduce uncertainty.[36] While our research did not focus on this issue, we believe that there must be a balance between front-end planned activities and ongoing iteration during the NPD project, between making "final" decisions early and intentionally keeping open parallel alternatives, and between establishing product development targets through analysis and working by instinct alone.[37]

DIAGNOSING FRONT-END ACTIVITIES

Based on our study findings, we propose that companies evaluate their front end on degree of formality and the integration of activities. The dimensions—formality and process integration—can be measured on a checklist (see Table 3.2). The items are derived from previous research and our case study findings on the need for formality and integration at the front end. The diagnostic statements evaluate the explicitness and formality of front-end practices. The statements on integration document how well these and other front-end activities are integrated.

A senior business-unit manager, such as the vice president of R&D, chief technology officer, or director of NPD, should assess business practices and then calculate the score of the business unit,

Table 3.2. Checklist for Diagnosing the Front End.

▼

Formality of Front-End Process	Integration of Activities
1. Customer and market information is used early on to set scope for product (target markets, customer segments, features, price). 2. Core team jointly reviews product concept, and senior management formally approves. 3. Early concept and other feasibility prototypes are planned, tested, and completed at front end so that there are no surprises later. 4. Product definition is explicitly developed and documented. 5. Major supplier and tooling considerations are explicit at front end. 6. Manufacturing, distribution, and logistics requirements are planned; product concept is modified to reflect process and logistics constraints. 7. Need for new technology for products is clearly stated. 8. Project targets (time, cost, quality) and relative priorities are clear. 9. Resource requirements are formally defined. 10. Roles and responsibilities for tasks and communications for core team are clear and well executed. 11. Roles for executive review team are clear and well executed (review criteria, decision responsibility, ongoing interaction with core team).	1. There is a clear vision of product lines and platforms for specific markets. 2. R&D and NPD have matching agendas and plans. 3. Balance is sought and achieved among multiple NPD projects belonging to different platforms/product lines (for example, risks, novelty). 4. Project priorities are consistent with product strategy, portfolio plans, and resource availability. 5. Resource allocations consider multiple project requirements and their relative priorities and pre-existing project commitments. 6. Early identification of technical and organizational interfaces is done for systems products so that development can proceed smoothly. 7. Core front-end team includes representatives from manufacturing, logistics, and after-sales service, apart from engineering and marketing. 8. Staffing policies and project-specific staffing are consistent with the product strategy. 9. Need for new innovations is anticipated so that extensive innovation is not required during the product development process. 10. If there is uncertainty on any dimensions—for example, technology or markets—organization has carefully planned alternative approach.

counting a check for any item as one point. The sum of the scores on the formality statements gives the formality score; the sum of the integration statements, the integration score. The manager can then map the score on each dimension on the front-end capability map (see Figure 3.2).

The mapping indicates how well (or poorly) a business unit is doing along the two dimensions of formality and integration. Our research indicates that world-class companies score eight or more on both dimensions. Companies that score three or less on either dimension have a deficient front end and are likely to have major problems with their product development efforts. Senior management needs to find ways to improve these efforts; the checklist is a first step to understanding where and what to improve. What is more difficult is to understand *how*. In the next section, we discuss how companies and business units can plan a transition to a better-managed front end.

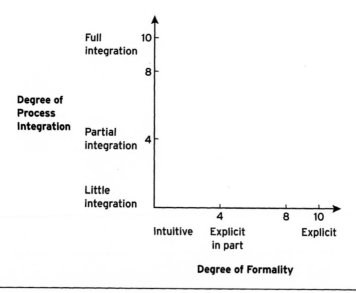

Figure 3.2. The Front-End Capability Map.

MANAGING THE TRANSITION

All the companies we studied were moving toward a more explicit, integrated front end. They were trying to build complementary capabilities to support the critical go/no-go decisions and development plans for new product concepts. Yet each was taking a different path at a different rate.

Stages of Evolution

We see three stages in the product development front end, not including the stage in which a company has no formal front end— the preemergent stage.[38] The next stages are "awareness," "islands of capability," and "integrated capability" (see Figure 3.3). The triggers to reach the awareness stage from the preemergent stage are typically growth, additional product line complexity, or competitive pressures for either more product innovation or lower product

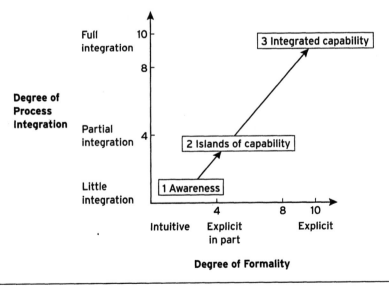

Figure 3.3. Stages in the Transition to a Mature Front End.

development costs. In any case, at the awareness stage companies recognize the significance of the front end but have little capability associated with it. They score poorly on both the formality and integration dimensions, as did companies B, E, and H in our sample.

Islands of Capability (Stage Two). Our study suggests that most leading product innovators are at the islands of capability stage, including companies A, C, D, I, J, and K. These companies realize the potential of having a well-managed front end and have some of the required capabilities, but inconsistently. Missing are many elements of front-end process integration. Companies find it easier to improve the formality of this process than to address the subtle gaps in integration.

How can companies evolve from awareness to islands of capability? That depends on what the business unit has already achieved and what capabilities it needs, given its industry and company. We identified two broad approaches to achieving stage two. First, those companies that have barely begun to understand the importance of the front end—for example, company H—should recognize that product development is a senior-management responsibility. Managers should carry out several structured activities, such as the diagnostic test. Second, those companies that recognize the importance of the front end—such as companies B and E—should formally and systematically conduct various front-end activities. Those activities include having an explicit product definition, estimating technology requirements early, and planning resources.

Integrated Capability (Stage Three). Front-end product development integration, the hallmark of stage three, is quite rare. We believe that most companies don't understand that this stage is significant in terms of required capabilities, and achieving it takes concerted effort. At the few companies with this degree of process integration—companies F, G, and, to some extent, J—analysis and decisions have been both explicit and rigorous, and all front-end activities are managed as a single process. Stage-three companies execute NPD projects better and faster than their competitors and are more likely to introduce a winning product. One can honestly say of these companies that "well begun is more than half done."

How can companies make a transition from islands of capability to integrated capability? Some stage-two companies have much of the required formality but not necessarily the degree of integration to yield substantial benefits. Most stage-two companies should focus on understanding the various dimensions of integration. Among our sample, we identified three clusters of companies that required somewhat different approaches to get to stage three. These three clusters represent generic front-end states and problems that many companies face.

While companies in the first cluster, A and K, have passed stage one, they still have a long way to go. They need to focus closely on senior-management involvement in creating a product vision. Improvements in front-end formality and integration, while not easy, will be easier if the product development group can understand its purpose better.

Companies C and D make up the second cluster. These companies will realize improvements from refinements in the front-end process. They need to make their front-end activities more explicit and, in particular, understand how to better manage their technology and resource requirements. Once they progress on these dimensions, they can focus more on cross-functional and integration problems.

The third cluster of companies, I and J, were the most advanced among the stage-two companies. Front-end explicitness is not their main problem. Instead, their challenge is to work on cross-project issues and technological uncertainties. By having close ties among strategic planners and project personnel, they will understand the links among projects and anticipate matches or mismatches between future market needs and current technology and product plans. They need to establish closer connections between their R&D and product development groups so that they can anticipate overall technological progress and product-specific technological uncertainty.

Sustaining Stage Three. Clearly, reaching stage three is not easy; even those companies that have achieved it continue to require improvements. Changes in competition, technologies, tools, and organization structures and relationships may need changes in at least some front-end practices.[39]

How can companies F and G improve? We found that these companies had minor deficiencies at their front ends (by using the diagnostic test in Table 3.2). Yet the companies have potential for improvement. For example, knowing what to finalize and approve in product concept and definition, and what to keep flexible and open to change, is important. Achieving a proper balance calls for more than just personal intuition and tacit understanding. Making explicit the connections between product requirements and internal technology development remains an elusive capability. And maintaining continuous links among business-unit vision, product strategy, technology, and new products is an ongoing challenge. Managers at stage-three companies need to evaluate and apply innovations such as developing carefully planned product architectures and platforms or adapting a front-end process—such as Cooper's—to deal with the dynamics of current technological, market, and organizational realities.[40]

CONCLUSION

Most companies have unnecessarily fuzzy front-end systems. The best way to integrate the front-end process is to use an overall systems perspective and thoroughly assess the current state of the front end. Fixing what appears to be broken requires the ability to see the interrelatedness of issues and the development of a coherent agenda.

We caution against oversimplification: not all companies should adopt the same front-end solution, and most will need to adopt more than one. For example, we found that companies used executive reviews in different ways with mixed success; some case study companies changed the role of the executive review group for different products. In general, company size, decision-making style, operating culture, and frequency of new product introduction are some factors that are critical to a preferred front-end solution. We discourage companies from importing a particular process or procedure that has worked well for others unless their contexts are clearly similar.[41]

Managing to become less fuzzy means integrating seemingly disparate but related strategic and operational activities, typically crossing functional boundaries. The solution must be balanced with the emerging realities of business and the environment. With proper diagnosis, consensus, and commitment, companies can enhance product development performance over the long term.

APPENDIX

We conducted our research between April 1994 and April 1995.[42] Of the sixteen companies invited to participate, eleven accepted. We chose companies based on whether they had a product-generation process and if they had NPD processes for one to eight years. Our final sample includes seven U.S. and four Japanese companies (all Fortune 500 companies or their equivalent in Japan) in various industries ranging from consumer packaged goods to electronics to industrial products (see Table 3.3 for more information on the specific industries). There are seven U.S., six Japanese, and two European business units (we interviewed managers at multiple business units at two companies). Business-unit size ranged from $300 million to $2.5 billion in annual sales, and six hundred to twenty thousand employees; company sizes ranged from $2 billion to \$55 billion, and twenty thousand to three hundred thousand employees. Further, we classified the companies as "active" or "neutral"; the active sites participated very closely in the research, and we had open access to them. At the neutral sites (companies B, E, G, and K), we had only one opportunity to get the data directly, that is, only one visit or series of interviews. Naturally, the data from these companies are less detailed, although we obtained the essential information.

We adopted an exploratory and "action-oriented" approach because we iterated among data collection, analysis, and feedback. We conducted our research at three to four company sites, analyzed data, presented partial results to a group of participants at "dissemination" workshops, wrote reports for their review, revised our knowledge base and conceptual models, and went on to the next case sites. Thus, implicitly and by design, we adopted the grounded theory approach.[43]

We spent more than two hundred hours interviewing more than seventy-five managers. On average, for each active site, we spent between eight and forty hours interviewing from three to twenty-five managers; for each neutral site, we spent eight to fifteen hours interviewing up to eight managers. We held four days of dissemination workshops with more than twenty-five different managers from several research companies. We interviewed managers (ranging from functional managers to company president) from marketing, R&D, software development, engineering, manufacturing, field service, finance, accounting, strategic planning, product management, NPD process owners, and corporate/business-unit general management.

For most of the case sites, we used secondary data collection in an effort to understand the industry and company background. We then adapted our basic research and interview questions to match the company profile. Thus most of the interviews were largely unstructured to support our exploration of the relatively undefined nature of the front end of product development.

Table 3.3. Descriptions of Sample Companies.

▼

Business Unit Code	Ownership	Core Businesses	Level of Analysis (Multiple products and/or NPD process)
A	United States	Equipment for publishing industry	NPD process and two specific product projects
B	Japan	OEM for systems devices (for example, printers, PCs, software drivers) and major electronic components	NPD process
C	United States, Germany	Specialized health-care equipment	NPD process
D	United States	Consumer packaged goods	NPD process
E	United States	Pharmaceuticals	NPD process
F	United States	Medical products	NPD process and two specific product projects
G	Japan	Super, mainframe, and midrange computers	NPD process
H	United States	Office equipment	NPD process and four specific product projects
I	Japan	Variety of electronics products from micro devices to printers to notebook computers	NPD process at corporate level and in three separate business units and one specific product project
J	United States, Europe	Durable white goods, such as washers and cooking products	NPD process in two separate business units and three specific product projects
K	Japan	Production technologies and equipment business unit of major electronics company	NPD process

The basic unit of analysis for our cases was the process of the front end of NPD. However, due to access, confidentiality, time, and contrasts, we used several approaches to understand and evaluate the process. As Table 3.3 shows, our interviews took two different forms: (1) a study of individual NPD projects (multiple projects at each company) and (2) an in-depth study of business-unit practices with regard to the process adopted for the front end of NPD. (We included multiple business units at two companies because these business units were in widely different markets or technologies, or because they were perceived to have distinctive front-end NPD practices.)

Acknowledgments

This research was sponsored and supported by the Boston University Manufacturing Roundtable, School of Management, and a research grant from Seiko Epson Corporation, Japan. The authors acknowledge the cooperation of the U.S., Japanese, and European companies that participated. They also thank Professors Jinichiro Nakane and Hiroshi Katayama of Waseda University, Japan, and acknowledge the help of Paul Callaghan, doctoral student at Boston University, in data collection.

NOTES

1. The notion of the fuzzy front end and its importance was first introduced in P. G. Smith and D. G. Reinertsen, *Developing Products in Half the Time* (New York: Van Nostrand Reinhold, 1991). See also A. Khurana and S. R. Rosenthal, "Discovering the Shortcomings in the 'Front-End' of New Product Development: Findings from Cross-Industry Case Studies," Manufacturing Roundtable working paper (Boston: Boston University School of Management, 1996); K. B. Clark and S. C. Wheelwright, *Leading Product Development* (New York: Free Press, 1995); S. R. Rosenthal, *Effective Product Design and Development* (Burr Ridge, Illinois: Irwin, 1992);

A. K. Gupta and D. L. Wilemon, "Accelerating the Development of Technology-Based New Products," *California Management Review,* Winter 1990, *32,* 24–44; and R. G. Cooper and E. J. Kleinschmidt, "New Products: What Separates Winners from Losers?" *Journal of Product Innovation Management,* September 1987, *4,* 169–184.

2. See D. A. Schön, *The Reflective Practitioner: How Professionals Think in Action* (New York: Basic Books, 1983), p. 266.

3. H. K. Bowen, K. B. Clark, C. A. Holloway, and S. C. Wheelwright, "Development Projects: The Engine of Renewal," *Harvard Business Review,* September-October 1994, *72,* 110–120. For a business process view, see T. Davenport, *Process Innovation: Reengineering Work Through Information* (Boston: Harvard Business School Press, 1993), chapter 11.

4. See Cooper and Kleinschmidt, "New Products"; Gupta and Wilemon, "Technology-Based New Products"; Smith and Reinertsen, *Developing Products;* Rosenthal, *Effective Product Design and Development;* and Clark and Wheelwright, *Leading Product Development.* For a study on factors explaining "good" product definition, see G. Bacon, S. Beckman, D. Mowery, and E. Wilson, "Managing Product Definition in High-Technology Industries: A Pilot Study," *California Management Review,* Spring 1994, *36,* 32–56. Of the key factors for new product development success identified by Bacon, Beckman, Mowery, and Wilson, and other researchers, several pertain to front-end issues: product-core competence fit, senior manager responsibility for new product development planning, clear understanding of user needs, explicit description of product concept and definition, careful planning, specifying contingency plans, and resource planning. For purposes of description and understanding, we divide Bacon, Beckman, Mowery, and Wilson's interpretation of product definition into product strategy, product definition, and project definition, primarily because these activities involve different analytical and implementation approaches. See also W. E. Souder, *Managing New Product Innovations* (Lexington, Massachusetts: Lexington Books, 1987); Booz Allen & Hamilton, *New Product Development in the 1980s* (New York: Booz Allen & Hamilton, 1982); and R. Rothwell and others, "Sappho Updated—Project Sappho Phase II," *Research Policy,* 1974, *3*(3), 258–291.

5. We first identified a series of operational problems encountered in new product development and linked them to activities and practices at the front end. For that analysis see Khurana and Rosenthal, "Shortcomings in the 'Front-End.'"

6. Bacon, Beckman, Mowery, and Wilson, "Managing Product Definition"; Gupta and Wilemon, "Technology-Based New Products." While there has been limited research on the front end, researchers who study NPD often include some NPD success factors that pertain to the front end. See, for example, Smith and Reinertsen, *Developing Products;* Rothwell and others, "Sappho Updated"; and R. G. Cooper and E. J. Kleinschmidt, "Determinants of Timeliness in Product Development," *Journal of Product Innovation Management,* November 1994, *11,* 381–396.

7. Roberts and Fusfeld call a set of foundation-type activities "critical functions for enhanced innovation." They portray project-specific activities as a six-stage process starting with preproject activities. See E. B. Roberts and A. R. Fusfeld, "Staffing the Innovative Technology-Based Organization," *Sloan Management Review,* Spring 1981, *22,* 19–34.

8. M. McGrath, *Product Strategy for High-Technology Companies* (Burr Ridge, Illinois: Irwin, 1995).

9. These are the top three levels of the strategic hierarchy presented in McGrath, *Product Strategy.* McGrath describes product strategy in a four-level hierarchy starting with strategic vision and then proceeding to product platform strategy, product line strategy, and, finally, individual projects.

10. Bacon, Beckman, Mowery, and Wilson, "Managing Product Definition."

11. McGrath, *Product Strategy;* and R. G. Cooper and E. J. Kleinschmidt, "New Product Performance: Keys to Success, Profitability, and Cycle Time Reduction," *Journal of Marketing Management,* September 1995, *11,* 315–337.

12. McGrath, *Product Strategy;* Cooper and Kleinschmidt, "New Product Performance"; D. G. Ancona and D. F. Caldwell, "Beyond Boundary Spanning: Managing External Dependence in Product Development Teams," *Journal of High-Technology Management Research,* 1990, *1*(2),

119–135; and D. G. Ancona and D. F. Caldwell, "Bridging the Boundary: External Process and Performance in Organizational Teams," *Administrative Science Quarterly,* December 1992, *37,* 634–665.

13. Selected research on these issues includes K. B. Clark and T. Fujimoto, *Product Development Performance* (Boston: Harvard Business School Press, 1991); K. Imai, I. Nonaka, and H. Takeuchi, "Managing the New Product Development Process: How Japanese Companies Learn and Unlearn," in *The Uneasy Alliance: Managing the Productivity-Technology Dilemma,* R. Hayes, K. Clark, and P. Lorenz, eds. (Boston: Harvard Business School Press, 1985), pp. 337–375; L. Dwyer and R. Mellor, "Organizational Environment, New Product Process Activities, and Project Outcomes," *Journal of Product Innovation Management,* March 1991, *8,* 39–48; and D. Dougherty, "Interpretive Barriers to Successful Product Innovations in Large Firms," *Organization Science,* May 1992, *3,* 179–202.

14. Cooper and Kleinschmidt, "New Product Performance."

15. The creation of product concepts is discussed in C. M. Crawford, *New Products Management,* 3rd ed. (Burr Ridge, Illinois: Irwin, 1991). Customer requirements should drive all product design and development, including the creation of product concepts. There is a growing body of information on how such requirements ought to be obtained and translated into product requirements. One familiar technique for translating customer requirements into product attributes is quality function deployment. See J. R. Hauser and D. Clausing, "The House of Quality," *Harvard Business Review,* May-June 1988, *66,* 63–73; and G. L. Urban and J. R. Hauser, *Design and Marketing of New Products,* 2nd ed. (Upper Saddle River, New Jersey: Prentice Hall, 1993).

16. Bacon, Beckman, Mowery, and Wilson, "Managing Product Definition."

17. Bacon, Beckman, Mowery, and Wilson, "Managing Product Definition"; and K. M. Eisenhardt and B. Tabrizi, "Accelerating Adaptive Processes: Product Innovation in the Global Computer Industry," *Administrative Science Quarterly,* March 1995, *40,* 84–110.

18. R. H. Hayes, S. C. Wheelwright, and K. B. Clark, *Dynamic Manufacturing* (New York: Free Press, 1988); Dwyer and Mellor, "Organizational Environment"; and R. Cooper, "Third-Generation New

Product Processes," *Journal of Product Innovation Management,* January 1994, *11,* 3–14.

19. See Rosenthal, *Effective Product Design and Development;* Smith and Reinertsen, *Developing Products;* Cooper, "Third-Generation New Product Processes"; and R. G. Cooper, "Stage-Gate Systems: A New Tool for Managing New Products," *Business Horizons,* May-June 1990, *33,* 44–54.

20. Bacon, Beckman, Mowery, and Wilson, "Managing Product Definition"; and Cooper and Kleinschmidt, "New Product Performance."

21. For a description of phase review systems, see Cooper, "Stage-Gate Systems"; and Rosenthal, *Effective Product Design and Development,* chapter 2. See also M. E. McGrath, M. T. Anthony, and A. R. Shapiro, *Product Development Success Through Product and Cycle-Time Excellence* (Boston: Butterworth-Heinemann, 1992).

22. An alternative approach that is emerging in the best companies is based on platform planning and emphasizes that product opportunities are related to the development of product platforms. See McGrath, *Product Strategy;* and M. H. Meyer, P. Tertzakian, and J. M. Utterback, "Metrics for Managing Research and Development," working paper 3817 (Cambridge, Massachusetts: MIT Sloan School of Management, 1995).

23. S. C. Wheelwright and K. B. Clark, *Revolutionizing Product Development* (New York: Free Press, 1992). Several product development researchers have raised the issue of roles, for example, project managers (Wheelwright and Clark, *Revolutionizing Product Development*), and core team and executive reviews (McGrath, Anthony, and Shapiro, *Product Development Success*). However, our interest is in looking at how these roles influence the front end of NPD and what challenges arise as a result of the interactions among these roles.

24. In some companies that do platform planning in a serious way, one can visualize the development of a platform concept or architecture also as a front-end deliverable.

25. Meyer, Tertzakian, and Utterback, "Metrics."

26. Wheelwright and Clark, *Revolutionizing Product Development.*

27. Ancona and Caldwell, "Beyond Boundary Spanning"; and Ancona and Caldwell, "Bridging the Boundary."

28. Clark and Fujimoto suggest that in such cases, there is often "little or no attention to integrating a clear sense of customer expectations into the work of the product development organization as a whole." See K. B. Clark and T. Fujimoto, "The Power of Product Integrity," *Harvard Business Review,* November-December 1990, *68,* 107–118.

29. Though not all platforms or product lines can plan for multiple releases at frequent intervals, proactive planning of product releases a few years ahead is desirable. For example, Sony does not necessarily plan multiple releases but achieves the same objective by freezing the product design early on. It then begins work on the next product model concurrently to incorporate changes in customer needs or technology. See Meyer, Tertzakian, and Utterback, "Metrics"; McGrath, *Product Strategy;* S. Sanderson-Walsh and M. Uzumeri, "Managing Product Families: The Case of the Sony Walkman," *Research Policy,* September 1995, *24,* 761–782; and P. R. Nayak and J. P. Deschamps, *Product Juggernauts* (Boston: Harvard Business School Press, 1995).

30. See, for example, R. R. Kamath and J. K. Liker, "A Second Look at Japanese Product Development," *Harvard Business Review,* November-December 1994, *72,* 154–170.

31. K. A. Howard, "Postponement of Packaging and Product Differentiation Lowers Logistics Costs," in *Globalization of Technology, Manufacturing, and Service Operations,* A. K. Chakravarty, ed., symposium proceedings (New Orleans: Goldring Institute, A. B. Freeman School of Business, Tulane University, January 7–8, 1994).

32. Apparently, such redundancy is at the heart of Toyota's development success. See A. Ward, J. K. Liker, J. J. Cristiano, and D. K. Sobek II, "The Second Toyota Paradox: How Delaying Decisions Can Make Better Cars Faster," *Sloan Management Review,* Spring 1995, *36,* 43–61. In the context of design, simultaneously working on multiple subsystem/component alternatives generally leads to a faster product development cycle. We suggest that the same is true for planned and anticipated redundancy in the face of technological or other risks.

33. Other interrelationships that have been mentioned in previous research, for example, Bacon, Beckman, Mowery, and Wilson, "Managing Product Definition," and used at several case study sites

include the need for strategic alignment between product development efforts and overall business strategy, the direct links between product definition and project planning, the close association of project planning and staffing policies, and the need to modify the roles and responsibilities of key organizational members as a function of project complexity and size.

34. P. Lawrence and J. Lorsch, *Organizations and Environments* (Burr Ridge, Illinois: Irwin, 1969); and Clark and Fujimoto, *Product Development Performance*.

35. D. Dougherty and E. H. Bowman, "The Effects of Organizational Downsizing on Product Innovation," *California Management Review,* Summer 1995, 37, 28–44.

36. Ward, Liker, Cristiano, and Sobek, "Second Toyota Paradox"; and M. Iansiti, "Shooting the Rapids," *California Management Review,* Fall 1995, 38, 1–22.

37. This notion of balance also reflects our agreement with an article on balancing instinctive and fully analytical decision making. See A. Langley, "Between 'Paralysis by Analysis' and 'Extinction by Instinct,'" *Sloan Management Review,* Spring 1995, 36, 63–76.

38. In the "preemergent" stage, a company has no formal front end, nor does it perceive the need for one; none of the companies we studied fell into this category. This situation is common either in start-up companies in which a few principals make product development decisions informally or in business units where structured product innovation is not yet the basis for competition. NPD activities for such organizations are tightly integrated, but often a few senior managers do this tacitly.

39. See, for example, S. L. Goldman, R. N. Nagel, and K. Preiss, *Agile Competitors and Virtual Organizations: Strategies for Enriching the Customer* (New York: Van Nostrand Reinhold, 1995).

40. See Meyer, Tertzakian, and Utterback, "Metrics"; McGrath, *Product Strategy;* and Sanderson-Walsh and Uzumeri, "Managing Product Families." For a proposed new model of the stage gate system, see Cooper, "Third-Generation New Product Processes."

41. A full description of why a company should adopt more than one front-end solution, and what these solutions might look like, is

beyond our scope. While we do not yet have a full map of "compatible contexts," some of the contingencies we have discovered are radicalness of product, maturity of industry, experience of the business unit with formal front-end processes, small or large firm, and entrepreneurial or conservative firm.

42. In addition to the eleven cases directly involved in this research, we also draw on and cite examples from prior knowledge of several cases of NPD projects that the second author researched in 1989 to 1991. See S. R. Rosenthal, *Effective Product Design and Development* (Burr Ridge, Illinois: Irwin, 1992).

43. B. Glaser and A. Strauss, *The Discovery of Grounded Theory: Strategies for Qualitative Research* (Hawthorne, New York: Aldine de Gruyter, 1967); and K. M. Eisenhardt, "Building Theory from Case Research," *Academy of Management Review,* 1989, *14*(4), 532–550.

CHAPTER FOUR

The Product Family and the Dynamics of Core Capability

MARC H. MEYER
JAMES M. UTTERBACK

W hy is it that some firms introduce distinctive new products time and time again, when so many other firms are far less able to generate new products? More specifically, some firms, while strong in product design, fail to gain commercial reward, but their more successful counterparts exhibit the right mix of capabilities in implementation, manufacturing, and distribution as well as product design. Much current management thought addresses developing single products as rapidly as possible. Product development when seen from this perspective has two essential problems: redundancy of both technical and marketing effort and lack of long-term consistency and focus. We will argue for a broader approach to managing new products.

Concentrating at the level of the product family, and more specifically on the development and sharing of key components and assets within a product family, is the vital issue. The benefit of examining elements shared by products within a family is that firms will

First published in the Spring 1993 issue of *MIT Sloan Management Review.*

then develop the foundation for a range of individual product variations. At an even broader level, one can examine relationships between product families themselves to achieve even greater commonality in both technologies and marketing. For an existing product family, renewal is achieved by integrating the best components in new structures or proprietary designs to better serve evolving customer needs. Integration improves all products within the family. Diversification can be achieved by building on and extending capabilities to build the foundations of new but related product families. For example, Hewlett-Packard built on a foundation of core capabilities in scientific instruments to create families of computers and peripherals, and also to enter into the medical systems business. Similarly, Canon built on its copier and facsimile machine platforms to create laser printer and scanner businesses.

Figure 4.1 portrays a set of products and their relationships over time that we believe is conducive to sustained success. Each generation of a product family has a platform used as the foundation for specific products targeted at different or complementary market applications ("platform development family A," products 1 through 4). Successive generations refresh older platforms with improved designs and technologies ("new-generation platform family A," products 1 through 6). Starting work on the next product platform while completing specific products based on the current platform helps the company maintain product leadership. In terms of creating new businesses, new product families branch from existing ones, expanding on their technical skills, market knowledge, and manufacturing capabilities ("platform development family B"). Thus the development of new technologies is focused. Market extensions are related. High levels of customer recognition are the cumulative effect of a robust product family. These factors all contribute to growth.

Deliberately building product families rather than single products requires management of a firm's core capabilities.[1] Quinn, Doorley, and Paquette view the firm as an intellectual holding company in which products and services are the application of the firm's

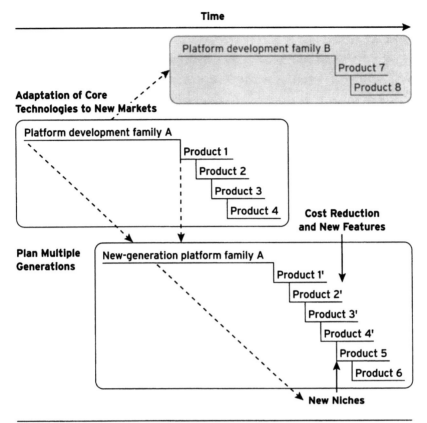

Figure 4.1. The Product Family Approach to New Product Development.

knowledge assets. By targeting and focusing on the best of these assets, a firm can dominate its rivals.[2] Core capabilities cannot be divorced or viewed separately from the actual products that a company makes and sells on a daily basis. Core capabilities are the basis of products. Nondistinctive capabilities lead to nondistinctive products. Strong capabilities lead to strong product families because these capabilities are embodied in the people and assets applied to building a company's new products.

Our purpose in this chapter is to synthesize the two central concepts of the product family and core capabilities. Many managers with whom we have worked in the past have expressed a strong desire to understand better the evolution of their product families and leverage achieved from underlying architectures and designs. Many have also wanted to identify more clearly the core capabilities of their organizations and how these capabilities have also changed over time. To address both needs, we have developed a method to map product families and assess their embodied core capabilities. We will apply this method to three product families developed by a large corporation for the electronic imaging market and then use that application to more broadly consider how firms may better manage the development of new products.

DEFINING THE PRODUCT FAMILY

What is a product family? What are those characteristics and properties shared by and therefore common to a series of related products grouped into a family?

The term *product platform* was used earlier in its common meaning: encompassing the design and components shared by a set of products. A robust platform is the heart of a successful product family, serving as the foundation for a series of closely related products. For example, Chrysler has just released three new lines of cars, the Chrysler Concorde, Eagle Vision, and Dodge Intrepid, based on a common platform in which all share the same basic frame, suspension, and drive train. New products are refinements or extensions of the platform. For example, Chrysler's forthcoming upscale New Yorker model will be based on a longer version of the new platform.

We will call products that share a common platform but have specific features and functionality required by different sets of customers a product family. A product family typically addresses a market *segment,* while specific products or groups of products within the family target *niches* within that segment. The commonality of technologies and markets leads to efficiency and effectiveness in manufacturing, distribution, and service, where the firm tailors each general resource or capability to the needs of specific customer groups.

The technology embodied in a product family has two key parts: the design and the implementation of the design. Design groups dedicated to new product platform research create basic designs, standard components, and norms for subsystem integration. Implementation teams create different product models, integrating component technologies to achieve specific product goals.[3, 4]

To illustrate the ideas of the product family, platforms, and extensions of platforms as products, consider Sony's Walkman. Sanderson and Uzumeri catalogued all products introduced in the portable tape cassette segment.[5] Sony introduced more than 160 variations of the Walkman between 1980 and 1990. These products were based on a platform that Sony refreshed with four major technical innovations.[6] The company combined these major innovations with incremental improvements to achieve better functionality and quality, while lowering production costs. Sony's trademark is virtually synonymous with the portable cassette player.

Black & Decker's power tool business pursued a deliberate strategy to share major elements of product platforms across different product families.[7] In 1970 the company had hundreds of products. The products used more than thirty different motors, sixty different motor housings, and dozens of different operating controls. Further, each of the hundreds of power tool products had its own unique armature. Management determined that in order to remain competitive, it would have to decrease its cost of goods sold by about a third in the coming decade. Black & Decker created a plan to design and manufacture product families based on shared components and modules. Nearly $20 million was allocated to the effort. First, the company developed a hexagonal, copper-wire-wrapped motor field with standard electrical plug-in connections that would serve all its power tools.[8] Engineers designed standard motor housings and controls as well as a more standardized, adhesive-bonded armature. The company tackled each product family in succession (drills, jigsaws, sanders, and so on). The results were dramatic: product costs were reduced by 50 percent, market share rose from 20 percent to a dominant share, and the number of competitors declined from more than twenty to three. The case also shows the extent to which product families can share technical designs and components, an understanding of market requirements, and production capabilities.

MAPPING PRODUCT FAMILIES

Individual products are therefore the offspring of product platforms that are enhanced over time. Product families and their successive platforms are themselves the applied result of a firm's underlying core capabilities. In well-managed firms such core capabilities tend to be of much longer duration and broader scope than single product families or individual products.

We believe that the product family can be used as a basis for assessing the dynamics of a firm's core capabilities—in other words, how these capabilities grow, decline, and integrate with one another over extended periods of time. The first step is to *map* the chronology of a product family. The following pages will describe our method as we applied it to three product families in a large corporation engaged in the electronic imaging business.

Figure 4.2 shows a product family map. The general application of the products shown has been to reproduce computer screen images onto various presentation media. We refer to them as a *horizontal market* application in that they are general-purpose solutions for different customer groups in different industries that nonetheless have a common need.

In order to map this product family, we assembled a study group of ten people, all actively involved in the family development for many years and representing business, technology, and marketing functions. Producing the map required several intensive meetings. The top half of Figure 4.2 is the summary, and the bottom half the detail, showing the market introduction and termination date for each product. The product family is represented in four hierarchical levels:[9]

▼ The product *family* itself. Figure 4.2 shows one product family.

▼ *Platforms with a family* are encapsulated in large rectangles in the top half of Figure 4.2. There were four basic product platforms in that family: two platforms generated internally (one analog, the other digital) and two acquired from vendors as private-labeled products ("OEM initiatives").

▼ *Product extensions* are denoted by oval forms starting at the beginning of the research and ending with the cessation of active marketing of platform-based products. "Skunk works" projects, having no commercial product offspring, can be the first iteration of a product platform and provide important technological and market knowledge for subsequent platform extensions. The first product platform in Figure 4.2 has had two successive platform extensions.

▼ Specific *products* (numbered here to disguise real product names) are placed at and numbered in order of their market introduction dates and, in the bottom half of the figure, extend out to the date of marketing termination.

Product family maps convey a sense of continuity or the lack thereof in product development. For example, in Figure 4.2 there have essentially been three overlapping streams of development: analog-architecture products, products resold from other vendors (called "OEM initiatives"), and the current digital-architecture products. All have been carried forward by different groups in the company. The original development team chose not to abandon its initial

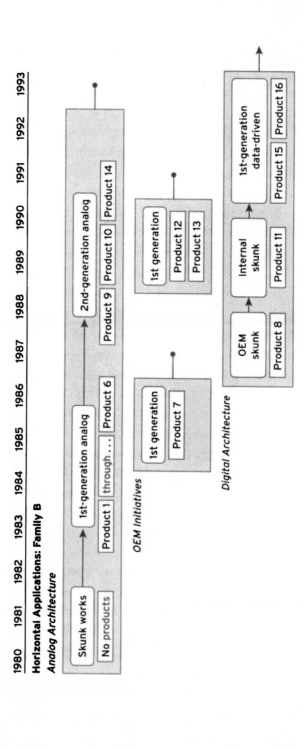

Horizontal Applications: Family B

Analog Architecture

1980 1981 1982 1983 1984 1985 1986 1987 1988 1989 1990 1991 1992 1993

Skunk works
No products

1st-generation analog
Product 1 | through... | Product 6

2nd-generation analog
Product 9 | Product 10 | Product 14

OEM Initiatives

1st generation
Product 7

1st generation
Product 12
Product 13

Digital Architecture

OEM skunk
Product 8

Internal skunk
Product 11

1st-generation data-driven
Product 15 | Product 16

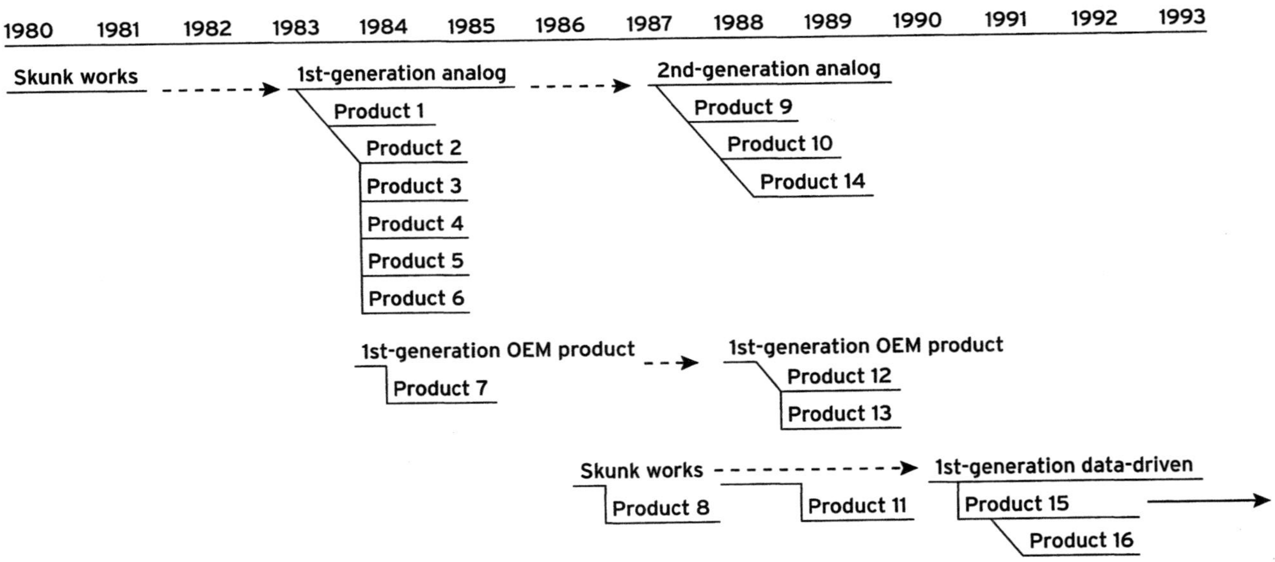

Figure 4.2. Product Family Map—Two Alternate Representations.

analog platform in favor of the newer digital platforms being introduced by competitors. Its products became obsolete. Seeing that this was happening, management tried to shortcut its lack of effective products with two private-label initiatives that were early digital systems. Meanwhile, two product champions resurrected the company's internal technical initiative by recruiting engineers from corporate research to create a new digital platform. The result, after four years of determined technical effort and marketing development, has been the delivery of what many would call world-class products.

Figure 4.3 includes the product family map already described as well as maps for two other, related businesses in the same company that addressed different areas of electronic imaging. Family A is a turnkey system made for a specific industrial vertical market. It is sold primarily through the company's own direct sales force and requires systems integration at the customer's site. Family B contains the horizontal electronic imaging applications already described. The company sells these products through distribution channels. Family C consists of peripherals and components sold through a number of different channels; they have been aimed at both industrial and consumer market segments. Management selected these three families for us to study because they represented different points along the spectrum from making components to building turnkey systems and therefore provided a good test of mapping product families and assessing core capabilities.

Assessing Core Capability

The product family idea serves as a basis for assessing the evolution of a firm's core capabilities. Figure 4.4 presents a detailed core capability assessment for family B. Figure 4.5 represents a summarization of that detail. We generated similar charts for the other two families. The charts have four basic parts:

▼ The product family map as a legend is plotted against time in both charts. Key product events serve as anchors for subsequent data gathering and analysis.[10]

▼ In Figure 4.4 the product family team's strengths are assessed in relation to existing competition for specific core capabilities within four basic dimensions: product technology, understanding of customer needs as reflected by products sold at that time, distribution, and manufacturing.[11] The solid line running across the measurement strips is a mean of responses from team members, the details of which will be described shortly.

▼ Figure 4.5 summarizes the means for responses for the core capabilities within the four basic dimensions.

▼ Figure 4.5 also shows a final summary of core capability strength as embodied within the product family.

All four parts show the ebb and flow of core capabilities over time for the product family.

The process of gathering data started with a group meeting of the product family team members.[12] At this initial meeting, the team defined the product families, groups, generations, and specific products under a product scope established earlier by the study's executive sponsors. This process required several iterations, using recollections of product histories, and archived project documents to create product maps. We also noted key products events, some made by the company itself and others by its competitors. These served as anchors for gathering information and then presenting it.

The study team was then reconvened in a second series of meetings to identify the general product technologies, the major customer segments, the distribution channels used over time, and the key manufacturing processes required for the product.[13] These are the specific core capabilities embodied in a product family and constitute the vertical legend running down the left side of Figure 4.4.

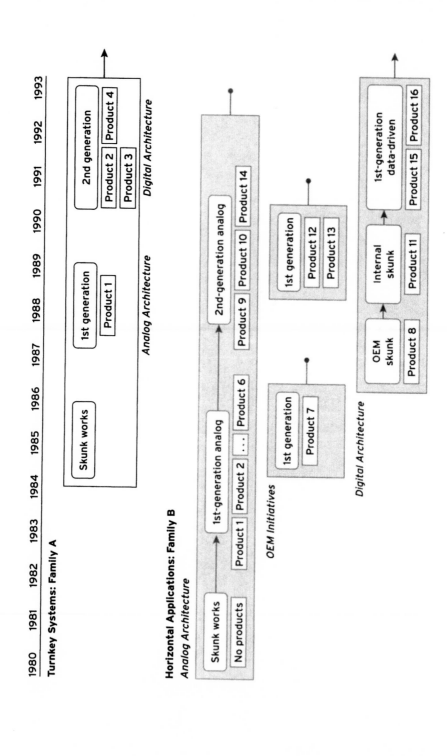

1980 1981 1982 1983 1984 1985 1986 1987 1988 1989 1990 1991 1992 1993

Turnkey Systems: Family A

Skunk works	1st generation	2nd generation
Product 1	Product 2
	Product 3
	Product 4

Analog Architecture — *Digital Architecture*

Horizontal Applications: Family B

Analog Architecture

| Skunk works | 1st-generation analog | 2nd-generation analog |
| No products | Product 1 | Product 2 | ... | Product 6 | Product 9 | Product 10 | Product 14 |

OEM Initiatives

1st generation	1st generation
Product 7	Product 12
	Product 13

Digital Architecture

OEM skunk	Internal skunk	1st-generation data-driven
Product 8	Product 11	Product 15
		Product 16

Peripherals: Family C
Analog Architecture

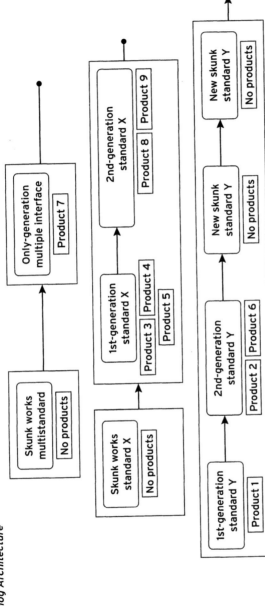

Figure 4.3. Three Product Family Maps.

Family B

Analog Architecture

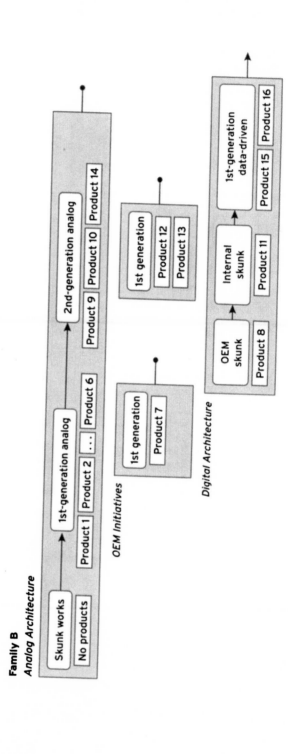

OEM Initiatives

Digital Architecture

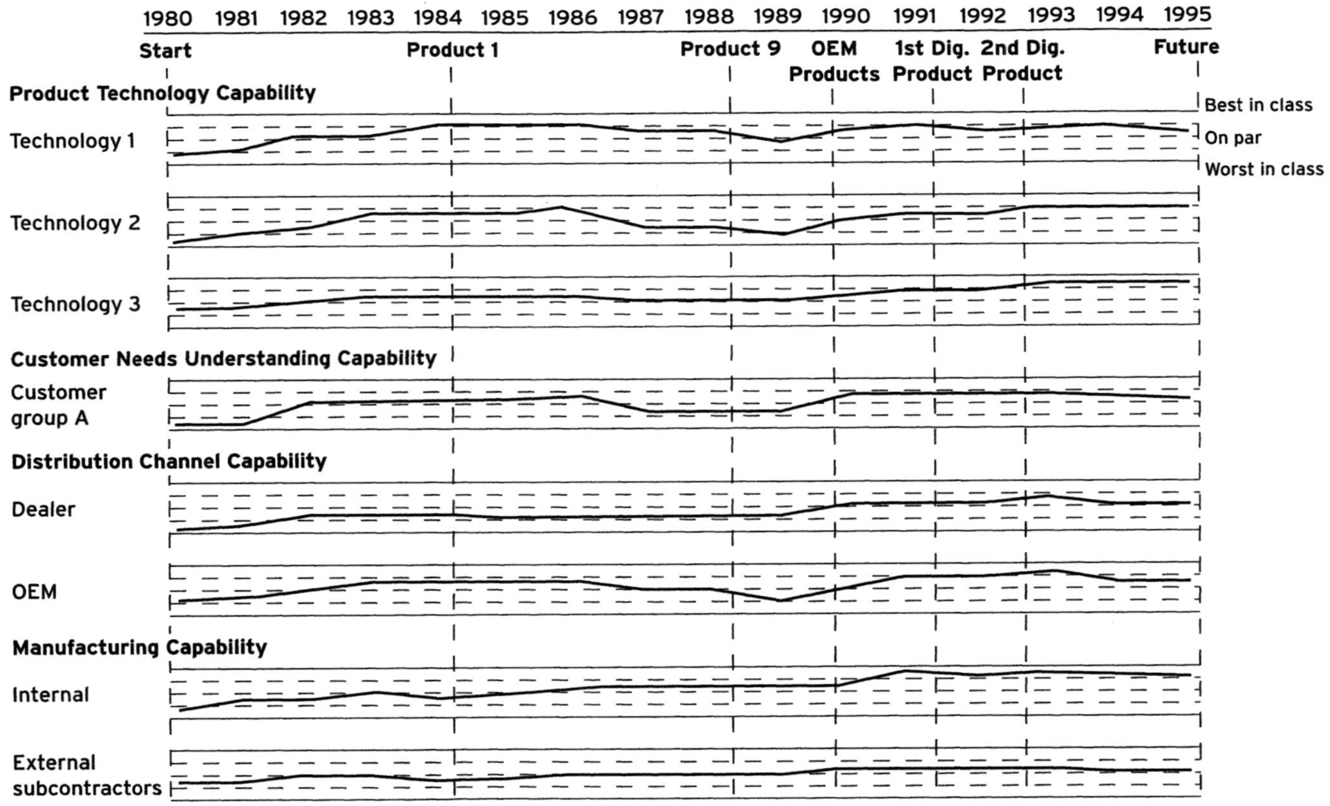

Figure 4.4. Core Capability Assessment for Family B.

Family B
Analog Architecture

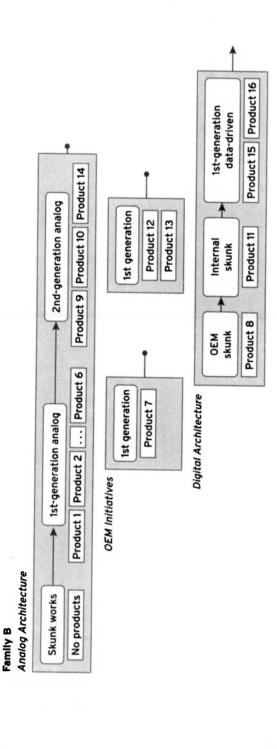

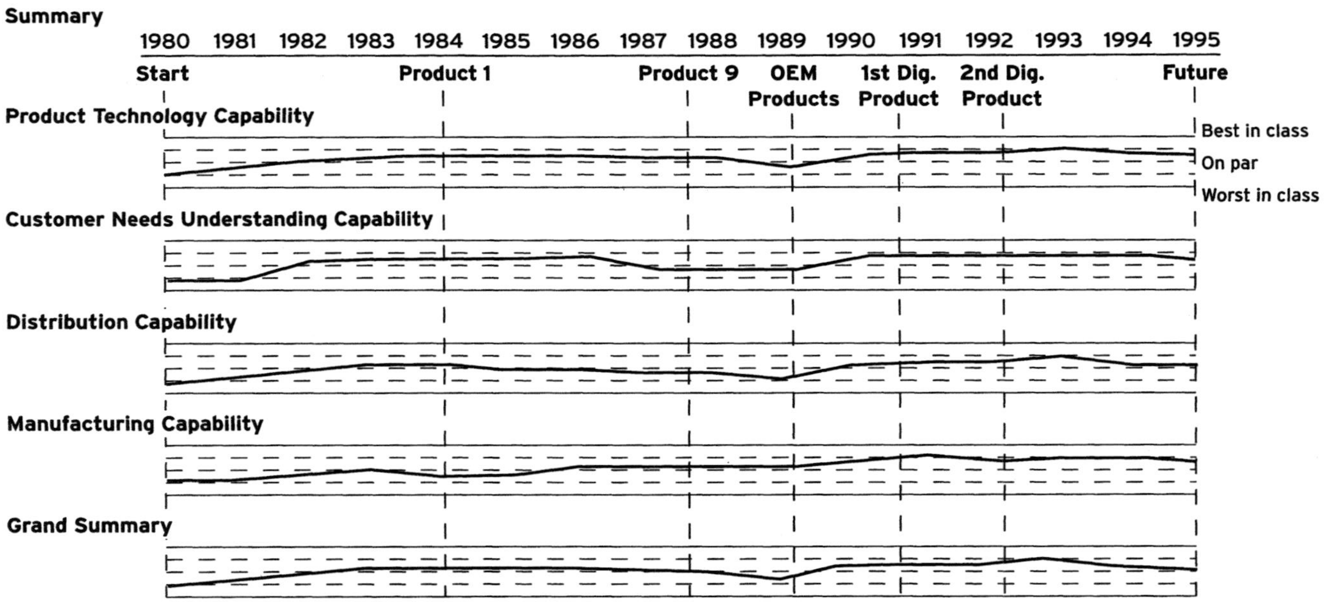

Summary

	1980	1981	1982	1983	1984	1985	1986	1987	1988	1989	1990	1991	1992	1993	1994	1995	Future
	Start				Product 1				Product 9	OEM Products	1st Dig. Product		2nd Dig. Product				

Product Technology Capability

Customer Needs Understanding Capability

Distribution Capability

Manufacturing Capability

Grand Summary

Best in class

On par

Worst in class

Figure 4.5. Summary Core Capability Assessment for Family B.

Our model posits that *generic* core capabilities in any product family exist in product technology, market understanding, and so on; the team defines the specific core capabilities within each of these areas. For example, the respondents who provided data for family B developed a consensus that three basic technical capabilities were central to their products. These technologies were higher-level groupings of more numerous individual technologies. Participants must determine the appropriate level of grouping using their understanding of the technologies employed in a product family. Examples of technological core capability categories from this company and others where we have applied the method include "PC graphics hardware," "signal processing" or "circuit packaging" or "networked computing," and "applications software development." Since the purpose of the study is to facilitate *managerial* analysis and action, too much detail will obfuscate major trends in the past and a firm's needs in the future.

Figure 4.4 also shows that family B had one major industrial customer group. The company sold the products through independent dealers and original equipment manufacturers. The team felt most comfortable combining specific manufacturing processes into one "internal manufacturing" core capability, and relationship management with suppliers and manufacturing subcontractors into an "external subcontractors" capability.[14]

We produced blank survey forms for each product family. These forms appeared exactly as shown in Figure 4.4 but with the measurement strips left empty for respondents to complete. Each measurement strip has five levels. These levels represent the degree of capability (from best in class to worst in class) *relative to competitors at that time,* for each of the years in the product family's history as perceived by respondents.[15] This assessment method can be further anchored by having participants identify competitors that at different points in time represented "best in class" or close to it for each area of core capability. Competitors' names are simply inserted at the appropriate point along each capability measurement strip. (We could not include the names of best-in-class competitors for family B in Figure 4.4 and still keep the case adequately disguised.)

Measurement strips can be extended into the future to learn a team's expectations. In fact, in other firms where we have applied the method, managers have included new areas of core capability that a product family will require in the future or, in other words, that appear as measurement strips starting in 1994 or 1995.

Respondents then completed the survey forms, using the same response scale for all core capabilities. We instructed them to indicate levels of strength relative to existing competitors for capabilities for only those years when they had worked on the product family. We also asked respondents to assess capability strength for the key product anchor points and then fill in the intervening years for which they had knowledge. Figure 4.4 shows average responses.[16]

Figure 4.5 summarizes the company's capabilities with unweighted means.[17] The bottom of Figure 4.5 shows a grand average of these capabilities.

Figure 4.6 shows the core capability assessments for all three product families in the study. We use the width of line and shading to represent levels of strength in core capability, so the reader can more quickly and clearly surmise meaning. The core capability embodied in family A has gradually increased over the years to a moderate level of strength. Family B experienced strong initial strengthening, then a strong decline, and, more recently, an even stronger rebound in its embodied core capabilities. The company has yet to build significant core capability in family C.

This method for identifying and assessing core capabilities is flexible. As already noted, each firm will identify those areas of core capability most important for each product family studied. Further, while the managers in families A, B, and C chose to treat each area of core capability as equal in importance, other companies may wish to assign different weights to different capabilities for computing averages. These weights can be adjusted to accommodate changes

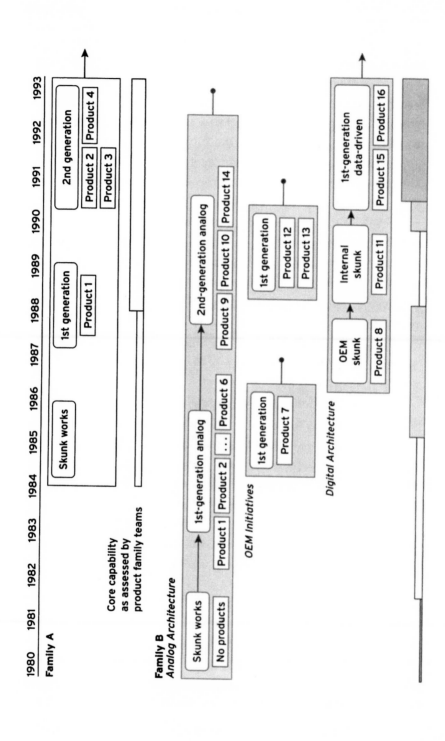

Family C
Analog Architectures

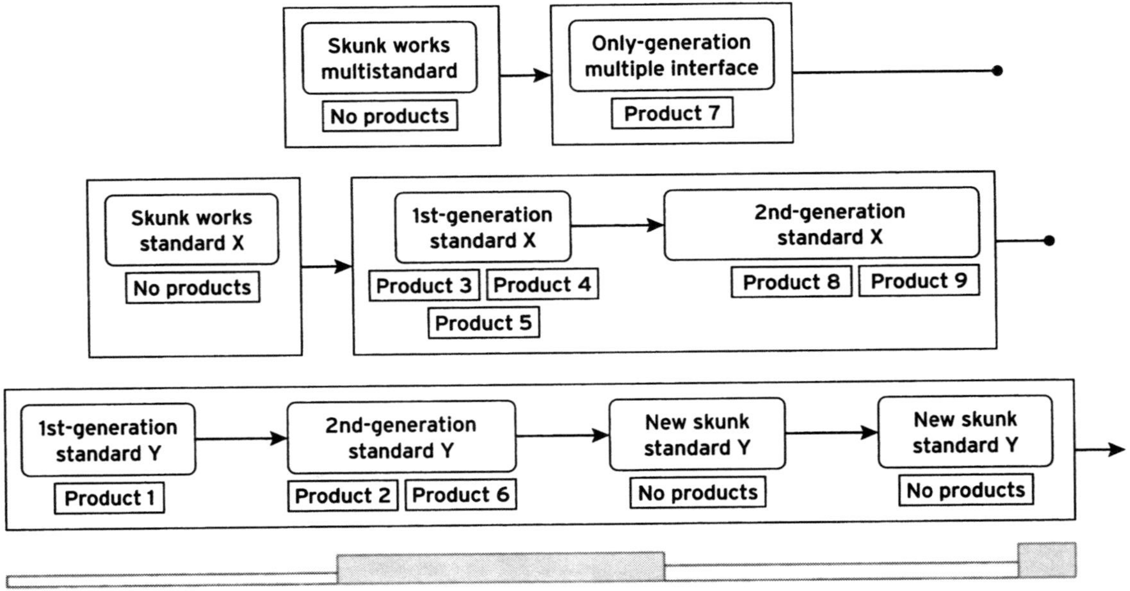

Skunk works multistandard
No products
Only-generation multiple interface
Product 7
Skunk works standard X
No products
1st-generation standard X
Product 3
Product 4
Product 5
2nd-generation standard X
Product 8
Product 9
1st-generation standard Y
Product 1
2nd-generation standard Y
Product 2
Product 6
New skunk standard Y
No products
New skunk standard Y
No products

Figure 4.6. Core Capability Assessments for Three Product Families.

in the relative importance of core capabilities over time. Further, we have used the same survey forms with long-term customers, which provides a way to validate a team's self-assessments and to gain new perspectives on benchmarking its competencies.

CORE CAPABILITIES AND PERFORMANCE

Higher levels of core capability should be associated with sustained success, be it in terms of product development effectiveness, financial performance, or learning and employee satisfaction.[18]

We asked divisional management of the sponsoring company to provide their assessment of the *success of the product family over its history relative to other new business developments undertaken by the company at that time.* Using a scale representing levels of performance, six senior vice presidents completed a measurement strip chart for each product family, basing their assessments on financial return.[19] We asked them to assess product families only for those years in which they had actively monitored and otherwise participated in the management of the product family. We plotted an average of these responses in Figure 4.7.[20]

Data for core capabilities and performance are compared in Figure 4.8, using width of line and shading to convey degree. Higher levels of core capability have tended to precede and then coincide with higher levels of performance. For example, family B gained moderate levels of core capability in 1985, and better performance came in 1987. The obsolete analog platform in family B for the two-year period between 1987 and 1989 did not significantly depress performance because customers were not quick to abandon the familiar product. However, participants indicated that the new digital platform arrived just in time in 1990. By 1991 the product family achieved very high levels of performance. Family A achieved moderate levels of overall core capability in 1988; better performance followed in 1989. Family C's levels of embodied core capability and performance have also been closely matched, that is, poor, over the course of ten years. The history of these three product families appears to support a cause-and-effect relationship between core capability and performance.[21]

Achieving high levels of capability can be expected to have less impact in declining markets. We have completed a similar analysis for an electronic capital equipment company where, despite continuously growing core capability in its traditional mainstream product line, declining market conditions (slower growth and more competitors) have nonetheless yielded poorer performance relative to prior years. This company must find new market applications for its core technologies.

Market dynamics temper the relationship between core capability and performance. We asked each family study team to indicate changes in the rate of market growth,[22] the level of competition,[23] and the effective product life cycle for their product families.[24] Figure 4.9 (pp. 116–117) shows the results for family B. For all three product families, market growth rates in target markets are now moderate to fast, and competition has intensified. Product life cycles have also shortened.

USING CORE CAPABILITY ASSESSMENT TO IMPROVE A PRODUCT FAMILY

A company must continue to invest in renewing product platforms, particularly for markets with accelerating rates of product introduction and competitive intensity. For example, if management does not continue to invest to renew family B's platform, the "dip" experienced before will probably occur again.

How is management to choose which requests to satisfy fully or whether the resources requested are indeed sufficient? Many, if not most, firms allocate resources by individual product effort on an annual basis. Further, allocation requests tend to be summarized

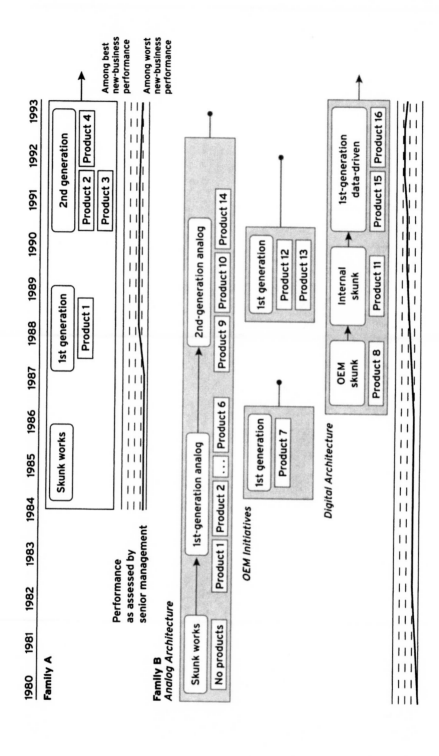

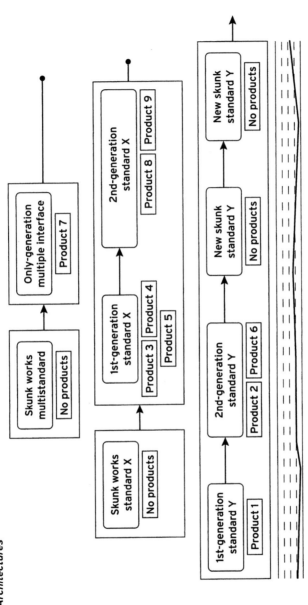

Family C
Analog Architectures

Figure 4.7. Performance Assessments for Three Product Families.

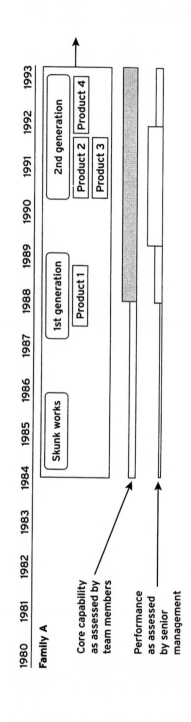

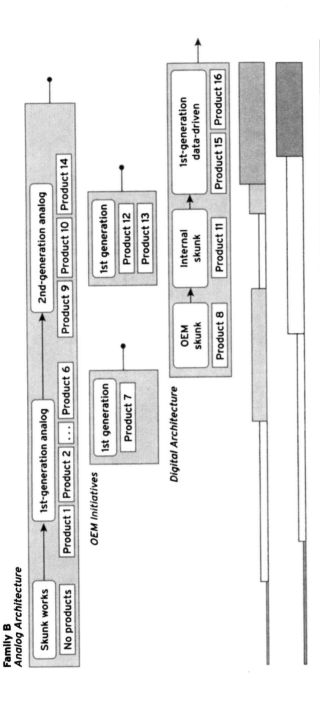

Figure 4.8. Core Capability and Performance for Three Product Families.

(continued)

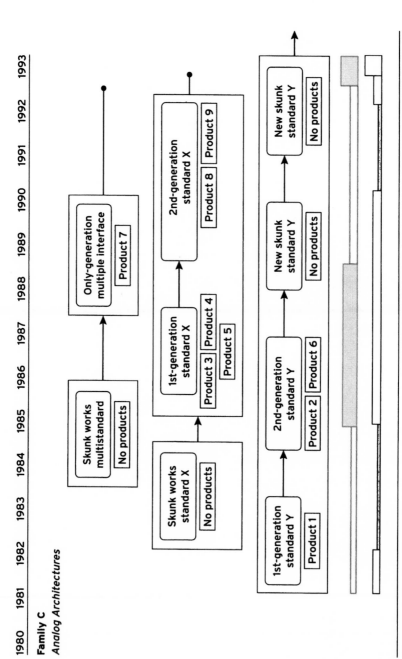

Figure 4.8. Continued.

by functional area (R&D versus marketing versus manufacturing). Single-product funding impedes the development of a core for product families and therefore inhibits creation of the type of leverage that we have discussed throughout this chapter.

What does a firm need to do to achieve best-in-class status in technology, market knowledge, distribution, manufacturing, and service? Product family maps combined with core capability assessment may be useful in this regard.

For example, Figure 4.10 (p. 118) shows the core capability assessments for product technologies in family A. While the first two technologies have risen above the industry average, the third (applications software development) continues to be well below par. The company must address this area of weakness to be more successful. Specific areas of need in the other product families also emerged from these more detailed core capability assessment charts.

EXPLAINING THE EBB AND FLOW OF CORE CAPABILITIES

Core capabilities are inherently dynamic. They result from the efforts of individuals and are thus affected by the organization of teams, the selection of products and markets, and the nature and quality of those markets. Once gained, competence can be readily lost. Ill-considered managerial policies and approaches can destroy hard-won capabilities, impede learning, hurt the effectiveness of product development, and ultimately, damage the profitability of the company. Our work suggests this and illustrates what managers intuitively know and feel.

Four fundamental inhibitors of core capability creation have emerged as common themes in our work.

Lack of Patience
Using unrealistic, short time horizons for the development of new businesses invariably leads promising technical and marketing

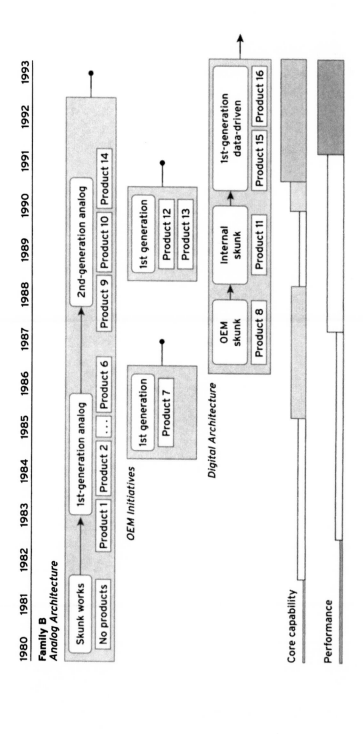

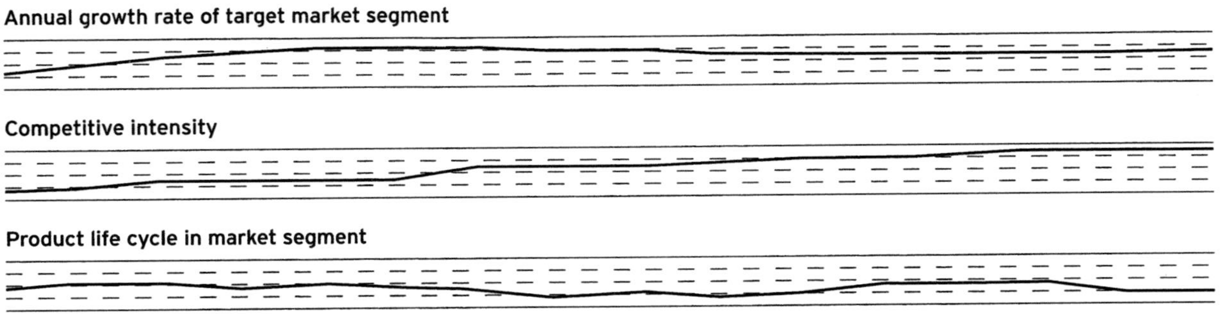

Annual growth rate of target market segment

Competitive intensity

Product life cycle in market segment

Figure 4.9. Core Capability, Performance, and Market Assessments for Family B.

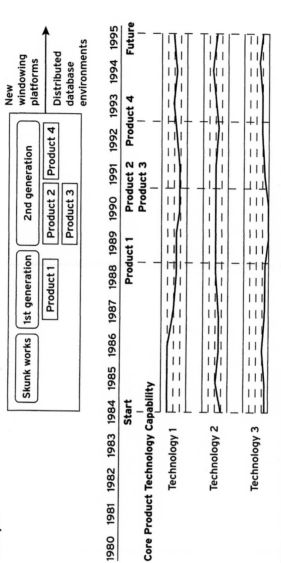

Figure 4.10. Identifying Problems in Family A's Product Technology Capabilities.

development efforts to be killed before capability, visible on the horizon, is realized and exploited. How long should it take to achieve excellence in the relevant core capabilities in a new area?

A visual presentation of a product family powerfully conveys the nature of the embodied core capabilities, how painstakingly they may be gained, and how quickly lost. Of the three product families studied, the company achieved competitive levels of capability in only one family, and in that case, only after approximately ten years. This experience is by no means atypical. Other studies have produced time ranges from seven to twenty years.[25]

Failure to Adopt Innovations and New Architecture

Technological discontinuities can quickly make a company's products obsolescent.[26] Radical technological innovation in an industry can make any given capability irrelevant. In fact, companies often get trapped in their earlier successes.[27] Thomas Edison dramatically improved the efficiency and reliability of carbon filaments in lightbulbs when his business was attacked by more efficient but expensive metal filaments. Later he was forced to spend large sums to license metal filament technology from these same competitors to replace his own carbon filament capability and create a new lightbulb platform for his company. Other firms have consistently looked forward. In workstations, for example, Sun Microsystems abandoned more quickly than its competitors complex instruction set processing (CISC) to embrace a simpler, more elegant, reduced instruction (RISC) architecture.

Planned renewal of product platforms combined with sustained development of core capabilities is a defense against technological surprises and obsolescence. We have observed that early planning and development of new product platforms must also be coupled with high levels of modularity in designs and emphasis on layering technologies within an overall product architecture. Modularity in designs allows a firm to more readily focus on critical areas of proprietary technology to advance internally. Modularity also allows a firm to upgrade components with newer and better variations from suppliers.

Coasting on Success

Management can dissipate the firm's capabilities by failing to invest in product and manufacturing technology required to maintain competitive distinctiveness. Members of our study groups called this the "coast mentality." Once a product family reaches high levels of success, management allocates only maintenance-level resources and shifts resources to other product families in earlier stages of development. Maintenance is a strategy prone to disaster.

The coast mentality is probably more a result of a portfolio management approach to new product development than anything else: diversify, spread risk, and invest by stage of maturity. Portfolio management leads large corporations to have too many irons in the fire. Rather than produce many successful products, the portfolio approach yields many mediocre products.[28] Strategic focus and aggressive reinvestment are essential to rapidly changing markets with high levels of technological change.

Breaking Up Design Teams

The staffing of business and technical teams has a strong bearing on the development of core capabilities. Surely core capabilities cannot be developed or maintained if key individuals do not have the chance to work with one another in a concentrated way for extended periods of time. In many companies, while management brings multifunctional "hit teams" together to design and complete a product, once that product is finished, management disbands the team and assigns its personnel to other high-priority product efforts.

Perhaps there is another way. Is it possible for firms to keep the heart of a multifunctional design team together for at least a generation of a product family? Momentum would then build behind a product platform that meets customers' needs and is amenable to effective manufacturing and sales. At the same time, management can rotate people into the development effort more frequently to implement the product platform and create specific variations using the latest skills and techniques.

MANAGING TOWARD A BETTER FUTURE

Companies can manage toward a better future by thinking in terms of the product family, product platforms, and the policies required to enrich core capabilities. Management must fashion planning horizons and financial commitments toward periods longer than current practice in many companies. Management must also have multifunctional design teams stay together longer than current practice. The more diverse a corporation's various businesses, the greater will be the pressure not *to do these things*.

The common understanding of product platforms focuses on technology and designs. We propose a broader definition (see Figure 4.11). A successful product family requires a clear and deep understanding of target customers' need for the product, how they will use it, and how the customer will integrate the product within their technical and business infrastructures.[29] Further, while product technology and market understanding are usually most important, in some situations, competences in manufacturing or distribution or service will explain success more than other factors.[30] For example, in a paper pulp manufacturer the rate of new product introduction is low. However, within its long-lived product family of pulp variations, the rate of continuous improvement in manufacturing quality and costs can be high, making its manufacturing core capabilities the keys to success. Similarly, a large retailer might well find its capabilities in logistics, selling, and customer service the levers of competitiveness since it neither creates nor manufactures its own products.

Current Product Applications

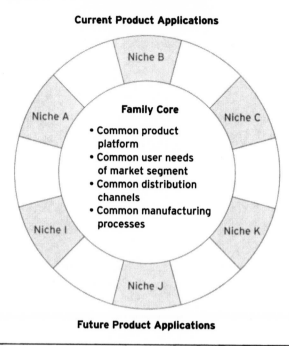

Future Product Applications

Figure 4.11. The Product Family: Core and Product Applications.

The idea that a product family requires a multidimensional core is summarized in a framework for managing successive development efforts in Figure 4.12. Product families consist of cores on which products are based to address specific market niches. Different functional aspects of the core undergo substantial improvements on a periodic basis. Platforms are improved. New manufacturing processes are used. The firm may implement new techniques and technologies to improve service. It can improve or add new channels of distribution. All such improvements to the family's core raise the effectiveness of the individual products within the family. If a company can enhance the capabilities undergirding the current family core, the result should be better products. Conversely, if core capabilities dissipate, families will lose their competitive edge and their products will fare poorly. Ideally, the percentage of the platform's contribution to individual products should increase from generation to generation based on the principles of modularity and technology layering in design.

For the product family idea to have impact, we believe that the firm must consider several basic steps. First, management must transform product planning into product *family* planning that includes, over several generations, ways in which its platforms and other aspects of its core must change in the form of specific product variations and their market applications. Second, management must adapt its budgeting to multiyear planning for related products. In many companies individual new product efforts compete for resources. To our way of thinking, a company must try to consolidate these individual efforts into basic product families. Each family management requests *multiple-year* commitments from senior management based on its plans; one major part is for core development, and the other major part is for the completion and marketing of specific products.

A disciplined approach to developing and extending product families presents a compelling basis for achieving rapid delivery cycles in the creation of new products. If one adopts this approach to making new products, then a strategy for "speed management" emerges. A company must be patient and forward thinking in developing product platforms and other dimensions of the family core. The completion of a strong platform then facilitates the far more rapid development of specific product variations. In fact, rather than release a single new product, the firm may simultaneously introduce many products, each aimed at a specific market niche. Concurrently, the company must begin designing the product platform for the next generation of the family and consider changes to its basic manufacturing, selling, and service capabilities.

Product obsolescence is inescapable. The issue is who takes control of the process. Winning companies retire their own products rather than let competitors do it for them. Methods such as ours will help management to see its past activities more clearly and to better plan the future.

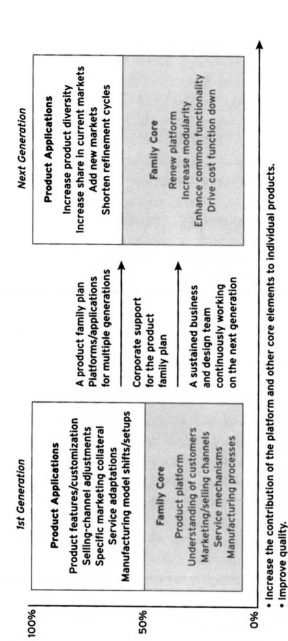

1st Generation

Product Applications

Product features/customization
Selling-channel adjustments
Specific marketing collateral
Service adaptations
Manufacturing model shifts/setups

Family Core

Product platform
Understanding of customers
Marketing/selling channels
Service mechanisms
Manufacturing processes

A product family plan
Platforms/applications
for multiple generations

Corporate support
for the product
family plan

A sustained business
and design team
continuously working
on the next generation

Next Generation

Product Applications

Increase product diversity
Increase share in current markets
Add new markets
Shorten refinement cycles

Family Core

Renew platform
Increase modularity
Enhance common functionality
Drive cost function down

100%

50%

0%

- Increase the contribution of the platform and other core elements to individual products.
- Improve quality.
- Product refinement cycle time is continuously shortened.
- Marketing emphasizes good products today, better ones tomorrow.

Figure 4.12. The Product Family Infrastructure and Product Applications.

Acknowledgments

The authors wish to thank the Center for Innovation Management Studies at Lehigh University and MIT's Leaders for Manufacturing Program and International Center for Research on the Management of Technology for their support of the research reported in this chapter.

NOTES

1. D. Teece, "Profiting from Technological Innovation: Implications for Integration, Collaboration, Licensing, and Public Policy," *Research Policy*, 1986, *15*, 285–306; and C. K. Prahalad and G. Hamel, "The Core Competence of the Corporation," *Harvard Business Review*, May-June 1990, pp. 79–91.

2. J. B. Quinn, T. L. Doorley, and P. C. Paquette, "Technology in Services: Rethinking Strategic Focus," *Sloan Management Review*, Winter 1990, pp. 79–87.

3. Sanderson posited that "virtual designs" serve as the basis for a series of "product realizations" within particular generations of a product family. See S. W. Sanderson, "Cost Models for Evaluating Virtual Design Strategies in Multicycle Product Families," *Journal of Engineering and Technology Management*, 1991, *8*, 339–358.

4. R. Henderson and K. Clark, "Architectural Innovation: The Reconfiguration of Existing Product Technologies and the Failure of Established Firms," *Administrative Science Quarterly*, 1990, *35*, 9–30.

5. Sanderson, "Cost Models."

6. The four major innovations were miniature stereo headphones, miniature super flat motors, disk drive mechanisms, and small, rechargeable nickel-cadmium batteries.

7. A. Lehnerd, "Revitalizing the Manufacture and Design of Mature Global Products," in *Technology and Global Industry: Companies and Nations in the World Economy*, B. R. Guile and H. Brooks, eds. (Washington, D.C.: National Academy of Engineering Press, 1987), pp. 49–64.

8. By simply varying the length of the motor field, power from 60 to 650 watts could be achieved.

9. Wheelwright and Clark employ a similar framework in their book on product development. See S. C. Wheelwright and K. B. Clark, *Revolutionizing Product Development* (New York: Free Press, 1992).

10. Events and years to anchor data gathering and analysis over a span of time have been used to study and illustrate that successful R&D teams pursue a number of alternative technical solutions before arriving at final solutions. See T. J. Allen, *Managing the Flow of Technology* (Cambridge, Massachusetts: MIT Press, 1977), pp. 13–26.

11. A fifth basic dimension, service, has been made part of our research with other companies.

12. For family A, seven individuals participated in the study; for family B, ten individuals; for family C, nine.

13. We settled on these four dimensions of core capability based on the literature. We are also examining core capabilities for data gathering and analysis.

14. In our work with other firms, managers have chosen to identify specific manufacturing processes as core capabilities for data gathering and analysis.

15. The metric used to assess capability was as follows: 5 = best in class—industry leadership; 4 = above par; 3 = on par; 2 = below par; 1 = worst in class.

16. The underlying databases for these studies can be quite large. For example, over a thousand data points were gathered for the horizontal application family alone. We computed standard deviations to examine the variance in responses among participants for each core capability. These have been left out of this chapter to simplify the presentation.

17. In our work for other firms, participants have requested that we weight certain core capabilities more heavily than others to reflect their importance in the products studied.

18. Prahalad and Hamel, "Core Competence"; and Quinn, Doorley, and Paquette, "Technology in Services."

19. The scale for performance was as follows: 5 = among the most successful new business development efforts in the company; 4 = above

par; 3 = on par; 2 = below par; 1 = among the least successful new business development efforts in the company.

20. In another study at the same company, we have gathered data on individual product performance. Grouping individual products into their respective families provided a cross-check on the validity of the executives' relative assessments. Cross-checks for earlier years were not feasible because performance data for individual products were not recorded.

21. We are presently applying this method to a number of other product-developing firms in order to gather sufficient data to generalize the finding reported here with meaningful statistics.

22. The scale for market growth was as follows: 5 = greater than 25 percent per year—rapid growth; 4 = greater than 10 percent and less than 25 percent—fast growth; 3 = greater than 5 percent and less than 10 percent—moderate growth; 2 = greater than or equal to 0 percent and less than 5 percent—slow growth; 1 = less than 0 percent—contracting market.

23. The scale for level of competition was as follows: 5 = many competitors, with several dominant firms; 4 = many competitors but no dominant firms; 3 = a few large competitors; 2 = a few small competitors; 1 = no competitors.

24. The scale for effective product life cycle was as follows: 5 = five or more years; 4 = four years; 3 = three years; 2 = two years; 1 = one year.

25. Sony spent approximately twenty years in basic research for the development of its video camera products. See M. Cusumano, Y. Mylonadis, and R. Rosenbloom, "Strategic Maneuvering and Mass-Market Dynamics: The Triumph of VHS over Beta," working paper 4091 (Cambridge, Massachusetts: International Center for Research on the Management of Technology, MIT Sloan School of Management, 1991).

26. W. J. Abernathy and J. M. Utterback, "Patterns of Innovation in Industry," *Technology Review*, 1978, *80*, 40–47; R. N. Foster, "Timing Technological Transitions," in *Technology in the Modern Corporation*, M. Horwitch, ed. (Cambridge, Massachusetts: MIT Press, 1986); W. J. Abernathy and K. B. Clark, "Innovation: Mapping the Winds of Creative Destruction," *Research Policy*, 1985, *14*, 3–22; and M. Tushman and P. Anderson, "Technological Discontinuities and

Organizational Environments," *Administrative Science Quarterly*, 1986, *31*, 439–465.

27. J. M. Utterback, *Mastering the Dynamics of Innovation: How Companies Can Seize Opportunities in the Face of Technological Change* (Boston: Harvard Business School Press, 1994).

28. M. H. Meyer and E. B. Roberts, "Focusing Product Technology for Corporate Growth," *Sloan Management Review,* Summer 1988, pp. 7–16; and Quinn, Doorley, and Paquette, "Technology in Services."

29. C. Freeman, *The Economics of Industrial Innovation* (Cambridge, Massachusetts: MIT Press, 1986); R. G. Cooper, *Winning at New Products* (Reading, Massachusetts: Addison-Wesley, 1986); and M. A. Maidique and B. J. Zirger, "The New Product Learning Cycle," *Research Policy,* 1985, *14,* 299–314.

30. J. M. Utterback, "Innovation and Industrial Evolution in Manufacturing Industries," in Guile and Brooks, *Technology and Global Industry,* 16–48; and E. B. Roberts and M. H. Meyer, "New Products and Corporate Strategy," *Engineering Management Review,* 1991, *19,* 4–18.

CHAPTER FIVE

Planning for Product Platforms

DAVID ROBERTSON
KARL ULRICH

I n 1987 Fuji introduced the QuickSnap 35 mm single-use camera in the U.S. market. Kodak, which did not have a comparable product of its own, was caught unprepared in a market that was destined to grow by more than 50 percent per year for the next eight years, from 3 million units in 1988 to 43 million in 1994. By the time Kodak introduced its first model almost a year later, Fuji had already developed a second model, the QuickSnap Flash. Yet Kodak won market share back from Fuji; by 1994 Kodak had captured more than 70 percent of the U.S. market.

The success of Kodak's response resulted in part from its strategy of developing many distinctively different models from a common platform. Between April 1989 and July 1990, Kodak redesigned its base model and introduced three additional models, all having common components and common production process steps.[1] Because Kodak designed its four products to share components and process steps, it was able to develop its products faster

---

First published in the Summer 1998 issue of *MIT Sloan Management Review.*

and more cheaply. The different models appealed to different customer segments and gave Kodak twice as many products as Fuji, allowing it to capture precious retail space and garner substantial market share.

The platform approach to product development is an important success factor in many markets. By sharing components and production processes across a platform of products, companies can develop differentiated products efficiently, increase the flexibility and responsiveness of their manufacturing processes, and take market share away from competitors that develop only one product at a time. For example, in the auto industry, firms taking a platform approach enjoyed market share gains of 5.1 percent per year, while firms pursuing a single-model approach lost 2.2 percent market share per year.[2]

The platform approach is also a way to achieve successful mass customization—the manufacture of products in high volumes that are tailored to meet the needs of individual customers.[3] It allows highly differentiated products to be delivered to the market without consuming excessive resources.

In this chapter we define what we mean by a "platform," describing the benefits and challenges of platform planning. We articulate three ideas underlying the platform approach to product development and present a method for planning a new platform of products. Finally, we provide recommendations for managing the platform-planning process.

FUNDAMENTALS OF PLATFORM PLANNING

Platform planning poses both opportunities and difficulties for companies. Basic to the effort is understanding what a product platform consists of. We define a platform as the collection of assets that are shared by a set of products. These assets can be divided into four categories:

▼ *Components*—the part designs of a product, the fixtures and tools needed to make them, the circuit designs, and the programs burned into programmable chips or stored on disks

▼ *Processes*—the equipment used to make components or to assemble components into products and the design of the associated production process and supply chain

▼ *Knowledge*—design know-how, technology applications and limitations, production techniques, mathematical models, and testing methods[4]

▼ *People and relationships*—teams, relationships among team members, relationships between the team and the larger organization, and relationships with a network of suppliers

Taken together, these shared assets constitute the product platform. Generally, platform products share many, if not most, development and production assets. In contrast, parts standardization efforts across products may lead to the sharing of a modest set of components, but such a collection of shared components is generally not considered a product platform.[5]

Benefits of Platform Planning

Companies that engage in successful platform planning realize benefits in many areas. They have greater ability to tailor products to the needs of different market segments or customers. The platform approach reduces the incremental cost of addressing the specific needs of a market segment or of an individual customer, enabling market needs to be more closely met.

Companies can reduce development cost and time. Parts and assembly processes developed for one model do not have to be developed and tested for the others. This benefit applies to new products developed from the platform and to updated products. They can also reduce manufacturing cost. When producing larger volumes of common parts, companies achieve economies of scale. Companies can also reduce production investment. Machinery, equipment, and tooling, and the engineering time needed to create them, can be shared across higher production volumes. Companies can simplify systemic complexity. Cutting the number of parts and processes lowers costs in materials management, logistics, distribution, inventory management, sales and service, and purchasing.[6]

Another benefit is lower risk. The lower investment required for each product developed from a platform results in decreased risk for each new product. Companies will also improve service. Sharing components across products allows companies to stock fewer parts in their production and service parts inventories, which translates into better service levels and/or lower service costs.

Challenges of Platform Planning

Companies developing platform products must meet the needs of diverse market segments while conserving development and production resources. The effort involves two difficult tasks. First, product planning and marketing managers address the problems of which market segments to enter, what the customers in each segment want, and what product attributes will appeal to those customers. Second, system-level designers address the problem of what product architecture should be used to deliver the different products while sharing parts and production steps across the products. These two tasks are challenging because they are inherently complex and because their completion requires coordination among the firm's marketing, design, and manufacturing functions. Since these functional groups may be unaccustomed to working with each other, conflicts may arise over differing time frames, jargon, goals, and assumptions.

Furthermore, platform planning is difficult because of the many ways in which it can fail. We have observed two common problems in companies attempting to create product platforms.

First, organizational forces frequently hinder the ability to balance commonality and distinctiveness. One perspective can dominate the debate. For example, design or manufacturing engineers often prepare hard cost data showing how expensive it would be to create distinctive products, leading to products that are too similar from the customer's perspective. The resulting imbalance was illustrated (if perhaps inaccurately) by a *Fortune* cover photo showing "look-alike" Chevrolet, Oldsmobile, Buick, and Pontiac automobiles.[7] Alternatively, the marketing function may argue convincingly that only completely different products will appeal to the different market segments and that commonality is penny wise and pound foolish.

Second, even when platform planning takes place with a balanced team committed to working together, the process can get bogged down in details, resulting either in the organization giving up or in products lacking character and integrity.[8]

PLATFORM PLANNING IN THE AUTO INDUSTRY

We believe that the platform-planning method we describe next is applicable to many types of products. To illustrate the method, we use an example from the auto industry: the design of an instrument panel, or dashboard. A critical part of a new car's design, an instrument panel plays several important roles. It provides structural support for heating, ventilation, and air conditioning (HVAC) ducts; components; switches; gauges; audio components; storage areas (such as the glove compartment); airbags; and tubing and wiring. The instrument panel also must help absorb the shock of a front or side collision and help prevent the car body from twisting during normal driving. Finally, the instrument panel plays an aesthetic role: the look, feel, and even smell of an instrument panel can affect the appeal of the car and distinguish one car from another. (The instrument panel example is drawn from our experience with a major auto manufacturer; for the sake of clarity, we have minimized technical details.)

Balancing Commonality and Distinctiveness

At a fundamental level, product variety is valuable in the market-place, yet it is usually costly to deliver.[9] The sharing of assets across products allows companies to manage the trade-off. Platform planning balances the need for distinctiveness with the need for commonality. Three ideas underlie the platform-planning process:

1. Customers care about distinctiveness; costs are driven by commonality. Customers care whether the firm offers a product that closely meets their needs; they are not particularly concerned about how many parts a collection of products has in common. Closely meeting the needs of different market segments requires distinctive products. At the same time, the cost of a firm's internal operations is largely driven by the level of parts held in common among a collection of products and is not directly related to how distinctive those products are in the marketplace.

We use the term *differentiating attribute* (DA) to denote a characteristic that customers deem important in distinguishing between products. Two products are distinctive from one another if the values of the DAs that characterize the products are noticeably different. For example, interior noise level is a DA for automobiles. Customers generally expect different values of this DA for different kinds of vehicles, such as audible cues from the engine in sporty vehicles but near silence in luxury vehicles.

We use the term *chunk* to refer to the major physical elements of a product, its key components, and subassemblies.[10] A set of products exhibits high levels of commonality if many chunks are shared. At many car companies, for example, the engine compartment is treated as a chunk that may be shared across several vehicles.

Although DAs and chunks are related (interior noise level, a differentiating attribute, is influenced by insulation, a chunk), they reflect two very different ways of describing a product. DAs reflect the level of distinctiveness as perceived by the external customer; chunks reflect the level of commonality as perceived within the firm.

2. Given a particular product architecture, a trade-off exists between distinctiveness and commonality. Consider a pair of products. If these products shared 100 percent of their parts, they would have commonality but no distinctiveness. If these products shared no parts, they would have no commonality but could have an arbitrarily high level of distinctiveness. As the percentage of common parts increases from 0 to 100, the distinctiveness of the two products declines to zero. For example, the instrument panels for two different automobile models could be arbitrarily distinctive if they shared no parts. A manufacturer might share several parts of the instrument panel, such as mounting screws and small brackets, with little loss of distinctiveness. As more and more parts, such as gauges, environmental controls, and audio systems, are shared, the two instrument panels lose more and more distinctiveness. Of course, if every part were common, the two panels would be indistinguishable.

The trade-off between distinctiveness and commonality is represented in Figure 5.1. Two products that are very distinctive and share few parts correspond to scenario A; two products that are less distinctive and share many parts correspond to scenario B. For a given product architecture, product designers face a trade-off between distinctiveness and commonality. Conceptually, this trade-off can be thought of as constraining the distinctiveness and commonality of a pair of products to fall along the curve, architecture 1.

3. Product architecture dictates the nature of the trade-off between distinctiveness and commonality. Although a trade-off exists between distinctiveness and commonality, the nature of the trade-off can be influenced by changing the product architecture. The curve, architecture 2 in Figure 5.1, results in a trade-off in which slight efforts at commonality mean drastic reductions in distinctiveness (scenario C). It is also possible, as illustrated by architecture 2, that even with no parts in common, two products may not be viewed as completely distinct. In the ideal case, the product architecture presents the company with a trade-off in which a relatively high level of commonality can be achieved without much

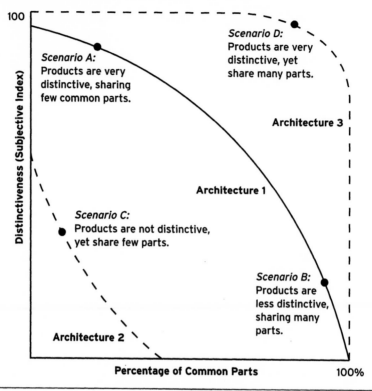

Figure 5.1. Trade-Off Between Distinctiveness and Commonality.

sacrifice in distinctiveness and distinctiveness declines slowly as commonality is increased. This situation is represented by architecture 3 and scenario D.

For example, consider the two different instrument panel designs shown in Figure 5.2. One architecture consists of a tubular metal structure over which a contoured plastic skin is assembled; the other consists of a curved plastic panel with metal reinforcements integrally molded as part of the structure. The first designs are called "modular"; the second, "integral."[11] In the first case, the underlying metal structure can be common across instrument panels A and B, while the plastic skin can be different. This commonality results in relatively little loss of distinctiveness. In the second case, an attempt to standardize one of the integral metal-plastic panels leaves the two vehicles with similar exterior appearances for the dashboard, a large decrease in distinctiveness.

Another type of architecture that is important to consider in platform planning is the production architecture. The production architecture defines the range of products that can be produced. For example, if the different models of a new platform of cars are to be assembled and painted on the same production line, then the structure of the production line will determine the range of possible

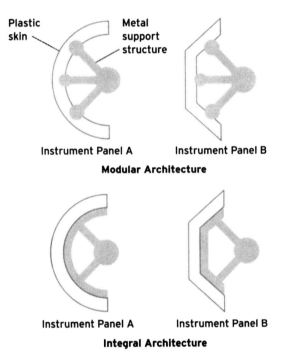

The modular architecture allows the same support structure to be used in two different instrument panel designs. (Illustrative instrument panel designs shown in cross-section.)

Figure 5.2. Modular and Integral Architectures for an Instrument Panel.

heights and widths, the allowable sizes of the different systems in the car (for example, how big or small the dashboard, seats, and other systems can be), and the assembly sequence of the car. This production architecture is not a fixed constraint, but the cost of revising it may be significant.

THE PLATFORM-PLANNING PROCESS

Platform planning is a cross-functional activity involving at least the firm's product marketing, design, and manufacturing functions. In most cases, platform planning is best carried out by a core team of representatives from each function. For large development projects each representative should in turn be supported by an experienced staff.

We advocate a loosely structured process for platform planning focused on three information management tools (see Figure 5.3):

▼ The product plan
▼ The differentiation plan
▼ The commonality plan

The three plans are top-level summaries of deeper analyses by members of the extended platform-planning team, but they explicitly display the degree to which coherence has been achieved among product strategy, market positioning, and product design. The goal of the platform-planning process is to achieve coherence among the three plans. The process of platform planning is likely to be iterative. The team begins by constructing the three plans and then works iteratively to achieve coherence among them.

Establish Product Plan
The product plan for the collection of products encompassed by the platform specifies the distinct market offerings over time and usually comes from the company's overall product plan. In a product

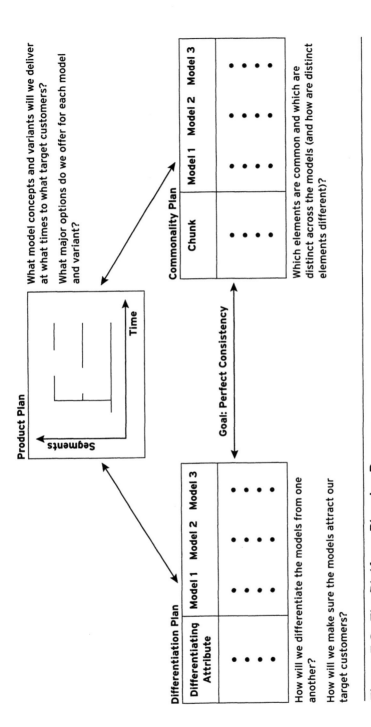

Figure 5.3. The Platform-Planning Process.

plan for a new platform for a sporty coupe, a family sedan, and a family station wagon, the two axes of the chart correspond to the segments of the marketplace and to time (see Figure 5.4). The timing and segment of each planned product are indicated by location. The genealogy of the products is indicated by links.

The product plan is supported by a top-level description of each product. This description contains the customer profile (needs, psychographics, and demographics) and a basic business plan (expected sales volumes and selling price range). The product plan indicates major models but does not show every variant and option.

The product plan is linked to several other issues and pieces of information:

▼ Availability of development resources
▼ Life cycles of current products
▼ Expected life cycles of competitive offerings

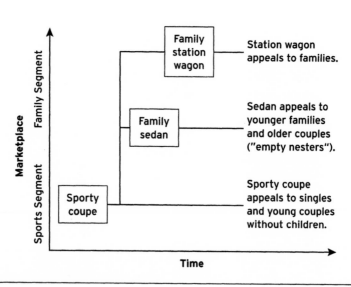

Figure 5.4. The Product Plan.

▼ Timing of major production system changes
▼ Availability of product technologies

The product plan reflects the company's product strategy. Some companies choose to issue several products simultaneously; others choose to launch products in succession.

Specify Each Product's Differentiating Attributes

DAs are the dimensions of the product that are meaningful to customers. The differentiation plan indicates the target values of the DAs for each product in the plan (see Table 5.1). The first column of the table shows the values of the DAs; the second and third columns show the critical DAs for each product in the product plan; and the fourth column gives an approximate assessment of the relative importance to the customer of each DA. A common pitfall in platform planning is to become bogged down in detail. We generally find that the best level of abstraction for platform planning results in no more than ten to twenty DAs. In the beginning of the process, these DAs focus on the overall properties of the product. As the planning process evolves, the work shifts to the system level, and the DAs become increasingly detailed.

On the first pass the differentiation plan represents the ideal case of each product's differentiation for maximum appeal to customers in the target segments. On subsequent iterations the ideal case is adjusted to respond to the need for commonality.

The values of the DAs for competing products serve as a useful benchmark for differentiation and can be entered in additional columns of the matrix. However, the team must avoid a focus on existing competing products at the expense of anticipating the future market.

Objective metrics are particularly useful for representing the target values of the DAs when such metrics are widely accepted as meaningful in the marketplace (for example, miles per gallon for automobiles). When such metrics are not available, direct comparisons may be useful (for example, "similar to a Lexus ES 300").

Table 5.1. The Differentiation Plan.

▼

Differentiating Attributes	Sporty Coupe	Family Sedan/ Station Wagon	Importance to Customer
Curvature of window glass	More curvature	Straight, vertical	• • •
Styling of instrument panel	Evocative of English roadster	Highly functional	• • •
Relationship between driver and instrument panel	Driver sits low to ground, distant from steering wheel, with seat reclined	Driver sits higher, closer, more upright	• • •
Front-end styling	Shorter nose; vehicle appears to attack the road	Longer nose, more substantial look	• • •
Colors and textures	Darker colors and mix of leather and textiles	Practical surfaces and colors	• •
Suspension stiffness	Stiff, for improved handling	Softer, for improved comfort	• •
Interior noise	Some engine noise desirable, 70 decibels	Noise minimized, 60 decibels	•

Quantify Commonality Across Products

The commonality plan describes the extent to which the products in the plan share physical elements. The plan is an explicit accounting of the costs associated with developing and producing each product (see Table 5.2). The first column of the table lists the critical chunks in the product. To manage complexity the team should limit the number of chunks to roughly the number of DAs—no more than ten or twenty. The remaining columns identify the products in the plan, according to the timing of their development, and the four metrics used in the commonality plan.

For example, consider the first row of the commonality plan in Table 5.2, the HVAC system. The sporty coupe requires forty-five

Table 5.2. The Initial Commonality Plan.

Instrument Panel Chunks	Sporty Coupe				Family Sedan/Station Wagon				Comments
	Number of Unique Parts	Development Cost ($ millions)	Tooling Cost ($ millions)	Manufacturing Cost	Number of Unique Parts	Development Cost ($ millions)	Tooling Cost ($ millions)	Manufacturing Cost	
HVAC system	45	$4.0	$9.0	$202	35	$3.8	$7.5	$200	Duct work and support structure different; share motors and other components
Dash cover and structure	52	$4.0	$7.0	$123	48	$3.8	$6.5	$120	Share some brackets and components
Electrical equipment	115	$4.0	$2.2	$420	65	$2.0	$2.1	$430	Share switches, wiring, and central module
Cross-car beam	12	$2.0	$2.0	$35	12	$2.0	$2.0	$35	Cross-car beam entirely different
Steering system and airbags	26	$2.0	$0.1	$200	26	$2.0	$0.1	$195	All components different
Instruments and gauges	16	$1.0	$0.2	$22	13	$0.8	$0.2	$20	Can share some instruments
Molding and trim	10	$0.4	$0.2	$11	10	$0.4	$0.2	$10	All molding and trim different
Insulation	3	$0.2	$0.2	$8	1	$0.1	$0.0	$10	Change insulation in coupe to let in more engine noise
Audio and radio	8	$0.2	$0.0	$300	0	$0.0	$0.0	$300	Same radio option in all vehicles
Total	287	$17.8	$20.8	$1,321	210	$14.9	$18.5	$1,320	

unique parts, $4 million in development cost, and $9 million in tooling cost; it has a unit manufacturing cost of $202. To then produce the HVAC system for the sedan and wagon requires an additional thirty-five unique parts, $3.8 million in development cost, and $7.5 million in tooling cost. The unit manufacturing cost of the HVAC system for the sedan and wagon is $200.

For different product contexts the relative importance of these metrics may vary. For example, in some settings tooling cost may be insignificant and may be dropped from the plan. In other settings other metrics may be important. For example, development time may be the most important metric for a product because of the potential loss of market share for being late to market. In this case, a time metric could be added to the commonality plan.

The values of these metrics are estimated because actual values cannot be determined until the products have been designed and produced. Note that, with the exception of unit manufacturing cost, the values in the commonality plan are incremental, assuming the preceding products are developed and produced. If the sequence of products in the product plan changes, the incremental values may also change. The commonality plan in the example considers the incremental parts and costs associated with producing the sedan and station wagon after the sporty coupe.

Underlying the commonality plan are the basic engineering design concepts for the product. In most cases, engineering layouts of each product are created to support the estimation process. Once the values of the metrics are estimated, the total values for each product and for each chunk can be added.

Iteratively Refine the Plans

Given the objective of maximizing market presence, a company would most likely want to enter many segments with many products and replace them all regularly. Given the objective of capturing a large fraction of each segment, the company would attempt to ideally position the product with respect to the values of the DAs.

Given the objective of minimizing development cost, tooling investment, and complexity, a large fraction of all the products in the plan would be identical. Typically, of course, these three objectives conflict. For most product contexts an unconstrained product plan and an unconstrained differentiation plan lead to high costs. For this reason iterative problem solving is required to balance the need for differentiation with the need for commonality. After completing the commonality plan, the team may return to the differentiation plan and modify the target level of differentiation on DAs that are particularly critical drivers of product costs. After reviewing the costs of effectively differentiating a product for a particular segment, the team may decide that it is simply infeasible to consider that product part of the platform.

Conceptually, this iterative activity involves both moving along the distinctiveness-commonality curve and exploring alternative product architectures with different associated trade-off characteristics (see Figure 5.1). Several practices can help companies achieve coherence across the three plans:

1. *Focus on a few critical DAs and chunks.* The relationship between the DAs and the chunks can be shown on a matrix (see Figure 5.5). The first column shows the DAs, and the column heads going across the matrix show the chunks. A cell of the matrix is filled when the DA and the chunk associated with that cell are interrelated (that is, when variation in the DA is likely to require variation in the chunk). Because the exact relationships between chunks and DAs depend on the final product architecture, the matrix is approximate and representative of the team's best estimates.

The matrix is most useful when the DAs are arranged in order of decreasing value of variation to the customer and when the chunks are arranged in order of the decreasing cost of variation. When organized this way, the DAs and chunks in the upper-left portion of the matrix whose corresponding cells are filled have special significance. These are the important DAs and costly chunks that

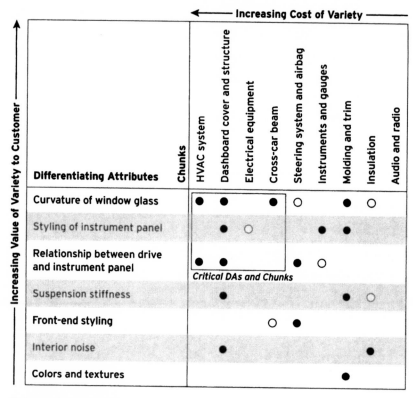

Figure 5.5. The Relationship Between Differentiating Attributes and Chunks.

are interrelated. These elements are the critical few on which platform planning is focused.

The chunks that are not related to important DAs should be rigorously standardized and incorporated into the platform. Variation in these chunks does not offer value in the marketplace. Furthermore, the valuable DAs that are not related to costly chunks can be varied arbitrarily without incurring high cost and so should be varied directly in accordance with market demands.

2. *Search for architectural solutions to apparent conflicts.* In our example the initial architecture of the instrument panel involved reusing only a few HVAC components, gauges, switches, wiring, brackets, fasteners, and other components. The initial commonality plan (see Table 5.2) shows that the development and tooling costs for the sedan or wagon would be $5.2 million less than for the coupe, reflecting savings from commonality in the initial design approach. However, the engineering team set out to develop an alternative architecture that would allow for greater reuse of components.

The first area that the team examined was the most expensive: the HVAC system. Team members realized that by designing the duct system using a modular architecture, they could reuse many HVAC components. They designed a system in which the ends of the ducts varied across models, while the main ducts and the mixing box that connects them could be reused (see Figure 5.6). They also realized that with some careful packaging, they could reuse the support structure for the entire instrument panel. The changes resulted in additional savings of $10.4 million in development and tooling costs (see Table 5.3, p. 150).

The second area they examined was the cross-car beam. They found that even though the coupe's instrument panel was narrower than the others on the platform, they could standardize the attachment points of the dashboard cover and structure and reuse most of the cross-car beam components. The only change that was required was a main beam that was six centimeters shorter. This resulted in another $3.8 million of development and tooling savings (see Table 5.3).

Finally, the team examined the electrical equipment and steering system. Team members found that while the airbag itself had to be tuned differently for the different models, they could reuse the housing, sensors, and control module. They could also reuse the expensive combination switch (which controls the turn signal, wiper washer, and headlight switches) if the dashboard cover was styled

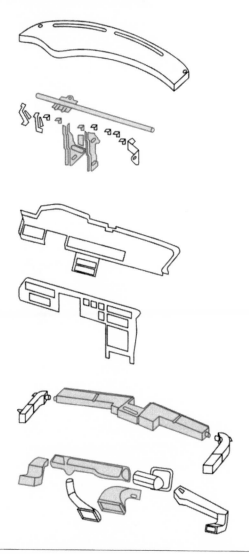

Figure 5.6. Design for Dashboard Cover and Structure and HVAC Components.

Note: Common components are shaded. Components highly visible to the customer are differentiated; invisible components are common.

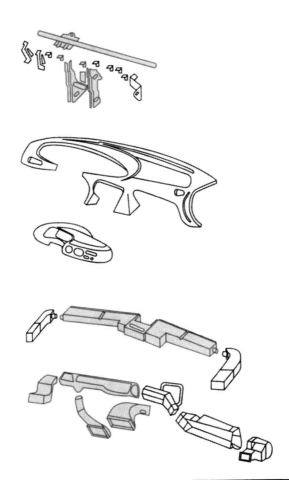

Table 5.3. The Revised Commonality Plan.

Instrument Panel Chunks	Sporty Coupe				Family Sedan/Station Wagon				Comments
	Number of Unique Parts	Development Cost ($ millions)	Tooling Cost ($ millions)	Manufacturing Cost	Number of Unique Parts	Development Cost ($ millions)	Tooling Cost ($ millions)	Manufacturing Cost	
HVAC system	45	$4.0	$9.0	$196	8	$0.4	$0.5	$195	Share all but ends of ducts
Dash cover and structure	52	$4.0	$7.0	$123	48	$3.8	$6.5	$120	All new shape and structure for coupe
Electrical equipment	115	$4.0	$2.2	$412	30	$0.5	$0.0	$415	Share wiring, control module, and combination switch
Cross-car beam	12	$2.0	$2.0	$33	1	$0.2	$0.0	$33	Change horizontal beam length
Steering system and airbags	26	$2.0	$0.1	$196	21	$1.0	$0.0	$192	Change only steering wheel and cover
Instruments and gauges	16	$1.0	$0.2	$22	13	$0.8	$0.2	$20	Share gauge mechanisms
Molding and trim	10	$0.4	$0.2	$11	10	$0.4	$0.2	$10	All molding and trim must be different
Insulation	3	$0.2	$0.1	$8	1	$0.1	$0.0	$10	Change insulation in coupe to let in more engine noise
Audio and radio	8	$0.2	$0.0	$300	0	$0.0	$0.0	$300	Same radio option in all vehicles
Total	287	$17.8	$20.8	$1,301	132	$7.2	$7.4	$1,295	

correctly and if different covers were used for the switch arms. Between the electrical equipment and steering system, these actions saved an additional $4.7 million over the initial plan.

In addition to savings in fixed costs, the variable costs of producing components also fell because the volume of the components increased. Suppliers offered an average 5 percent price discount in return for standardizing components. The discount resulted in an annual savings of $9 million.

The team could have achieved further savings by using a common dashboard cover. However, the dashboard cover is absolutely critical in differentiating the two products. Therefore the team chose to sacrifice commonality, even at substantial cost, because of the market value of the resulting distinctiveness.

3. *Express costs and benefits in terms of profits.* To keep the problem-solving discussions productive, the team should use a common language. The best approach is to focus on the impact of choices on platform profitability. The group iteratively refining the differentiation plan must focus on the impact of decisions on market share and link share points to profitability. The group refining the product architecture should link product costs to profitability. Only when both groups are working from the same profitability model can they discuss constructively the bottom-line trade-offs between commonality and distinctiveness.

In an ideal world, a company wants to explicitly optimize the platform to achieve maximum profits. While some current research efforts are directed at this objective, explicit profit maximization is hard for at least three reasons.[12] First, data are scarce, especially data related to the value of a particular DA. Second, decomposing the value of a product into the value of individual DAs is difficult. Third, much of the problem-solving activity in platform planning involves creative design problem solving on the choice of product architecture, for which there are no structured optimization techniques. For this reason our underlying assumptions are that a correct answer is unlikely, that providing a clear way of displaying information helps, and that the team should work for a solution that is good enough. The key to making the process a success is to avoid "analysis paralysis"; the goal is to obtain data that support quick, creative problem-solving iterations.

4. *Become as sophisticated as possible in describing DAs.* The ability to describe DAs well is vital to platform planning. Understanding how customers view products and what distinguishes one product from the next is a difficult task. By describing DAs clearly and in detail, teams can better understand the linkage to the chunks of a product. Developing an understanding of DAs that are holistic (that is, that arise from the entire product as a system) is especially critical.[13]

A good example of careful DA definition comes from Lotus Engineering.[14] To describe the handling characteristics of its cars, Lotus uses sophisticated and vivid terms. These terms help Lotus better connect a car's handling characteristics to the components that determine them. For example, among Lotus's attributes are:

▼ *Umbrella*—the feeling that a car is descending after coming over the crest of a hill. A car has motions that make a driver feel that it is flying off the road and motions that bring it closer to the road; a car with good umbrella will have twice as many motions closer to the road than motions off the road.

▼ *Nibbling*—the series of quick back-and-forth movements that happen when a car goes over a series of bumps.

▼ *Standing up*—the feeling that the rear end of the vehicle is rising. The back end of a car that stands up feels like it rises more than it falls as it goes over bumps and hills.

These DAs allow the different groups at Lotus to better understand what to differentiate and how. By describing carefully how the attributes should be different, the team can more exactly determine specifications for the chunks of a car.

MANAGING PLATFORM PLANNING

Top management should play a strong role in the platform-planning process for three reasons: (1) platform decisions are among the most important a company makes, (2) platform decisions may cut across several product lines or divisional boundaries, and (3) platform decisions frequently require the resolution of cross-functional conflict.

Platform planning determines the products that a company introduces into the market during the next five to ten years or beyond, the types and levels of capital investment, and the R&D agendas for both the company and its suppliers. Because of the impact of platform decisions, they warrant significant top-management involvement.

Top management's participation is also needed because making good platform decisions requires making complex trade-offs in different business areas. For example, making an instrument panel slightly less stylish could hurt the appeal to certain target segments, yet improve commonality and manufacturability. Or a product plan that requires spinning five products off a common platform may turn out to be unrealistic and have to be revised.

Different functions within the firm have different perspectives during product development. Some functions, such as sales, market research, marketing, and styling, concentrate on those product characteristics that the customer experiences while using the product. Other functions, such as engineering, production, and after-sales service, may be more focused on the product cost. When designing a new platform, the functions that focus on the customer features of the product are often in conflict with groups that care about the parts and production processes. Top managers should recognize that the various functions may fundamentally disagree about the goals of the platform and that their perspective may be required to achieve the best solutions.

When organizing a platform-planning project, top managers should

▼ Put someone in charge of each plan (the product plan, the differentiation plan, and the commonality plan) and someone else in charge of driving the whole process.

▼ Make sure that all key functions are involved—engineering, market research, manufacturing engineering, industrial design, and so on.

▼ Set up two support teams. One team estimates the value of differentiation or the cost of a lack of differentiation. The other team estimates the costs associated with a given level of commonality.

▼ Spend time building a high-performing team. The planning process is difficult, involving many different functions that are not accustomed to working together. Time spent during the early phases clarifying objectives, building consensus, and creating a true team can pay off handsomely during the later phases of the process.

▼ Set targets for the total cost of the platform, based on past performance or on benchmarked results. These cost targets will help prevent the activity from resulting in too little commonality.

Once the project is organized, top management should

▼ Help everyone understand that, while there is a trade-off between commonality and variety, it is not a zero-sum game. All functions may take a while to learn that choosing the right architecture can do much to balance commonality and distinctiveness. Working together can help improve the platform products from everyone's perspective.

▼ Drive for quick, approximate results, not for slow, perfect answers. Challenge the company to experiment quickly with different architectures, evaluating them on the basis of their ability to achieve commonality and distinctiveness. The secret to platform planning is not deep, detailed analysis but fast, creative problem solving.

▼ Push for facts, not someone's "gut feel." Management should ask for and receive the best possible data on customer needs, size of segments, and cost of differentiation before making decisions. This is not to suggest that analyses should be detailed, bulletproof research papers. Rather, the analyses, however approximate, should be based on the best facts available, not on personal hunches.

▼ Don't insist on total agreement and perfect resolution of all issues; ask for design solutions that everyone agrees are good enough on all dimensions and very good relative to the few critical competitive dimensions.

▼ Start at the top level of the product and then iteratively refine the plan in greater and greater detail. For example, in developing a new car, platform planning would first be directed at the overall vehicle and the twenty or so top-level chunks. Then planning would be directed at each chunk and its constitutive components.

▼ Make the process a living one. The way in which platform planning is implemented is (and should be) different in every company. One key to successful platform planning is continuing evaluation and improvement of the process. A static, regulated implementation of the planning process is doomed to fail.

▼ Evolve the planning process into the next phase. As planning nears completion, more and more members of the team that will execute the next phase of the project should be involved to ensure they understand and agree with the major decisions already made.

▼ Use the results to drive the improvement agenda for the company. What should research work on? Where does production need to be more flexible? What are other customer segments? What dimensions of the product do the customers really care about? How can the product technology be made more robust so that it can be used in many platforms?

CONCLUSION

In many industries the standard for minimum acceptable product development performance is high and rising fast. It is no longer possible to dominate large markets by developing one product at a time. Increasingly, good product development means good platform development.

To develop good platforms a company must carefully align its product plan, its differentiation plan, and its commonality plan through an iterative planning process. No longer can the product planning group throw its plan over the wall to other groups; planning must be a cooperative process involving all groups and guided by top management. Just as good product engineering involves up-front consideration of manufacturing issues, good platform planning requires up-front consideration of marketing, design, and manufacturing issues.

Much academic and industrial attention has been concentrated on product strategy and on product development and project execution. Little emphasis, however, has been placed on coordinating the development of the set of products that realize a product plan. Platform planning fills that gap. Yet platform planning is difficult: teams may achieve high commonality but fail to differentiate the products; teams may differentiate the products but create products with excessive costs; or teams may create viable platform plans that are subsequently never realized.

The planning tools in this chapter provide a common language that a company's marketing, design, and manufacturing functions can all understand. The platform-planning process we present gives them a method for applying these tools that captures all critical elements of the process and achieves coherence among the product, differentiation, and commonality plans.

Acknowledgments

We would like to thank Per-Ola Karlsson, Glenn Mercer, Jeff Sinclair, and Karl Swartling from McKinsey & Company for their contributions and the many McKinsey clients who helped develop the ideas in this chapter.

NOTES

1. K. B. Clark and S. Wheelwright, *Leading Product Development* (New York: Free Press, 1996).

2. K. Nobeoka and M. A. Cusumano, "Multiproject Strategy and Sales Growth: The Benefits of Rapid Design Transfer in New Product Development," *Strategic Management Journal*, March 1997, *18*, 169–186; and K. Nobeoka and M. A. Cusumano, "Multiproject Strategy, Design Transfer, and Project Performance: A Survey of Automobile Development Projects in the U.S. and Japan," *IEEE Transactions on Engineering Management*, November 1995, *42*, 397–409.

3. B. J. Pine II, *Mass Customization: The New Frontier in Business Competition* (Boston: Harvard Business School Press, 1993); B. J. Pine II, B. Victor, and A. C. Boynton, "Making Mass Customization Work," *Harvard Business Review*, September-October 1993, *71*, 108–111; and E. Feitzinger and H. L. Lee, "Mass Customization at Hewlett-Packard: The Power of Postponement," *Harvard Business Review*, January-February 1997, *75*, 116–121.

4. For an interesting discussion of the strategic role of knowledge platforms, see D. J. Kim and B. Kogut, "Technological Platforms and Diversification," *Organization Science*, May-June 1996, *7*, 283–301.

5. M. L. Fisher, K. Ramdas, and K. Ulrich, "Component Sharing: A Study of Automotive Brakes," working paper (Philadelphia: Department of Operations and Information Management, Wharton School, University of Pennsylvania, 1996).

6. For an example of the magnitude of these costs, see K. Ulrich, D. Sartorius, S. Pearson, and M. Jakiela, "Including the Value of Time in Design for Manufacturing Decision Making," *Management Science*, April 1993, *39*, 429–447.

7. "Will Success Spoil General Motors?" *Fortune*, August 22, 1983.

8. K. B. Clark and T. Fujimoto, "The Power of Product Integrity," *Harvard Business Review*, November-December 1990, *68*, 107–118.

9. K. Lancaster, "The Economics of Product Variety," *Marketing Science,* Summer 1990, *9*(3), 189–206.

10. This usage is increasingly common in industrial practice and is consistent with that used in K. Ulrich and S. Eppinger, *Product Design and Development* (New York: McGraw-Hill, 1995).

11. K. Ulrich, "The Role of Product Architecture in the Manufacturing Firm," *Research Policy,* May 1995, *24,* 419–440.

12. V. Krishnan, R. Singh, and D. Tirupati, "A Model-Based Approach for Planning and Developing a Family of Technology-Based Products," working paper (Austin: University of Texas, 1998).

13. K. Ulrich and D. Ellison, "Customer Requirements and the Design-Select Decision," working paper (Philadelphia: Department of Operations and Information Management, Wharton School, University of Pennsylvania, 1997).

14. H. Lees, "Word Perfect: How Do You Accurately Describe What a Car Feels Like to Drive?" *Car Design & Technology,* August 1992, pp. 54–57.

PART TWO

Innovating with the Outside

CHAPTER SIX

Ally or Acquire?
How Technology Leaders
Decide

EDWARD B. ROBERTS
WENYUN KATHY LIU

There are four phases in the life cycle of a technology, and for each there are appropriate ways of partnering with outsiders. Increasingly, the challenge for managers is to recognize which phase each of their products is in and decide what kinds of external partnerships are most likely to facilitate speedy development. Each product a company is juggling may be in a different phase, and because the partnerships developed for one phase of a given technology could serve a different purpose in another phase of another technology, partnerships must be handled with care. Despite the complexity that comes with the need to manage a variety of alliances, Microsoft and others are demonstrating that it can be done successfully.

The most dramatic change in global technological innovation—the movement toward externally oriented collaborative strategies that complement internal R&D investments—began more than a decade ago.[1] Today companies use alliances, joint ventures,

---

First published in the Fall 2001 issue of *MIT Sloan Management Review.*

licensing, equity investments, mergers, and acquisitions to accomplish their technological and market goals over a technology's life cycle. How can companies decide when to use which form of partnership? In part, by understanding the externally focused technology-life-cycle model.[2]

THE TECHNOLOGY-LIFE-CYCLE MODEL OF ALLIANCES AND ACQUISITIONS

Understanding the role of alliances and acquisitions in the technology life cycle starts with understanding the cycle's four stages: the fluid phase, the transitional phase, the mature phase, and the discontinuities phase.[3] The first three were identified in the 1970s by James M. Utterback (see Figure 6.1). He later added a fourth, discontinuities, stage. Each stage is shaped by changes in the character and frequency of innovations in technology-based products and processes and by market dynamics (see Table 6.1).

The Fluid Phase

In the fluid phase the earliest pioneering products enter the market for that technology amid a high level of product and market uncertainty.[4] For example, CDs that use fluorescent technology are now entering the market for digital data storage, but it is too soon to tell if that technology will win out over DVDs—or other concepts. With the technology in flux, organizations seeking to increase data storage capacity (say, the military or the movie industry) hesitate to place R&D bets on a single technology. (In an earlier time period Exxon Enterprises found eight alternative computer storage technologies equally attractive for investments during a fluid phase of emerging technology.)

The fluid stage also is characterized by a high rate of growth in market demand. Barriers to entry are low; companies with proprietary technologies can enter with ease. There is little brand loy-

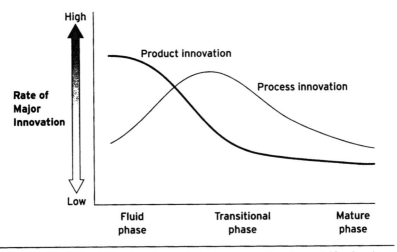

Figure 6.1. The Utterback Model of the Technology Life Cycle.

alty; customers seek functionality and quality instead. Direct competition among existing companies is relatively low, so profit margins are high. The bargaining power of suppliers is low because the materials and equipment used to make the products are general in nature.

Today, as product life cycles in high-tech markets shrink, new technology needs quick acceptance. Hence managers of companies in the fluid stage should pursue aggressive outward-licensing strategies to promote their technologies. For example, after Sun Microsystems introduced scalable processor architecture reduced-instruction-set computing in 1989, the company licensed it to twenty-one hardware manufacturers and software developers, including IBM, Novell, and Toshiba. And after introducing its Java technology in 1995, Sun made thirty-two Java licensing agreements in two years.

Start-up companies often adopt variations of traditional licensing. For instance, open-source software creators make their source

Table 6.1. Characteristics of the Four Technology Phases.

	Fluid Phase	Transitional Phase	Mature Phase	Discontinuities Phase
Dynamics of the phase	• Uncertainty in products and markets • High rate of product innovation and high degree of process flexibility • Fast-growing demand; low total volume • Greater importance of product functionality than brand names • Little direct competition	• Appearance of dominant design • Increased clarity about customer needs • Increased process innovation • Importance of complementary assets • Competition based on quality and availability	• Strong pressure on profit margin • More similarities than differences in final products • Convergence of product and process innovations	• Invasion of new technologies • Increasing obsolescence of incumbents' assets • Lowered barriers to entry; new competition • Convergence of some markets as new technologies emerge
Priorities	• Development and preservation of technology (with a focus on product development and aggressive patenting) • Promotion of proprietary technology as industry standard	• Realignment of technological capabilities with the dominant design • Continued exploration of technological opportunities • Pursuit of a growth strategy (through aggressive capacity building or by establishing a close relationship with suppliers and customers)	• Cost control throughout the value chain • Strong customer focus • Lean and efficient organization	• A need for incumbents to identify new technologies and realign core competencies • An option for incumbents to exit the market • Attackers' need to gain market recognition • Attackers' need to focus on product development

	Fluid Phase	Transitional Phase	Mature Phase	Discontinuities Phase
Strategic alliances	• Formation of alliances to promote technology as the industry standard • Adoption of licensing strategies (say, open-source licensing or aggressive licensing to users) • Formation of marketing alliances (with key players of the supply chain or with one industry leader) • Formation of technology alliances with established companies, often coupled with equity investments	• Winners' aggressive licensing to customers and to companies that lost the dominant-design battle • Formation of joint R&D ventures with companies in the market • Formation of marketing alliances; signing of supply agreements to guarantee consistent quality, price, and availability	• Formation of joint R&D ventures to share risks and costs of technology development • Formation of marketing alliances to attack latent markets or lure customers away from competitors • Manufacturing alliances to ensure availability of essential products • Open alliances with suppliers and customers	• Attackers' formation of marketing alliances to gain market recognition • Attacker agreements to supply technology leaders • Incumbents' acquisition of the disruptive technology through license agreements

(continued)

Table 6.1. Continued.

	Fluid Phase	Transitional Phase	Mature Phase	Discontinuities Phase
Mergers and acquisitions	• Acquisitions of start-ups by well-established technology companies from a more mature high-tech industry • Corporate equity investment by well-established high-tech companies	• Acquisitions of competitors by the winners of the dominant-technology battle • Acquisitions by established technology companies entering the market	• Horizontal mergers between companies with complementary products and services • Divestiture of manufacturing capabilities that are not essential • Acquisition of technology start-ups making products that would be difficult to develop in-house	• Possible equity financing for attacker from established technology companies • Established companies' move into new markets through acquisition of niche technology companies • Established companies' acquisition of enterprises that have related product capabilities • Divestiture of companies as priorities shift with market convergence

code available to independent programmers who then make compatible changes and share the results—an effective launch strategy for Linux and Apache, among other software products.

To enable a new product to reach customers quickly, high-tech companies in the fluid stage also form marketing alliances with key players in their supply chain. A difference from traditional marketing alliances is the current focus on speeding products to market. Business-to-business Internet companies, such as Allaire, Ariba, BroadVision, ChannelWave Software, Veritas Software, Vignette, and Webridge, allied with key channel players: solutions providers, application service providers, systems integrators, Internet service providers, and consulting companies.

Among the new kinds of alliances, those organized to establish standards are increasingly important. Indeed, in 1999 and 2000 most prominent computer companies participated in one standards alliance or more (see Table 6.2). Such alliances involve not only the promotion of the technology but also its further development—often among competitors. For example, in the high-profile Trusted Computing Platform Alliance of 1999, five competing computer giants joined forces to create standards for better security solutions.

During the fluid stage well-established technology companies often acquire start-ups. The acquired companies get access to a wider range of resources, and the acquirer gains critical competitive technologies that would have been costly to develop in-house. Another attractive alternative is to form an R&D alliance with a start-up while also making minority equity investments in it. Such strategic alliances allow established companies to keep pace with change while building high-level managerial connections and operational links that can lead to later acquisitions.

The Transitional Phase

The transitional phase of a technology life cycle starts with the emergence of a dominant design. As product and market uncertainty

Table 6.2. Recent Standards Alliances in the Computer Industry.

▼

Date	Participants	Objective
Jan. 13, 1999	Adaptec, Compaq, Hewlett-Packard, and IBM	To create a new input/output standard
Apr. 26, 1999	Dictaphone, eDigital, IBM, Intel, Norcom Electronics, Olympus America, and Philips Electronics	To develop a standard for the way voice commands and information are transmitted and received by mobile devices
Oct. 18, 1999	Compaq, Hewlett-Packard, IBM, Intel, and Microsoft	To develop security standards for hardware and software used in e-commerce
Dec. 14, 1999	Akamai Technologies, Allaire, BroadVision, Exodus Communications, Finian Software, Network Appliance, Network Associates, Novell, Open Market, and Oracle	To create a standard that connects multiple Web functions on any Internet access device
Feb. 8, 2000	3Com, Cisco Systems, Extreme Networks, Intel, Nortel Networks, Sun Microsystems, and World Wide Packets	To develop standards and technology for 10-gigabit Ethernet networks

Source: Techweb, http://www.techweb.com.

lessen and R&D efforts become focused on improving the dominant technology, design cycles shrink.

During the transitional phase industry demand grows rapidly, customers require quality products and timely delivery, and barriers to entry become even lower if the dominant design is easily accessible. Companies must realign themselves with the new standards and pursue an aggressive growth strategy.[5] To signal their commitment they also should consider capital investment in production capacity. And to ensure product availability, they need supply and marketing agreements with customers. In the transitional phase companies often collaborate to improve the dominant design and develop new technological extensions, features, and applications through joint R&D. Typically, once they possess sufficient technological capabilities, companies of similar size join forces.

For increased market share and revenue growth, companies need to move quickly to develop or adopt the dominant design. Those with the dominant design pursue their advantage and collect royalties (as Texas Instruments has done most effectively) by aggressively licensing the product to other enterprises. Organizations that have lost the standards battle should adopt the standards quickly by getting a license to use someone else's discovery or through internal R&D. The growth potential in the transitional phase makes entry particularly attractive for companies in mature technology markets. When the PC industry was in transition, Japanese electronics giants—Hitachi, NEC, and Toshiba—invested heavily to enter the business. Mature companies seek to acquire businesses that either possess the dominant design or have the capabilities needed for quick adoption of the new standards.

Growing companies that possess the dominant technology may be able to make acquisitions of their own, thanks to the financial clout of their surging stock prices. Ideally, those acquisitions would have a strong strategic objective, and target companies would possess complementary technologies or an attractive customer base.

The Mature Phase

In the mature phase products built around the dominant design proliferate. R&D emphasis shifts from product innovation toward process innovation.

Because process innovations are inherently time consuming and expensive, many companies form R&D alliances to share the cost and risk. Last year's alliance between Fujitsu and Toshiba to codevelop one-gigabit dynamic random-access memory (DRAM) computer chips is a good example.

The high cost and risk of internal R&D make technology acquisitions attractive too. In some respects, an acquisition is better than an alliance, in which partners are also competitors and have equal access to the new technology. Acquisitions give the acquirer exclusive rights to the proprietary technology. Between 1993 and 2000 Cisco Systems spent roughly $9 billion buying more than fifty companies.[6] Cisco's technology acquisitions freed up important resources for an internal focus on core competencies.

During the mature stage of a technology's life cycle, the growth rate of market demand slows, but the total volume of demand expands. The once highly profitable market becomes commoditized, a direct result of cost reduction and excess capacity. There is fierce price competition and pressure on profit margins. The need to bring down cost and grow volume increases. Given the technological and capital requirements, entry is harder for outsiders. The key to surviving the mature stage is strong commitment to organizationwide improvement in efficiency. One way to reduce development cost is through cooperative alliances with suppliers—or even with competitors.

High-tech industries are notoriously cyclical, and companies that pursue manufacturing joint ventures in the mature stage have a better shot at controlling cost and guaranteeing availability and quality despite marketplace fluctuations. Marketing alliances are important, too, as competition intensifies and focusing on customers becomes critical. Marketing alliances help companies target the latent market, pursue competitors' customers, and expand into new geographical markets.

In high-tech industries horizontal mergers with complementary product lines are another popular method to reduce costs and obtain a stronger market position by offering more products and services. That was the apparent rationale when Compaq bought Digital Equipment Corp. (DEC) in 1998. Compaq, facing a saturated PC market, saw DEC as its key to expanding into the then more lucrative high-end server and service markets.

In the mature stage some companies divest noncore properties to alleviate pressures on earnings. In 1998 Texas Instruments, wishing to concentrate on its core digital-signal processing business, sold its facilities for manufacturing DRAMs to Micron Technologies. This also is the phase during which technology companies have the highest propensity to make equity investments and acquisitions and to form alliances for R&D, marketing, or manufacturing.

The Discontinuities Phase

The existing technology can be rendered obsolete by the introduction of next-generation technology (NGT), a more advanced technology, or converging markets. During the discontinuities stage the marketplace is volatile. A new market develops, taking demand away from the old market. As many previous barriers to entry (incumbents' specialized production facilities, their investments in R&D, and their technology portfolios) lose their force, the likelihood of new entrants is high. The technology in the field gradually turns toward the fluid phase of a new technology life cycle. The process of technological evolution starts again.

Because technological discontinuities can render a company's competitive ability obsolete, companies must adjust business strategies. When NGT increases system performance, it may either destroy or enhance company competencies.[7] If existing producers initiate the NGT (an uncommon scenario in high-tech industries), it is competence-enhancing to them. Even if the market conditions for their mainstream product deteriorate, the new technology may provide first-mover advantage. Companies that are first to increase capacity can capture near-monopoly rents. A one-month time-to-market advantage can dramatically increase the product's total profit margin. Marketing alliances and agreements to supply end users can accelerate the transition; they guarantee the new product's availability to high-end customers and alleviate the first mover's concern about uncertain market demand.

The definition of the technology's market becomes blurred as markets converge and horizontal mergers appear between attackers and incumbents. Companies with stronger financial bases become acquirers. For example, in an effort to stay ahead of the transition into Internet protocol networks, telecommunications giant AT&T purchased cable, telecommunications, high-speed Internet, and networking companies. At the same time, to focus on core competencies and avoid redundancy, AT&T made several divestitures. The company's joint R&D alliances and minority equity investments supported both capital and technology goals—without incurring the costs or risks of acquisitions. Such arrangements are popular between technology giants that have a need to collaborate. In May 1999 AT&T entered a critical alliance in which Microsoft put $5 billion into AT&T and supplied its Windows CE operating system to AT&T's set-top boxes. Similarly, Intel, having observed that networking and communications were displacing PCs as the opportunity for semiconductors, made fifteen acquisitions in those fields during 1999 and 2000 alone.

COMPANIES' DECISIONS TO ALLY OR ACQUIRE

A decision to ally or acquire depends not only on company-specific competencies and needs but also on overall market development and the company's position relative to its competitors (see Figure 6.2). Industry structure and critical success factors change as the underlying technology evolves over its life cycle and as competitive pressures vary. Companies are more inclined to form alliances as the technology becomes better defined and as competitive pressure increases. Then the number of alliances declines in the discontinuities phase, when consolidation decreases the total number of companies in the industry. The number of mergers and acquisitions is often high during the transition stage because established companies acquire start-ups to enhance their technology portfolios. As the dominant design becomes clear and technology becomes more mature, companies increase acquisition efforts to stay ahead of the competition.[8]

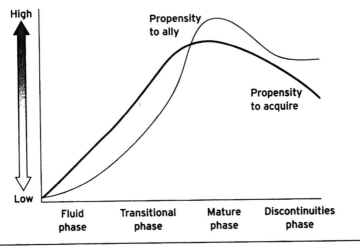

Figure 6.2. Propensity to Ally or Acquire.

MICROSOFT AND THE TECHNOLOGY LIFE CYCLE

Microsoft presents a good example of a company managing its external activities in sync with the underlying technological life cycle (see Table 6.3).

Microsoft's Fluid Phase (1975 to 1981)

When Microsoft was established in 1975 to provide software for the first PC, such software was relatively new and crude; direct competition was minimal. Throughout the late 1970s Microsoft focused on developing its PC software products and technology portfolio. It built strategic relationships with domestic and foreign computer manufacturers, choosing licensing as its principal collaborative mechanism for attracting new customers. During its first six-year period, sales grew at an average annual rate of 165 percent; revenue reached $16 million by the end of 1981.[9]

Aggressive licensing of its own versions of generic software products, such as Basic, Cobol, Fortran, and Pascal, helped Microsoft

Table 6.3. Microsoft and the Four Technology Phases.

	Fluid Phase	Transitional Phase	Mature Phase	Discontinuities Phase
Dynamics of the phase	• 165 percent growth rate • Poorly defined technology • Proliferation of products • Small niche market–the PC market • Limited competition	• 69 percent growth rate • Establishment of Microsoft's operating system as the industry standard • Competition from other application software companies • Market growth as technology is better defined	• 45 percent growth rate • Enormous software sales • More competition in the application software industry • Product upgrades and product development to meet customers' needs	• 32 percent growth rate • Slower growth of the current technology • Invasion of the Internet; converging markets • Market invasion by new companies with new Internet technologies • Need for incumbent to play technological catch-up
Priorities	• Rapid market recognition • Promotion of the technology as part of the dominant design for PCs	• Pursuit of growth strategy • Development of application software to run on Microsoft's operating systems	• Easy-to-use application software programs • Keeping pace with technology developments	• Development of new technologies • Attempt to get established in the new technology area

	Fluid Phase	Transitional Phase	Mature Phase	Discontinuities Phase
Strategic alliances	• Important strategic alliance with IBM • Aggressive licensing to commercial users and PC manufacturers	• Continued aggressive licensing to commercial users and PC manufacturers • Ongoing strategic alliance with IBM	• 36 joint ventures • Joint R&D ventures with PC hardware companies • Joint marketing agreements • Continued focus on licensing	• High level of alliance activity • 35 alliances, including several that had more than one objective (46 percent for joint R&D, 52 percent for joint marketing, 17 percent for licensing)
Mergers and acquisitions	• None	• Acquisition of Forethought, the developer of PowerPoint • No other mergers or acquisitions	• 2 equity minority investments (1 in competing operating system, 1 in applications) • 2 technology acquisitions • Slightly more activity than during the transitional stage	• Much activity • 26 minority equity investments • 15 equity investments since 1999, all Internet related • 15 companies bought, half Internet related, half application software technologies

attract the attention of the most powerful mainframe computer company, IBM. In 1980 Microsoft signed a contract to develop operating systems for IBM's first PC. The strategic partnership between the start-up and the established manufacturer was key in making Microsoft's operating system technology (MS-DOS 1.0) part of the dominant design for PCs. IBM quickly triumphed in the PC market, and as other computer manufacturers started to clone the IBM PC, they adopted Microsoft's operating system too.

Microsoft's Transitional Phase (1982 to 1987)

By 1982 Microsoft's MS-DOS was the dominant operating system for the dominant IBM PC. While Microsoft continued to improve the functionality of its operating systems, it also enhanced its efforts to develop products for specific customer needs. It broadened its technology base by adding application software programs to its portfolio. Its main objective was to create user-friendly operating systems and software programs for PC users. As the market for PC software grew, Microsoft continued its aggressive licensing strategy. In the first sixteen months that MS-DOS was on the market, it was licensed to fifty hardware manufacturers.[10] By retaining distribution rights to DOS, Microsoft benefited from the PC boom. And the continuing IBM alliance helped establish Windows as the standard operating system after MS-DOS.

Microsoft's strong stock performance after its 1986 initial public offering enabled the company to make its first acquisition in 1987—of Forethought, the developer of PowerPoint.

Microsoft's Mature Phase (1988 to 1994)

By 1988 Microsoft had developed a complete technology portfolio. It surpassed Lotus Development Corp. as the world's top software vendor. In the mature stage of its technology life cycle, Microsoft continued to develop and improve its operating systems and application software and to address PC users' needs for word processing, spreadsheet, and multimedia software. Sales grew an average of 45 percent annually. The growth rate was significantly lower than during the fluid and transitional stages, but overall sales volume was larger.

To strengthen its dominance in the high-growth software market, Microsoft participated in strategic partnerships and made key acquisitions. From 1988 to 1994 Microsoft entered thirty-six joint ventures and alliances, 61 percent of which involved joint R&D agreements.[11] More important, because it had partnerships with all seven of the leading computer hardware companies (and because twenty-one out of thirty-six joint ventures were exclusive partnerships), Microsoft was able to develop more-functional, user-friendly software.

Microsoft's Discontinuities Phase (1995 to 1999)

The Internet changed the industry's competitive landscape. Although it fueled the growth of the PC market, it also lowered the barriers to entry. Alternative devices appeared. From 1995 to 1999 Microsoft continued to improve the product lines that embodied its base technology. Meanwhile it began to develop Internet technologies to establish itself in the new growth market, introducing Internet Explorer 2.0 in 1995 in competition with leading Web browser Netscape Navigator. As it did with application software, Microsoft leveraged its effective operating system monopoly, bundling Internet Explorer with Windows in the hope that people would use something preinstalled in their PCs.

Microsoft provides a textbook case of a company facing technological discontinuity. As the incumbent, the company possessed deep financial resources and a strong customer base. However, it neither pioneered the Internet nor reacted immediately to it—and consequently fell behind its attackers in the technology and product arenas. Once aware of the seriousness of the threat, Microsoft increased its alliance and acquisition efforts. From 1995 to 1999 alone, it participated in thirty-five joint ventures. Joint marketing agreements mounted as the market became more volatile and Microsoft strove to maintain a strong relationship with customers.

With the dawn of the Internet and mobile technologies, Microsoft bought fifteen companies and, in four years, made twenty-six minority equity investments focusing on Internet-related technologies and application software.

THE RIGHT PARTNERSHIP ARRANGEMENT FOR THE RIGHT STAGE

Our life cycle model indicates that during the fluid stage companies focus on improving product functionality and gaining quick market recognition. Because Microsoft established an important strategic relationship with IBM in that stage, its operating system became the industry standard and Microsoft could proceed to an aggressive licensing strategy.

In the transitional stage, high-tech companies generally form joint R&D ventures, pursue aggressive licensing strategies to realign their technology portfolio, and sign marketing and supply agreements to guarantee consistent quality, price, and availability for their customers. Microsoft continued its licensing strategy, and its strategic alliance with IBM remained instrumental to growth.

In the mature stage of the technology life cycle, companies use numerous strategic alliances and acquisitions to share the risks and costs of technology development, ensure availability of essential products, and expand into latent markets. Collaborating with leading hardware companies in thirty-six joint ventures and alliances during its mature phase, Microsoft obtained access to the advanced technologies it needed.

The model anticipates that companies in the discontinuities stage will establish marketing and licensing agreements as well as joint R&D ventures. The phase also features a high level of product and market uncertainty, with technologies invading and markets merging. Thus, when the Internet changed the computer industry's competitive landscape, Microsoft turned increasingly to alliance efforts. Its thirty-five joint ventures helped maintain customer relationships and provide comprehensive solutions to clients. As of this writing, Microsoft also has made twenty-six minority investments and has acquired fifteen companies to address the challenge.

Clearly, Microsoft exemplifies our model of the externally focused technology life cycle. Unpublished life cycle case studies on Cisco and Compaq—plus statistical analyses of industry data—also lend support to our framework.[12] Nevertheless, additional empirical validation from many companies and industries is needed.

Ultimately, the model raises concerns for managers. It shows that a company should use, in a timely and appropriate way, every form of business development—alliances, joint ventures, licensing, equity investments, mergers, and acquisitions—in order to perform optimally over its underlying technology life cycle. But doing so requires integrated technology and market and financial planning that may be beyond most companies.

Furthermore, few companies seem to excel, with either organizational or managerial processes, in implementing even a portion of what is needed in business development. A subjective search for benchmarks finds Texas Instruments remarkably capable of carrying out profitable outbound licensing. Cisco excels in acquisitions. Intel and 3M do different but comparably effective jobs of corporate venture-capital investing. Millennium Pharmaceuticals in Cambridge, Massachusetts, has rapidly built a multibillion-dollar enterprise from alliances and joint ventures. But no one company seems to be outstanding at more than one mode of business development. The challenge is not beyond companies' reach, but in order to rise to it managers must understand the externally focused technology-life-cycle model, think about how it applies to their own situation—and learn to use partnerships that are targeted to a particular technology-life-cycle stage.

NOTES

1. E. B. Roberts, "Benchmarking Global Strategic Management of Technology," *Research-Technology Management,* March-April 2001, *44,* 25–36.
2. The authors appreciate the financial support of the global industrial sponsors of the MIT International Center for Research on the Management of Technology, as well as funding from the National Science Foundation to the MIT Center for Innovation in Product Development.
3. For a comprehensive literature review on different models of the technology life cycle, see P. Anderson and M. L. Tushman, "Technological Discontinuities and Dominant Designs: A Cyclical Model of Technological Change," *Administrative Science Quarterly,* 1990, *35,* 604–633. Further discussion of the model's evolution is provided by J. M. Utterback, *Mastering the Dynamics of Innovation* (Boston: Harvard Business School Press, 1994). Utterback's pioneering life cycle work, begun in the 1970s, is best summarized by his book. Following Utterback, Tushman and Rosenkopf propose a similar technology-life-cycle model with four stages: eras of ferment, dominant designs, eras of incremental change, and technological discontinuities. See M. L. Tushman and L. Rosenkopf, "Organizational Determinants of Technological Change: Towards a Sociology of Technological Evolution," *Research in Organizational Behavior,* 1992, *14,* 311–347. See also R. R. Nelson and S. G. Winter, "Simulation of Schumpeterian Competition," *American Economic Review,* 1977, *67,* 271–276; R. R. Nelson and S. G. Winter, "The Schumpeterian Tradeoff Revisited," *American Economic Review,* 1982, *72,* 114–132; G. Dosi, "Technological Paradigms and Technological Trajectories: A Suggested Interpretation of the Determinants and Directions of Technical Change," *Research Policy,* 1982, *11,* 147–162; N. Rosenberg, *Inside the Black Box: Technology and Economics* (New York: Cambridge University Press, 1982); D. J. Teece, "Profiting from Technological Innovation: Implications for Integration, Collaboration, Licensing and Public Policy," *Research Policy,* 1986, *15,* 285–305; D. J. Teece, "Capturing Value from Technological Inno-

vation: Integration, Strategic Partnering and Licensing Decisions," *Interfaces,* 1988, *18,* 46–61; and R. R. Nelson, "Recent Evolutionary Theorizing About Economic Change," *Journal of Economic Literature,* 1995, *33,* 48–90.

4. W. J. Abernathy and J. M. Utterback, "Patterns of Industrial Innovation," *Technology Review,* 1978, *80,* 40–47.

5. R. M. Henderson, "Underinvestment and Incompetence as Responses to Radical Innovation: Evidence from the Photolithographic Alignment Equipment," *RAND Journal of Economics,* 1993, *24,* 248–269.

6. www.cisco.com/warp/public/750/acquisition.

7. M. L. Tushman and P. Anderson, "Technological Discontinuities and Organizational Environments," *Administrative Science Quarterly,* 1986, *31,* 439–465.

8. We define "propensity to ally" as the likelihood that a company will participate in joint ventures and alliances. Several ways for post hoc measurement of a company's propensity to ally seem plausible—for example, by examining its total number of alliances normalized by sales. We define "propensity to acquire" as the likelihood that a company will make an acquisition, perhaps measured similarly by the total number of acquisitions normalized by sales.

9. www.microsoft.com.

10. www.microsoft.com.

11. Data from the Securities Data Company's joint-venture database. Many joint ventures involve multiple agreements.

12. W. Liu, "Essays in Management of Technology: Collaborative Strategies for American Technology Industries," Ph.D. dissertation (Cambridge, Massachusetts: Department of Political Science, MIT, 2000).

CHAPTER SEVEN

Outsourcing Innovation:
The New Engine of Growth

JAMES BRIAN QUINN

nnovate or die. That's a theme many senior executives support. How to keep ahead is the issue. With 2 billion new minds becoming innovation sources for our marketplaces between 1995 and 2010, no one company acting alone can hope to outinnovate every competitor, potential competitor, supplier, or external knowledge source around the world.[1]

But there is hope. Strategically outsourcing innovation— using the most current technologies and management techniques—can put a company in a sustainable leadership position. Leading companies have lowered innovation costs and risks 60 to 90 percent while similarly decreasing cycle times and leveraging the impact of their internal investments by tens to hundreds of times.[2] Strategic management of outsourcing is perhaps the most powerful tool in management, and outsourcing of innovation is its frontier.[3]

First published in the Summer 2000 issue of *MIT Sloan Management Review.*

THINKING ABOUT OUTSOURCING

First, consider the pharmaceutical industry, where independent biotechnology research adds one hundred gigabytes per day to the databases of the GenBank alone (the National Institutes of Health genetic sequence database, an annotated collection of all publicly available DNA sequences). No company can hope to keep ahead of such an outpouring by itself. Furthermore, at the applied research level, combinatory chemistry (designing, constructing, and testing new compounds in vitro at the molecular level) has reduced experimental cycle times by more than eight hundred times and lowered costs and risks by more than six hundred times (see Table 7.1). As a result, hundreds of small, sophisticated firms have entered the field as potential suppliers of innovation—radically changing the opportunities for outsourcing and restructuring the entire industry.

Next, consider both the large services industries, where most innovations are dependent on software, and the manufacturing world, which increasingly relies on embedded electronics. In both

Table 7.1. Shrinking the Time and Cost for Drug Development.

▼

Combinatory chemistry (designing, constructing, and testing new compounds at the molecular level) is one way that outsourcing innovation pays off.

	Traditional	Combinatorial	Improvement Multiple
Chemist time	3 months	3 months	N/A
Number of new compounds	12	10,000	833 times
Total cost	$90 million	$120 million	N/A
Cost per compound	$7,500	$12	625 times
Average time per compound	1 week	Less than 5 minutes	2,000 times

Source: "In Vivo, Making Combinatory Chemistry Pay," Booz Allen & Hamilton report (New York, 1997).

cases, a mere fifteen sequences of software can be combined in more than 10 trillion ways, each creating a potential new product or process. No internal R&D group can possibly predict, evaluate, or cover all possible designs or competitive positions. To prosper in this environment—even survive—companies need to systematically tap the capabilities of external knowledge leaders, not just for state-of-the-art products and services but also for the continuous innovation and evolution of ideas that will keep companies at the frontier of their industries.[4] Carefully pursued, the strategic outsourcing of innovation has led to the restructuring of industries as diverse as automobiles, aerospace, computers, telecommunications, pharmaceuticals, chemicals, health care, financial services, energy systems, and software.

A high-profile example of outsourcing for innovation is Cisco Systems, currently valued at $12.2 billion. In the early 1990s the company found that it could not rely on internal manufacturing or hiring capabilities to keep up with its 100 percent growth rate. Instead, it established long-term relationships with a few selected manufacturers and opened its systems, processes, and networks to them for joint equipment development. Today partners provide most of Cisco's component, hardware, and manufacturing innovation. About thirty vendors and service providers have recently joined the Cisco Hosting Applications Initiative to develop new technology for Cisco's routers and to optimize performance in hosted applications.

Why the Time Is Right for Outsourcing Innovation

The time is right for outsourcing innovation. Four powerful forces are currently driving the innovation revolution. First, demand (as defined by real gross national product in the world's largest and most rapidly growing economies) is doubling every fourteen to sixteen years, creating a host of new specialist markets sufficiently large to attract innovation.[5] Second, the supply of scientists, technologists, and knowledge workers has skyrocketed, as have knowledge bases and access to them. Software-based analytical, modeling, communications, and market feedback technologies have lowered costs and risks substantially, allowing many smaller enterprises to participate in emerging markets. Third, interaction capabilities have grown. Combined with the Internet and other information technology capabilities, interactions among technologies—including the biotech, computer, chemistry, environmental, and food fields—are growing exponentially. Fourth, new incentives have emerged. Lower tax rates, privatization, the relaxation of many national and international trade barriers, and the lower capital investments needed in many fields have meant greater incentives for entrepreneurs worldwide to develop and exploit advances in knowledge. New management techniques, software, and communications systems have enabled much better coordination of highly dispersed innovation activities.

OUTSOURCING THE TECHNOLOGY CHAIN

Depending on their capabilities and needs, many companies can profitably outsource almost any element in the innovation chain.[6]

Basic Research

For large pharmaceutical companies, outsourcing to universities, institutes, and government laboratories has long provided fundamental research knowledge for new product streams. In the 1950s Hoffman La Roche, through the La Roche Institute, was among the first to formalize such relationships, giving researchers support, independence, and facilities that few universities or independent laboratories could equal. Continuous long-term support to outside researchers is now such an industry standard that some preeminent internal-research companies have been criticized for not outsourcing enough. New large-scale independent collaborative efforts, such as the Human Genome Project and the Cochrane Collaboration (which is assembling and analyzing all the literature on roughly 1 million controlled studies about the effectiveness of different medical treatments), have made it almost impossible to keep up through internal efforts alone.

Early-Stage Research

Outsourcing early-stage applied and precompetitive research is critical in such industries as semiconductors (Sematech), aerospace (for systems modeling and new materials), computers (subatomic-particle phenomena and materials interactions), and foods (plant pathogens, nutrition and flavor enhancement, soils, and weather research). Eaton, a major equipment manufacturer, has long outsourced basic and early applied analysis and design of its gear mechanisms to the Illinois Institute of Technology, claiming a greater than 90 percent return over in-house sourcing.

Combinatory chemistry is now revolutionizing the pharmaceuticals and biochemistry industries. Millennium Pharmaceuticals, Inc. and 3D Pharmaceuticals, for example, have software models to build and analyze virtual chemicals that have demonstrated biological effects. They then can search for molecules with similar effects or combinatory possibilities, assisted by outsourcers who can rapidly build and test millions of possibilities using small-scale apparatuses and a few molecules of refined materials in vitro. Once a pathogen is identified, these companies can test thousands of compounds per day for activity that might destroy the pathogen or interrupt its path. After patenting the most promising compounds, they may present packages of attractive new products to their larger partners—to do testing on animals and humans, seek regulatory clearance, or handle large-scale manufacturing and distribution. Alternatively, the small companies may themselves outsource those activities to independent testing labs for further verification, refinement of results, or credibility before choosing between downstream alliances or proceeding in-house.

No single pharmaceuticals company can hope to match the sum of all the external enterprises innovating in its value chain. As knowledge bases from the Human Genome Project and from world-wide cellular and basic pathogen research explode, the interactive outsourced structure has become a model around which much of the industry is restructuring. Innovative companies focus on certain core activities and outsource not only product distribution but also basic research, combinatory chemistry, clinical trials, and field monitoring (see Figure 7.1).

Advanced Development

The outsourcing of advanced development and product innovation, especially for software and component innovation, has become de rigueur in industries where the most rapid and high-impact innovation occurs at the supplier level. For example, Boeing's defense operations (including recently merged McDonnell Douglas and Rockwell) just introduced two prototypes of its Joint Strike Fighter, built using only fifty-eight workers in its Palmdale, California, factory. With computerized modeling coordinating their activities, hundreds of suppliers developed and produced "snap-together" component modules—allowing Boeing to slash design and revision times and costs.[7]

By specializing, many suppliers have developed in-depth knowledge, skills, investment infrastructures, and innovative capabilities for their segment of the value chain—advantages that are well beyond those that any integrated enterprise could obtain. Dell Computer and Intel exploit different ends of the innovation-outsourcing spectrum. As an integrator, the $18.2 billion Dell, growing at 47 percent compounded for the last decade, outsources virtually all design and innovation for components, software, and nonassembly production. It invests heavily only in its core competencies (understanding customer needs, logistics, and component integration) and wherever it sees a unique opportunity for adding value. By outsourcing it avoids not just huge investments in facilities, inventory, and human resources but also development risks and investments. Opening up technical needs and production schedules

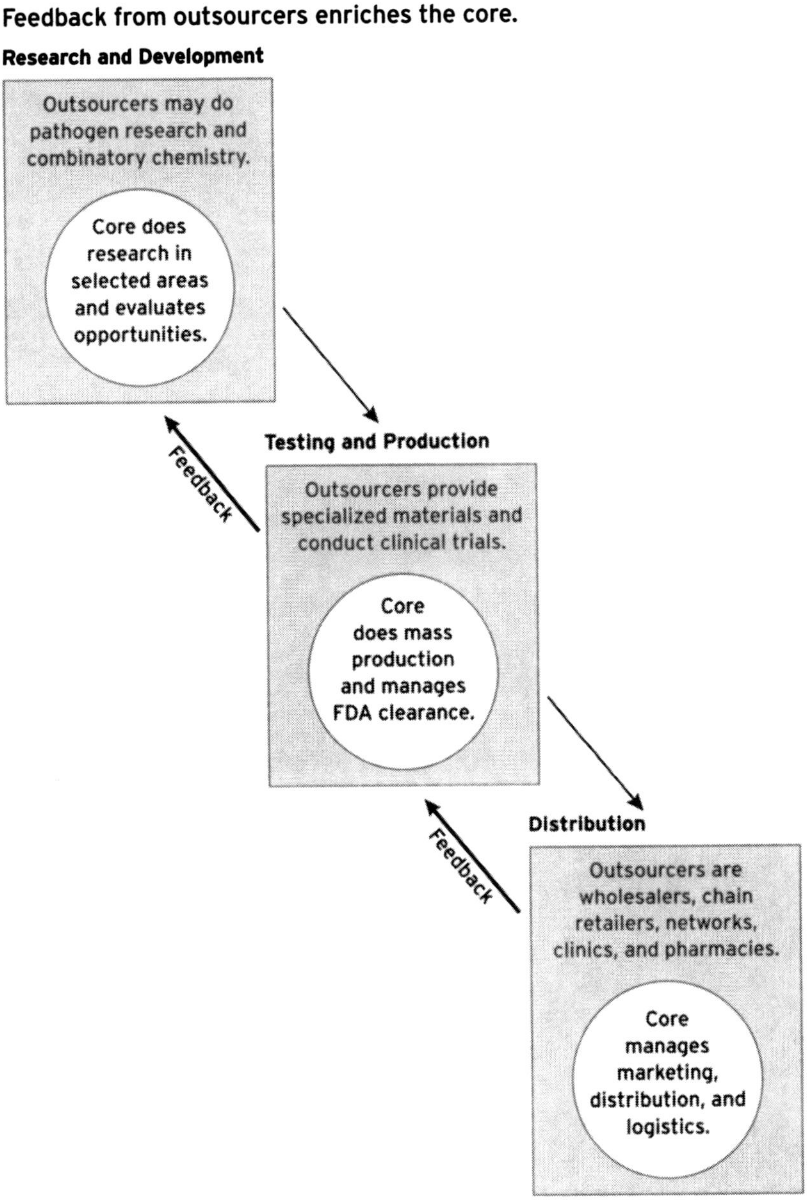

Feedback from outsourcers enriches the core.

Research and Development

Outsourcers may do
pathogen research and
combinatory chemistry.

Core does
research in
selected areas
and evaluates
opportunities.

Feedback

Testing and Production

Outsourcers provide
specialized materials and
conduct clinical trials.

Core
does mass
production
and manages
FDA clearance.

Feedback

Distribution

Outsourcers are
wholesalers, chain
retailers, networks,
clinics, and pharmacies.

Core
manages
marketing,
distribution, and
logistics.

Figure 7.1. Ways in Which the Pharmaceuticals Industry
Focuses on Core Competencies and Outsources Innovation.

to suppliers, Dell obtains the most current products with the shortest innovation and cycle times, often with direct shipments from suppliers to customers. Dell has chosen to outsource component production and innovation, keeping component integration, logistics, and customer understanding as in-house core competencies.

As a component supplier, Intel avoids end-product production and concentrates investments and formidable development capabilities on its specialized competencies. By doing so, the company has long been able to offer advanced microprocessors and complex integrated circuits to computer and system customers with a timing, quality, reliability, and cost that have given it a preeminent position in microprocessors.

Ford and Johnson Controls offer a similar pairing between core competence and outsourcing in autos. When Ford moved from being 70 percent insourced and vertically integrated to 70 percent outsourced during the Taurus introduction in the early 1980s, it feared losing its detailed knowledge about subsystems and its capacity to remain innovative. Instead, it found that suppliers often had much greater knowledge depth, could innovate faster and better, and could save Ford the investments and risks of supporting a full range of development activities.[8]

Other automakers followed suit. Now there is a high correlation throughout the industry between a company's degree of outsourcing, its innovativeness, and its product margins and return on investment.[9] In conjunction with Oracle and Commerce One, the Big Three automakers just announced an Internet-based parts exchange (estimated at $490 billion) to support outsourcing.[10]

Johnson Controls, the world's leading supplier of automotive interiors, concentrates only on certain subsystems and sells them to numerous customers. It can therefore support more depth than any integrated auto company in terms of technical knowledge, automated facilities, and a wide supplier network for interiors innovation. As economies of scale in component knowledge and technologies become more important, disaggregation offers many companies greater flexibility, lower costs, and higher rates of innovation—all at lower risk. Even Europe is beginning to exploit the opportunities, with the European Airbus integrators tapping into worldwide component innovation sources to change the entire performance position of Airbus.

OUTSOURCING BUSINESS PROCESSES

Even higher innovation returns can accrue from outsourcing entire business processes or process design activities that are not core competencies. Functional services, such as advertising, maintenance, and auditing, fall into that category. Increasingly, major systems— including logistics, worldwide accounting, energy supplies, real estate operations, and software systems development and operations—are also outsourced. Sophisticated specialist suppliers can arrive at solutions that fragmented internal sources could never even imagine—and they can implement those solutions rapidly without disruptive internal politics.[11]

For example, Enron Energy Systems has worldwide operations and multisourcing experience that enables it to handle a client's full energy management system efficiently (raw-material sourcing, conversion operations, equipment purchasing and maintenance, facility design and operations, and specialized personnel training). Most clients have dispersed such functions into many different locations and organizations. Enron can often implement solutions for energy supply and usage across internal divisions that might not perceive or have incentives to create such solutions—for example, jointly purchasing larger equipment, sharing facilities with outsiders, or optimizing plant design, maintenance, and energy use trade-offs. One of Enron's innovations involves first offering internal divisions stabilized energy costs through its sophisticated energy industry knowledge, financial modeling, and risk-sharing capabilities; and second, pricing energy on a per-unit basis (per room in hotels, per linear foot of production in manufacturing, or per square foot in offices) to fit the specific strategic cost-control needs of each division. Enron can offer solutions using purchased raw materials and equipment at economies of scale its customers can't touch. Another innovator, Trigen Energy Corporation, has invented processes that are more environmentally benign than most. For specific customers Trigen has increased energy conversion efficiencies from the national average of 35 percent to levels as high as 90 percent.

In corporate services (financial, logistics, maintenance, software, building design, auditing, real estate, human resources, and Internet services), external sources are the dominant innovators. The success of such sources is a function of their depth of expertise, their software and investment support, and the variety of their customer contacts (to enhance innovation opportunities). In comparison with internal counterparts in integrated companies, a Pricewaterhouse-Coopers or Arthur Andersen is more likely to come up with auditing innovations; Hay Management or Hewitt Associates with new performance-evaluation or incentive systems; and Vanguard, Merrill Lynch, or Alex Brown BT with innovative investment or retirement plan vehicles. Companies that use only internal sources instead of outsourcing such activities tend to cut themselves off from both a continuing stream of innovations and the opportunity to switch rapidly if a new value-added service appears. Proper outsourcing of entire business processes can speed and amplify major innovative changes.

Consider Royal Bank of Scotland (RBS). Under stress in a tight labor market, RBS wanted to shift its benefits package rapidly toward a new approach that would attract and retain highly qualified people. The bank worked with Hewitt Associates to design and implement the largest cafeteria-style flexible benefits plan in the United Kingdom. Through a "value account," employees could select, for example, different in-house benefit options, supplemental health coverage, or discounted vouchers for groceries, child care, or life insurance. RBS and Hewitt created innovative tax-free pay and added special plans for maternity leave, new hires, and termination. To speed implementation and enable continued innovation, RBS then outsourced much of the benefit management to Hewitt.[12]

Raytheon, based in Lexington, Massachusetts, provides outsourced technical support and rapid staffing throughout the United States and abroad. Using a robust and secure information technology network, it electronically connects its distance solutions unit to customer sites to develop, transfer, and coordinate internal and external solutions. Clients thus get faster solutions and avoid overloading local technical-labor markets.[13]

OUTSOURCING NEW PRODUCT INTRODUCTIONS

Outsourcing key phases of new product introduction speeds the process, lowers costs, and amplifies impact. For example, few companies other than the dot-coms have a deep competence in developing and operating the interactive sites needed for successful product introduction on the Internet. Many independent software houses, however, offer sophisticated Web site design capabilities. Recently companies such as Verio and Exodus, large independent service providers that connect customers to the Internet, have been capitalizing on opportunities to support such activities by acting as application service providers (ASPs). As a part of their services, ASPs provide specialized software applications and value-added services to their subscribers and other customers. In addition to providing Web access, they facilitate interfaces among innovators, Web design houses, large individual customers, and specialized market segments. The role of ASPs is evolving, not just as a hosting industry but also as an outsourcing industry that connects clients (especially small and midsize companies) to the most advanced software providers on a network basis.

A high percentage of all innovation occurs at the interface between innovative suppliers and customers—with customers making more than 50 percent of innovations on new products in many industries.[14] Many companies have found that proper attention to outsourcing interfaces upstream and cooperative relationships with distribution partners downstream both lowers innovation costs and enormously expands the value of innovation to customers. Such relationships have benefits for both initial product introduction and subsequent product modification.

Nonalcoholic beverage brands, such as Snapple and rapidly growing SoBe, outsource the mixing and bottling of their new product introductions; in so doing, they avoid huge investments, time lags, and risks. Pharmaceuticals companies outsource their clinical studies for objectivity, higher quality, and faster data collection from various sites. Quintiles Transnational Corporation at Research Park, North Carolina, offers outsourcing services and software to manage pharmaceuticals development, clearance, and introduction more effectively across diverse locations. And auto companies, to make new product introductions more responsive to customer demands and less subject to hunches, are modularizing their designs and accessories, reducing their response cycle times to four or five days, and creating partnerships both with dealers and with Internet operators such as Autobytel and CarsDirect.com in order to collect and analyze consumer preferences rapidly so that they can modify prices and offerings responsively.[15]

In medical devices, codevelopment—outsourcing to obtain specialized customer expertise—is common. In developing real-time microsurgical magnetic resonance imaging techniques, GE Medical Devices personnel worked directly with MIT's artificial-intelligence laboratories and surgeon researchers at Boston's Brigham and Women's Hospital. Together, they created new devices, along with improved scanning and feedback systems, to help surgeons position and wield instruments in difficult-to-access locations—with minimum trauma for patients and improved outcomes.[16] HP Medical

Products has long had relationships with hospitals that allowed live-in Hewlett-Packard observers to identify and solve problems that operating room and medical care personnel could not see while performing.[17] Benefits are shared among the participating parties.

Many innovators have found that all they have to do is interest a single buyer at Home Depot, Wal-Mart, or Circuit City, and they have immediate distribution and product support in the world's most sophisticated marketplaces. Such distributors can provide instant feedback on models or features that are having problems or are selling best. Thus downstream distribution outsourcing, coupled with the outsourcing of physical logistics to companies such as Federal Express or UPS, allows innovators to eliminate multiple phases of product introduction and focus on what they do best: creating. Furthermore, the Internet allows companies to deliver upgrades and service support directly to customers—or through intermediaries such as Synergys—without establishing dedicated service centers everywhere.

The classic examples are Dell, Cisco, and the dot-coms, which connect a component or subsystem supplier to their product or service platform, shipping many elements directly from supplier to customer. Many suppliers have internal knowledge capabilities, access to multiple upstream technology specialists, and contacts with downstream customer problems and innovations that the coordinating client cannot hope to duplicate.

Utilizing outsourcing fully can bring the costs and risks of innovation to new lows. It also mitigates a new reverse risk—that of a company becoming obsolete if it doesn't participate properly in outsourcing innovation both upstream and downstream.

MANAGING OUTSOURCED INNOVATION

How does a company manage in the new world? The best analogy is surfing. With many waves of change occurring at once, innovation surfers cannot be sure of riding the right one. So they position themselves where experience or intuition tells them many waves will be forming. They prepare themselves with the best equipment and training, including hundreds of hours of studying waves and other surfers. They learn to discern a likely surfing opportunity from the sea's random motion, seeking waves that build on the energy of previous waves until they can tell that a really big one is forming. They may test a few. When a truly attractive wave starts to form, they speed into the curl and try to adapt quickly to each shift for a long, fast (profitable) ride. Finally—and just as important—they recognize when the wave is fading and get off before it hits the beach. Using the same equipment and skills, they reposition and look for the new wave.[18]

In today's world attempting to build permanent marketing or production dominance is futile. But building up skill sets, platforms, and sensing capabilities can produce successive fast rides.[19] Companies must drop outmoded core competencies, learn from each ride, and develop a genuine scanning capability for future opportunities. Like Cisco riding the Internet router wave, they must keep in mind that the interacting power and shape of the waves are more important than an individual company's swimming abilities. In today's stormy markets high-level technical, market-scanning, sensing, and responsiveness skills—and a well-designed platform for continual innovation—are key.

Commitment to Exciting Goals

At the core of successfully managing outsourced innovation is an exciting vision that inspires internal and external people to work together with energy. Such visions are essential in outsourcing because daily line contact is impossible and technical people feel free to jump to wherever the action and rewards look most exciting.[20]

Jointly developed visions and figures of merit help create identity and make goals exciting and explicit. As one CEO said, "They can't just be my goals or 'the buyer's' goals. Unless the outsource and its people enthusiastically support and benefit directly from innovation, it is unlikely to happen." Before finalizing contracts, carefully investigating potential partners' records on innovation, attitudes toward innovation, treatment of innovative champions, and reward structures for innovation offers high payoffs. Some enterprises literally vibrate with a palpable sense of energy, vision, and delight in change. Others don't. If either the buyer or seller doesn't expect, drive, welcome, and reward change, innovation is unlikely.

Hay Management Group, a leading human resource outsourcing firm, notes that "the key to success is both sides getting the relationship right at the outset. There must be mutuality of interest, common objectives, and an agreed-on scorecard." Hay works with its clients in workshops to understand as clearly as possible each party's needs, desires, and worst fears. It then jointly establishes a "mirror image" scorecard and a two-way accountability system defining exactly which specific Hay and client employees are responsible for each major program goal. Hay notes that the effort "vastly decreases risks of outsourcing failure, increases client satisfaction, and lowers coordination costs."

Effectiveness requires both parties to embrace a shared platform—first, of goals or purposes and, second, of ethical principles or culture. It also requires that each party have a strong sense that the other is entitled to operate independently despite the interdependence of the relationship.[21] Although different from one another, Dell, Nintendo, MCI, Eli Lilly, Sony, Microsoft, Home Depot, 3M, Hewlett-Packard, and Wal-Mart are among the companies that have effectively established such relationships. As a result, outside inventors seek them out directly.

MCI's innovation management team seeks and implements associations with small groups and individuals developing services that could attach to the MCI network. Recently MCI's chief technology officer noted that the company had about twenty times as many professional technical people working full time at vendors' or partners' premises as it did in its own offices. Internally, MCI designed the overall operating system and did all specifications, process rating, operational procedures, and system testing. MCI controlled the system itself but recognized it could neither attract nor afford (on a full-time basis) all the required talent.[22] However, by offering adequate interface information, a reputation for fairness, a well-known brand name, nationwide distribution, and attractive profit prospects, MCI stimulated outside software and service innovators to design many new products for the company. (It is too early to appraise the future effect of the WorldCom merger.)

Making Sure Your Partners Benefit

To attract innovative cooperation, a company must have some capabilities to access desired markets that supplier-inventors cannot duplicate. That means developing best-in-world performance in a grouping of services, skills, or systems important to customers. It also means focusing on those genuine core competencies—and a few other essential competencies—that protect the core or are demanded by customers.[23] Those central activities define the way the company creates value for customers. They also provide essential bargaining leverage with suppliers and serve as a strategic block against suppliers or competitors wishing to bypass the company and move into its markets.

Consider the following example. Exploiting its powerful marketing, mass production, brand, and distribution capabilities, Nintendo offers outside game designers a low-investment opportunity to roll out their innovations worldwide. The company's complex presentation technologies and patents (as well as its massive marketing capabilities) prevent independents from attacking its markets directly. Although it creates some games itself, Nintendo focuses its resources on those core activities—and lets many outsiders create the games that have made more Japanese game designers into millionaires than any other company.[24] Any company can similarly benefit from outsourcing the activities that it cannot become best-in-world at performing—or that are peripheral to its strategic posture—to a best-in-world supplier. Figure 7.2 (using Sony as an example) illustrates this principle.

Core competence offers strategic focus; outsourcing offers continuous innovation and flexibility.

Outsourcers Sony Could Consider

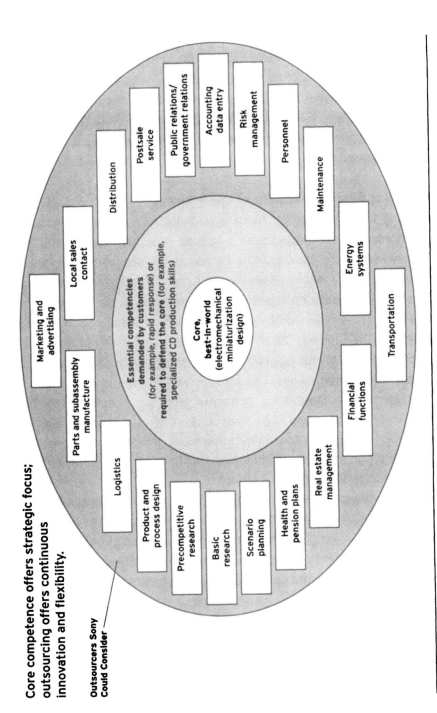

Distribution

Postsale service

Public relations/ government relations

Accounting data entry

Risk management

Personnel

Marketing and advertising

Local sales contact

Maintenance

Parts and subassembly manufacture

Essential competencies demanded by customers (for example, rapid response) or required to defend the core (for example, specialized CD production skills)

Core, best-in-world (electromechanical miniaturization design)

Energy systems

Logistics

Transportation

Product and process design

Precompetitive research

Basic research

Scenario planning

Health and pension plans

Real estate management

Financial functions

Figure 7.2. The Structure of Sony, an Outsourcing Company.

Every outsourcing opportunity offers possibilities to improve innovation. Leading professional outsourcers—real estate, human relations, software systems, or financial firms—are just as likely to come up with major innovations as specialized technical-research or product design houses are. That's how they maintain their own margins, satisfy customers' needs, and leverage their own intellectual resources.

Creating Internal Masters of the Process

To help find and develop the most talented outsourcing partners, some companies—for example, Chevron—use "process masters." Individual process masters (who are usually inquisitive and gregarious people with excellent specialist skills) and small groups of them become knowledge centers for all divisions in a company. Process masters identify and transfer to other parts of the company best-in-class internal innovations. They also find, benchmark, and track best-in-world external capabilities for the company's processes. Constantly prospecting, process masters are often sources of a high percentage of the innovative concepts entering organizations.[25] Chevron's process masters, through constant travel and networking, develop knowledge maps to guide other Chevron employees toward both internal and external expertise and help stimulate and facilitate the adoption of new solutions.

The biggest obstacle to adopting innovative ideas internally is to adjust traditional performance measures to reward implementation. By improving information about outsourcing possibilities, process masters help buttress senior managers with more objective checks against internal pressures to continue outmoded practices.

Developing Open, Interactive Software Models

Well-developed, open, interactive software models are at the core of most rapid innovation today.[26] Such models provide a constantly updated, accessible, visual, and dimensional view both of the system to which any innovation must adhere and of the performance that the innovation must surpass. The models also provide software hooks and defined interfaces that enable external designers to innovate independently.

Almost all new services—for example, in human resources or financial services, in product design or electronic commerce—are developed and tested collaboratively with customers through shared screens. Everyone shares enough interface, goal, and performance criteria for a variety of independents to operate individually and to propose totally new solutions that fit system needs and that can be tested quickly by the software model. Many others—including Boeing, Ford, and Millennium—do the same thing in the product world.

An example is NASA's Web-based, collaborative aeronautical-design system, called "Darwin." Darwin lets Ames Research Center, other NASA facilities, and industry partners come together in a virtual work space that is interconnected by NASA's secure nationwide Aeronet. Through broadband video links the parties compare their projections to actual test data while the test is going on. Experts estimate the system lowers design-stage costs for advanced aircraft by 80 to 90 percent.[27]

Structural Research Dynamics Corporation is one of many specialized software companies helping aerospace, auto, and mechanical equipment companies link their CAD-CAM or Catia (mechanical design) software to outside suppliers and customers worldwide. Built on Oracle databases, the software allows parties to interact (instantaneously or asynchronously) in either a visual or a formulaic mode to design parts, component subsystems, or styling features. Worldwide inputs offer many more opportunities for totally new insights, yet the software enforces the snap-fit dimensional discipline needed for manufacturing. Both quality and customer-accommodating inputs increase. The approach helps automakers assess thousands of possible engines, body configurations, and interiors in customer and performance tests that would otherwise be prohibitively expensive.

With such software models, participants in different time zones or work cycles can perform precisely and asynchronously. Three-shift, around-the-clock R&D has become common, decreasing cycle times by two-thirds, lowering development capital costs and risks by at least that much, and allowing the coordinating company to tap into the world's best minds for better results. Software—not new team concepts or personnel management models—is responsible for most of the increased speed and precision of today's innovation processes.

Establishing Audacious Goals: Figures of Merit

With the far-flung participation that software allows, companies need to ensure that they focus on innovation efforts. To do so, many adopt figures of merit, which define what winning performance really demands and specify technical-economic performance levels that are feasible but sufficiently high to shift customers from one provider to another.[28] In several studies on innovation, virtually all the top innovative companies (including Sony, Hewlett-Packard, Intel, Motorola, Du Pont, and Vanguard Securities) utilized figures of merit.[29] Company leaders would project known trend performance in the industry and set 30 to 500 percent higher performance targets—sufficiently high for customers to take risks, make changes, and invest in new solutions.

Figures of merit are exciting performance targets that induce innovators to rethink existing approaches and come up with something genuinely new. They can provide the focus, cohesion, and energizing goals needed for delegating to small, flexible, decentralized, self-coordinating internal or external innovation groups. In contrast, benchmark targets may merely stimulate copying best-in-class providers. Consider the case of Donna Dubinsky and Jeff Hawkins, who left 3Com to form Handspring and build the Visor handheld computer. To lure customers away from Palm Pilot, they set a target of superior performance and features—at "less than half" Palm Pilot's price and with appropriately rigorous goals for outsourced features.[30]

Concentrating on What Needs to Be Accomplished, Not on How to Get There

Once companies identify the most talented people and once those individuals have internalized figure-of-merit targets, the innovation process can be decentralized and outsourced to any desired level. Too often, however, buying parties insist on specifying what processes will be used (the *how*) rather than focusing on the desired result (the *what*). Some also install detailed process approvals and checkpoints. Such checks comfort the buyer but constrain innovators. True innovation is complex and tumultuous—full of spurts, frustrations, and sudden insights.[31] By insisting on overly detailed schedules, the buyer may prevent the very innovations it seeks. Because the supplier has greater knowledge in the area under development, attempting to manage suppliers rigorously is futile.

The norm for success in outsourcing innovation is continuous interactive tests and feedback about subsystem and system performance. A properly constructed governing software model offers the most objective possible program checks and feedback, from competing ideas and customers, about gaps the innovating supplier and the potential buyer should address. Software systems based on customer inputs (such as Kao's Echo) or interactive design software (Aavid's Fluent for flow-process design or CAVE for large-scale equipment demonstrations) help innovative suppliers understand customer issues in detail, lower the risk of creating a new product or process that will fail, assist clients in understanding and preparing for innovation, transfer knowledge smoothly to them, and provide the necessary comfort level to ensure use of the product.

Through interactive software, customers are "sold" on the innovation in advance on their own premises. The customer is closely involved in the innovation's development and becomes familiar with it. As a result, before money actually changes hands, the customer is anticipating the innovation and will resist other competing innovations. Because of the uncertainties always present, a company working with a number of innovating outsource partners should keep them all participating and competing as long as possible. With more innovators involved and critiquing ideas through interactive software, the company can decrease its performance and market risks, increase the probability of successful innovation, and obtain valuable product performance insights that otherwise might not surface.[32]

Using Software to Coordinate the Players

By forcing a common language, measurement system, and set of rules, software improves human communications, capturing and preserving knowledge with a precision, detail, and transferability that person-to-person communications and hard-copy reports cannot. Sophisticated electronic modeling and visual presentations offer an opportunity for companies to perform joint reviews with their outsourcers and to develop subtleties (microscopic views, extreme-environment scenarios, or simultaneous internal/external views) that would be too expensive or impossible to create with physical models.

Such capabilities allow joint design to move beyond traditional, physically interactive, culture-sharing teams to collaboration among diverse and independent entities that are physically dispersed and serve no single authority. That new model, which might be called "independent collaboration," is already common at the frontiers of biotechnology, software development, oceanographic and environmental research, nanotechnology, microbiology, new materials development, and sensor technologies, and it is used in the creation of financial tools or entertainment products.

Even for systems like the one Boeing used for its joint-strike fighter, which simultaneously involved thousands of participants worldwide, individuals remained in their own units working for their own goals, while benefiting from interactions with other units. Software can coordinate progress and results with exceptional precision and speed—despite the fact that most interactions are occurring at a distance. It allows specific, instantaneous, disciplined interactions, undiluted by personal, linguistic, or interpretive biases.

Sharing Gains from Surpassing Targets

Figures of merit, properly set, are based on the exponential gains in knowledge that are expected to flow from multiple suppliers and their outsource partners working together to improve performance. The amplified knowledge gains that come from network interactions and feedback are usually sufficiently large that returns from improved performance can be shared among all contributors—without hurting cost targets. But fixed targets are not sufficient. If a company offers to share with outsource partners any gains from exceeding the targets, it may realize entirely unexpected boosts in performance levels. That is what environmental regulators found when they moved from current best-technology standards to marketlike incentives that shared gains that went beyond initial targets. Because so much innovation is now in software and potential software is constantly evolving, companies that outsource have found that targets based on today's techniques are unproductively binding—and that bonuses for performance gains beyond initial targets offer much higher payoffs. Today "hedonic measures" (anticipating currently unspecifiable but expected total performance gains) augment directly foreseeable cost and gain measures so that managers can make the most of the learning that results from networks.

For example, DaimlerChrysler Corporation has standard contract clauses that specify continuous, measurable performance improvement levels beyond current targets in each year of a contract's life. In industries such as biotechnology, performance trends are hard to predict. But even there, cost improvements and future yields are often estimated based on an experience curve. Then they can be embedded in targets. Although neither buyer nor supplier knows how they can achieve the result, their experience indicates they can achieve it. In some companies—such as Dell and the dotcoms—performance levels are improving and costs are decreasing so fast for their outsourced segments that specifications and prices have to be changed almost daily and shipments made from suppliers directly to customers. These companies have had to create entirely new organization structures and information systems to deal with the constantly accelerating pace.

It is important that both parties agree on specific performance targets that are fair, few in number, easy to understand, and readily usable by the people doing the work. Although clients generally want an outsource provider to innovate and keep its operations at state-of-the-art levels, they may insist unrealistically that suppliers pass all gains from innovations to the buyer in their pricing, use the buyer's own practices to ensure consistency and quality, and bill professional inputs on an hourly basis instead of using value pricing or jointly shared innovation incentives. That approach is deadly. In a short time the buyer will lose the very things it is seeking from outsourcing—greater knowledge and innovative depth, access to the most up-to-date systems, highest quality at lowest cost, maximum flexibility, and no front-end investment. The highly successful CEO of a $4 billion outsourcing company has suggested a wiser approach, saying, "To encourage innovation, I won't worry about how much the provider makes from the transaction. . . . [But] I will constantly want to know how our relationship with the provider is making us more money than we would otherwise."

A Three-Point System of Information Exchange and Project Execution

To help monitor and implement the innovation-creating relationships they seek, many of the most successful companies we studied utilized three points of contact to form a system of information exchange and project execution. The first contact point is one in which a few top-level managers review developing opportunities, create exciting goals and challenging figures of merit, constantly realign existing strategic priorities as external environments change, and break bottlenecks that may occur at lower levels. The second contact point is where champions on both sides meet—people whose careers depend on the relationship's success. The third comprises numerous interactions among those who actually develop, produce, and operate the invention—the people who are often the first to spot new operating needs or technical opportunities and creatively solve problems. Interactions at that contact point help ensure that the valuable nuances of tacit knowledge about problems and processes get transferred when needed—and that the best vendor talent and sufficient urgency are applied to the project.

Communications and innovation are substantially enhanced if client and outsourcer share the same electronic model of products or processes and can work together asynchronously yet within the discipline the software imposes. That is especially important if multiple outsourcers must cooperate. For example, the Xerox Palo Alto Research Center (PARC) has found its Collabra software helpful in supporting multiple-knowledge-source interactions that rely on the concept of "WYSIWIS" ("what you see is what I see"). Everyone who works on a product utilizes the same software model and sees what everyone else sees. If one person makes a change, the other people see the change appear on their screens. Supplemented by PARC's Agnoter and Cognoter software, the system augments remote or same-room verbal communications, allowing different groups to create together and evaluate concepts instantaneously and with precision. By allowing others to observe and critique ideas, such software also prevents the contact people from becoming overly impressed by their partners' particularly articulate technical people or newest technical solution.[33]

Incentive Systems and Open, Compatible Information

Many innovative companies operate with highly decentralized organizations that feature only three organizational levels—the people at the top, the people doing the project, and, using open information systems, everyone else—and strong incentives adapted to the specific type of innovation sought. At the heart of successful innovation is a common, open-information capability that places all participants on the same footing in discussions. To develop their knowledge in depth, specialists normally work closely in units with others from their specialty. Like high school students returning to homeroom, they return to those units between project activities. But to solve particularly complex problems, they work in small project teams with specialists from other disciplines, sharing a common information base that is open to everyone. (Fire walls exist for highly secret or personal information.) With an open system people cannot argue that their ideas should prevail because they have proprietary information. Many consultants, software houses, financial services, and emerging high-tech companies use such open structures. By contrast, multilayered, divisional organizations—because they keep people and information in one silo away from the others—are an anathema to innovation. Generally, companies that are successful at innovating have porous organizations developed around three such contact centers, permitting maximum information exchange and avoiding endless approvals and communication delays. Flat organizations further amplify individual responsibility and flexibility—both of which are critical to fast-response, highly motivated innovation (see box, Some Advice on Managing Outsourced Innovation).

SOMEWHAT ORDERLY CHAOS

"Managed chaos" once described successful innovation processes within companies.[34] But with today's speed and numerous outside suppliers, the chaos is not so much "managed" as it is "somewhat orderly." No one manager or team controls the hurricane of worldwide supplier, customer, and competitor innovations; and yet the hurricane has some broadly predictable characteristics—for example, greater bandwidth, speeds, wireless capabilities, and interconnectivity. To keep up with the pace, leading organizations are reforming into circular, independent modes with knowledge centers that broadly match anticipated changes but little visible authority or ownership structure. The new structures are built on two

▼

Some Advice on Managing Outsourced Innovation

Don't ...	Do ...
... look at only relative internal capabilities.	... develop selected skills to be best in world.
... think of products as core competencies. (*Skills* are core competencies.)	... position your company to seize opportunities.
... expect opportunities to come to you.	... develop capabilities for scanning externally.
... assume you can outdesign the world.	... create a clear, exciting vision of the future.
... rely on your years of experience.	... manage relationships by using process masters.
... dictate details of processes or practices.	... evaluate suppliers' past innovation practices.
... set fixed current-best-practice targets.	... develop shared goals and figures of merit.
... try to capture all the gains.	... share incentives to perform beyond targets.
... overlook the importance of customers to the process.	... create open, interactive software models.
... make suppliers into subordinates.	... say what you want, not how to get it; then test interactively.
... tolerate vertical hierarchies.	... establish a three-point management focus.
... let internal politics isolate participants.	... reward those who make alliances work.

premises. First, those who have the necessary knowledge will work *with* but not *for* those who lack it; second, change is so constant that almost any structure is an impediment.

Using the somewhat-orderly-chaos model, companies such as MCI, Dell, Nintendo, and Amgen—as well as television networks and financial-services houses—let it be known that they are interested in new product or service concepts with certain defined characteristics, that they will use their infrastructures to introduce new products or services for inventors, and that they will share rewards fairly. Independent innovators, scientists, or service providers develop and test their concepts on a small scale until their probabilities of success, performance characteristics, and potentials are clear enough to permit them to approach the firm as a partner.

The independents may receive some early information or support from the potential partner in return for a right of first refusal. As the project passes some way points—points changing constantly with scientific, industry, and marketplace conditions—the independents may receive further guidance and support. If they then prove they can exceed established figure-of-merit targets, their innovations may become serious candidates for internal and beta-site testing against other finalists' proposals. From that group a final marketplace test will indicate which concepts should be commercialized, and profit- and risk-sharing incentives then take over. Most innovations do not progress along a predictable, linear path but one that is tumultuous and interactive. The process should be managed as such—with a focus on winning goals, incentives, and "whats," not "hows"—lest genuine innovation be stifled.

ADAPTING AND EXPLOITING THE INNOVATION

One of the more difficult problems of outsourcing innovation is adapting and exploiting innovation in internal operations. When the innovation is embodied in products, it may simply appear as a purchased component in the final assembly. Although CAE/CAD/CAM systems have reduced problems of physical fit, components often have software features that must be carefully integrated. Hence successful outsourcers insist on constant interactive development, disciplined by frequent software tests both before and after physical models are available. Software testing helps create an explanation of why things happen, and rapid, repeated testing in both physical and software simulations decreases the likelihood of unexpected problems.

In cases other than buying or developing innovative components for established product lines, many companies migrate toward more circular (and therefore simultaneous) organizational models, with units that act independently. They avoid hierarchical models that require ideas to pass in a sequence up and down an organizational ladder or across departmental barriers. Two circular, independent organizations are the starburst structure and the network, or spider's web, enterprise (see box, Circular, Independent Organizations).

Why Outsource Innovation?

Different structures, specifically matched to the strategic needs of each outsourcing project, can help enormously in stimulating, monitoring, and transitioning innovation in individual situations.[35] But there are some common reasons companies of any size are increasingly benefiting from outsourcing particular aspects of innovation.

Resource Limits. No single company can innovate better than the combination of all its potential direct, functional, component, and service competitors. Each potential supplier can tap into many more upstream technological sources and downstream customer problems and solutions. The combination of their capabilities can be overwhelming.

Specialist Talents. Companies may not have the motivation or depth of knowledge in all necessary technical fields. They may be short on managers who know how to stimulate innovation and who can tolerate its uncertainties, challenges, and risks.

▼

Circular, Independent Organizations

Starburst Companies

Companies operating in a starburst structure—such as MGM, Thermo Electron, and Vanguard Securities—differ from conglomerates or holding companies in that they have a cohesive, constantly renewed core that retains critical intellectual capabilities. The starburst structure works well for companies with very expensive and complex core competencies, many discrete products, and multiple independent markets. The central enterprise acquires, invests in, or forms an alliance with multiple downstream nodes. It supports the resulting ventures with knowledge, skills, or resources from its own core competence. Each node provides a continuing entrepreneurial presence to exploit innovation in its markets. Each may acquire, combine with, or outsource to other external units with complementary capabilities.

Thermo Electron, for example, has assembled a complex core of high-tech research specialists in materials, electronics, and thermal sciences, as well as a top management team of visionary technical and acquisition experts. As it internally develops or externally finds a new technical-market opportunity that fits its skills, Thermo Electron sets up a partially owned enterprise to exploit the concept—leveraging the innovation internally with management and continued R&D support and externally by financing the unit with its own alliances, independent debt, and equity financing. Using senior managers' skills, the new unit may do further acquisitions or outsourcing on its own.

A starburst's center generally maintains its competencies by charging a fee to the nodes as they become profitable. It usually manages the overall image and culture, sets broad priorities, selects key people, approves major capital and long-range plans, and raises capital for the nodes. Both the nodes and the center continuously scan upstream and downstream for new concepts and human resources.

The Starburst Organization

Starburst organizations work well for downstream outsourcing. The center contains a complex core competence. The nodes (N) are permanent entrepreneurial businesses in different markets. The nodes may be separate alliances or partially owned companies leveraged financially through direct external equity or debt guaranteed by the center.

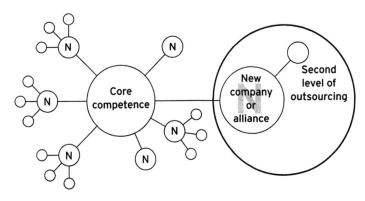

Network, or Spider's Web, Enterprises

When knowledge resides in many highly dispersed centers, is required for only a limited time and purpose, and must flow interactively among the multiple nodes, a network format of outsourcing is often the best choice.

For example, Arthur Andersen has knowledge specialists in its offices all over the world. To provide optimum solutions for clients, it may want regional, industry, and functional experts from many different locations to contribute. Using its computer-based human resource files, it can quickly identify the best talents and their availability. Many different locations and specialists can interact simultaneously across Andersen's secure intranet, quickly calling forth all necessary files and customer records and enabling

(continued)

▼

Circular, Independent Organizations (cont.)

partners in different locations to interact in real time in order to speed and improve solutions.

Such industries as energy, banking, semiconductors, biotech, textiles, real estate, and insurance now operate in a similar way. They frequently form temporary alliances to carry out a specific limited purpose: for example, joint research, product development, product introduction, flexible field support, or implementing an innovative, complex investment requiring high-level creative skills and interactions among many different specialized organizations.

Network organizations can be assembled quickly to simultaneously support high specialization, multiple geographical locations, and a disciplined focus on a single problem or set of customers. They can disperse risks and reduce investments for individual units. They can release the imaginations of many different innovators, multiply the number of opportunities for innovation, and exponentially increase the likelihood of revolutionary inventions.

Although networks are effective for rapidly identifying problems, discovering innovative solutions, or building up capabilities, they often present challenges when used for long-term, ongoing operations. Who owns what share of new innovations may be a problem. All participating organizations' goals and practices are rarely completely congruent, and a failure by one party to perform can seriously damage the others. Constant efforts to inculcate a maximum sense of shared interest, a clear understanding of and commitment to goals, and mutually compatible and reinforcing incentives are, of course, the essential starting points for any relationship.[1] As a result, many companies have those responsible

The Spider's Web Organization

Network, or spider's web, organizations (for example, Andersen Consulting) are used for lateral collaborations or outsourcing. Each node is a knowledge center yet must work intimately with other nodes to solve specific short-term problems. Individual nodes may operate quite independently when they are not directly participating for a specific purpose.

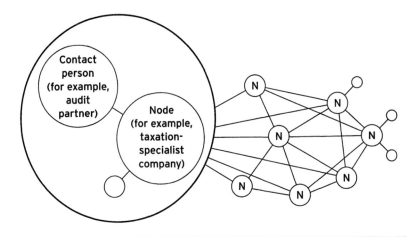

for key relationships in all units draw up a single, written common statement of goals, set of priorities, rules for interaction, and agreed-on monitoring, performance, measurement, and reward systems for their projects.

[1] J. B. Quinn, P. Anderson, and S. Finkelstein, "Leveraging Intellect," *Academy of Management Executive*, June 1998. The article develops in detail both the problems and management techniques associated with these and some of the other innovation organizational forms discussed in this chapter.

Multiple Risks. The company that outsources knows it cannot afford development risks for every desired innovation, whereas outsource suppliers can spread risks across multiple present and future customers. The company that outsources upstream and partners downstream significantly lowers its innovation adoption risk.

Attracting Talent. For a noncore activity a company may be unable to attract the most talented people to work in-house. Such workers tend to seek out the best specialist and innovation houses where their talents will be most recognized and rewarded.

Speed. Companies can get to market faster through outsourcing and avoid time delays in hiring, infrastructure development, and internal resistance to new ideas. Small companies that take in outsourced work can often be more flexible, nimble, and objective about new ideas than large companies, and they have fewer historical barriers to solutions. They must innovate to succeed—or die.

As innovative solutions become more complex—requiring more specialist knowledge and more specialized software support (while other economies of scale drop)—more deeply skilled, competing specialist outsourcers have appeared. Outsourcing offers increased opportunities for much faster and lower-cost innovation to companies that develop their core competencies and outsourcing-management practices properly. In fact, the supplier side of the process has become the major source of new high-tech jobs, new companies, and economic growth worldwide.[36]

Managers will need new strategies for surfing the opportunity waves around them. They will need to leverage their own resources to improve internal innovation practices and develop sophisticated outsourcing partnerships with those billions of new minds who can provide innovative support. And they will need to overcome the not-invented-here forces inside their own and their customers' companies. Developing the necessary management practices is not easy. But using only traditional internal innovation practices can be fatal.

ADDITIONAL RESOURCES

J. B. Quinn, *Intelligent Enterprise: A Knowledge and Service Based Paradigm for Industry* (New York: Free Press, 1992).

For current outsourcing data see www.CorbettGroup.com.

For strategic measurements see National Research Council, *Information Technology in the Service Society: A Twenty-First Century Lever* (Washington, D.C.: National Academy Press, 1994); and J. B. Quinn, R. Julien, and M. Negrin, "Strategic Outsourcing: Risk Management," *Global Focus,* in press.

For innovation practices see J. B. Quinn, J. J. Baruch, and K. A. Zien, *Innovation Explosion: Using Intellect and Software to Revolutionize Growth Strategies* (New York: Free Press, 1997).

For macro considerations see F. Cairncross, *The Death of Distance* (Boston: Harvard Business School Press, 1997).

NOTES

1. Forester Research and Access Media International estimate 140 million Internet users, doubling at least annually through 2005.
2. Figures are derived from interviews conducted between 1997 and 2000 with leading practitioners cited in this chapter.
3. The definition of "outsourcing" includes the relatively permanent purchase of goods or services in a particular category from a single source or multiple sources. "Innovation" is widely defined as the first reduction of a concept to useful practice in a culture.
4. J. B. Quinn, "Strategic Outsourcing: Leveraging Knowledge Capabilities," *Sloan Management Review,* Summer 1999, 40, 9–21. The article provides a complete framework and key practices for outsourcing state-of-the-art products and services.

5. United Nations, *Statistical Yearbook* (New York: United Nations, 1998).

6. The basic framework for strategic outsourcing was delineated in the following publications: J. B. Quinn, *Intelligent Enterprise: A Knowledge and Service Based Paradigm for Industry* (New York: Free Press, 1992); and J. B. Quinn and F. Hilmer, "Strategic Outsourcing," *Sloan Management Review,* Summer 1994, *35,* 43–55. The classic economist's statement of the rationale for outsourcing is R. Coase, "The Nature of the Firm," *Economica,* November 1937, pp. 386–405.

7. "A New Kind of Boeing," *Economist,* January 22, 2000, pp. 62–63.

8. H. Mintzberg and J. B. Quinn, "Ford Team Taurus," in *The Strategy Process: Concepts, Contexts, Cases,* 3rd ed. (Upper Saddle River, New Jersey: Prentice Hall, 1996).

9. R. D'Aveni and P. Ravenscraft, "Economies of Integration vs. Bureaucracy: Does Vertical Integration Improve Performance," *Academy of Management Journal,* October 1994, *37,* 1167–1206.

10. R. L. Simison, F. Warner, and G. L. White, "Big Three Car Makers Plan Net Exchange," *Wall Street Journal,* February 28, 2000, sec. A, p. 3.

11. Quinn, "Strategic Outsourcing," develops this concept, numerous examples, and management practices in depth.

12. T. Blackman, "Trading in Options," *People Management,* May 6, 1999, pp. 42–46.

13. Company documents.

14. E. von Hippel, *The Sources of Innovation* (New York: Oxford University Press, 1988).

15. "Business: Wheels and Wires," *Economist,* January 8, 2000, pp. 58–62.

16. W. Grimson, R. Kikinis, and F. Jolesz, "Image Guided Surgery," *Scientific American,* June 1999, *280,* 62–69.

17. For an excellent review of this and other techniques, see E. Wilson, "Product Definition: Assorted Techniques and Their Marketplace Impact," in *IEEE International Engineering Management Conference,* Institute of Electrical and Electronics Engineers (Piscataway, New Jersey: Institute of Electrical and Electronics Engineers, 1990), pp. 64–69.

18. This analogy was first suggested by S. Halsted, managing partner, The Centennial Group, 1998.

19. For a full analytical approach for operating in this mode, see R. D'Aveni, *Hypercompetition* (New York: Free Press, 1997).

20. "The Future of Work," *Economist*, January 29, 2000, pp. 89–92; and J. B. Quinn, P. Anderson, and S. Finkelstein, "Managing Professional Intellect: Making the Most of the Best," *Harvard Business Review*, May-June 1998, 76, 71–80.

21. K. Zien and S. Buckler, "From Experience: Dreams to Market: Creating a Culture of Innovation," *Journal of Product Innovation Management*, July 1997, 14, 274–287.

22. Interviews in support of National Research Council, *Information Technology in the Service Society: A Twenty-First Century Lever* (Washington, D.C.: National Academy Press, 1994).

23. These concepts were first published in J. B. Quinn, T. L. Doorley, and P. C. Paquette, "Technology in Services: Rethinking Strategic Focus," *Sloan Management Review*, Winter 1990, pp. 79–87; and J. B. Quinn, T. L. Doorley, and P. C. Paquette, "Beyond Products: Services Based Strategy," *Harvard Business Review*, March-April 1990, 68, 58–68. J. B. Quinn, J. J. Baruch, and K. A. Zien, *Innovation Explosion: Using Intellect and Software to Revolutionize Growth Strategies* (New York: Free Press, 1997) extends this concept to innovation outsourcing in detail.

24. "Nintendo of America" in Mintzberg and Quinn, *Strategy Process*.

25. R. Katz and T. Allen, "Project Performance and the Locus of Influence in the R&D Matrix," *Academy of Management Journal*, March 1985, 28, 67–87; and M. Tushman and P. Anderson, eds., *Managing Strategic Innovation and Change* (New York: Oxford University Press, 1996).

26. J. B. Quinn, J. J. Baruch, and K. A. Zien, "Software-Based Innovation," *Sloan Management Review*, Summer 1996, 37, 11–24; and Quinn, Baruch, and Zien, *Innovation Explosion*.

27. G. Arnaut, "Partners in Virtual Workspace," *Information Week*, December 16, 1996, pp. 70–77.

28. For a detailed development of the design and use of figures of merit, see Quinn, Baruch, and Zien, *Innovation Explosion*.

29. J. B. Quinn, *Logical Incrementalism* (Burr Ridge, Illinois: Irwin, 1980); Quinn, *Intelligent Enterprise;* National Research Council, *Information Technology;* and Quinn, Baruch, and Zien, *Innovation Explosion.*

30. W. Mossberg, "A Pilot Rival Organizes Your Life, Then Morphs into Something Else," *Wall Street Journal,* September 16, 1999, sec. B, p. 1.

31. The following major studies of innovation support this thesis: J. Jewkes, D. Sawers, and S. Stillerman, *Sources of Invention* (London: St. Martin's Press, 1958); T. Kuhn, *The Structure of Scientific Revolutions* (Chicago: University of Chicago Press, 1962); D. deSolla Price, "Of Sealing Wax and String," *Natural History,* January 1984, pp. 48–57; J. Diebold, *The Innovators: The Discoveries, Inventions, and Breakthroughs of Our Times* (New York: Dutton, 1990); and R. Root-Bernstein, *Discovering* (Cambridge, Massachusetts: Harvard University Press, 1991). See also the monthly series "Scientific Pathways" in *Science.*

32. The full logic for this is developed in Quinn, *Logical Incrementalism.*

33. Government R&D procurement offers an example of the need for both human and software interactions. Contract officers' personal knowledge was often necessary to overcome the slow bureaucratic review committees that are remote from the actual work. Yet they often unintentionally became "captured" by certain groups with exciting ideas. Software testing with independent observers helped ensure balance.

34. J. B. Quinn, "Managing Innovation: Controlled Chaos," *Harvard Business Review,* May-June 1985, *63,* 73–84.

35. Quinn, Baruch, and Zien, *Innovation Explosion,* chapter 8, illustrates many of the most common and useful forms and their associated incentive and performance measurement systems.

36. "The Future of Work," *Economist.*

CHAPTER EIGHT

How to Make Strategic Alliances Work

JEFFREY H. DYER
PRASHANT KALE
HARBIR SINGH

S trategic alliances—a fast and flexible way to access complementary resources and skills that reside in other companies—
have become an important tool for achieving sustainable competitive
advantage. Indeed, the past decade has witnessed an extraordinary
increase in alliances.[1] Currently, the top five hundred global businesses have an average of sixty major strategic alliances each.

Yet alliances are fraught with risks, and almost half fail. Hence
the ability to form and manage them more effectively than competitors can become an important source of competitive advantage.
We conducted an in-depth study of 203 corporations and their
1,572 alliances (see box, Research Design and Methodology, pp.
224–225). We found that a company's stock price jumped roughly
1 percent with each announcement of a new alliance, which translated into an increase in market value of $54 million per alliance.[2]
And although all companies seemed to create some value through
alliances, certain companies—for example, Hewlett-Packard,

First published in the Summer 2001 issue of *MIT Sloan Management Review.*

Oracle, Eli Lilly, and Parke-Davis (a division of Pfizer Inc.)—showed themselves capable of systematically generating more alliance value than others (see Figure 8.1).

How do they do it? By building a dedicated strategic-alliance function. The companies and others like them appoint a vice president or director of strategic alliances with his or her own staff and resources. The dedicated function coordinates all alliance-related activity within the organization and is charged with institutionalizing processes and systems to teach, share, and leverage prior alliance management experience and know-how throughout the company. And it is effective. Enterprises with a dedicated function achieved a 25 percent higher long-term success rate with their alliances than those without such a function—and generated almost four times the market wealth whenever they announced the formation of a new alliance.

HOW A DEDICATED ALLIANCE FUNCTION CREATES VALUE

An effective dedicated strategic-alliance function performs four key roles: it improves knowledge management efforts, increases external visibility, provides internal coordination, and eliminates both accountability problems and intervention problems (see Figure 8.2).

Improving Knowledge Management

A dedicated function acts as a focal point for learning and for leveraging lessons and feedback from prior and ongoing alliances. It systematically establishes a series of routine processes to articulate, document, codify, and share alliance know-how about the key phases of the alliance life cycle. There are five key phases, and companies that have been successful with alliances have tools and templates to manage each (see Figure 8.3, p. 226).

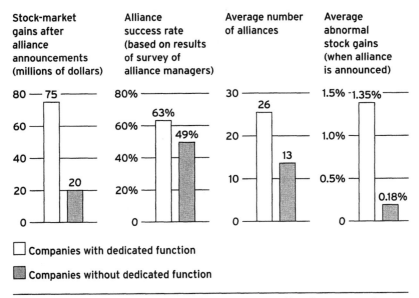

Figure 8.1. A Dedicated Function Improves the Success of Strategic Alliances, 1993–1997.

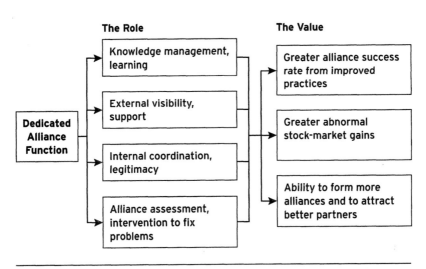

Figure 8.2. The Role of the Alliance Function and How It Creates Value.

▼

Research Design and Methodology

We conducted two types of research. From 1996 to 2000 we interviewed at companies such as Hewlett-Packard, Warner-Lambert (now part of Pfizer), Oracle, Corning, Lilly, GlaxoSmithKline, and others that were reputed to have effective alliance capabilities. We also interviewed executives at companies that did not have a dedicated strategic-alliance function, many of which have had relatively poor success with alliances. We conducted a survey-based study of 203 companies (from a variety of industries) with average revenues of $3.05 billion in 1998. The analysis of alliance success and stock market gain from alliance announcements is based on data from 1,572 alliances formed by the companies between 1993 and 1997.

To assess the long-term success of the alliances, we collected survey data on the primary reasons that each of the alliances was formed. We then asked managers to evaluate each alliance on the following dimensions:

▼ The extent to which the alliance met its stated objectives
▼ The extent to which the alliance enhanced the competitive position of the parent company

Many companies with dedicated alliance functions have codified explicit alliance management knowledge by creating guidelines and manuals to help them manage specific aspects of the alliance life cycle, such as partner selection and alliance negotiation and contracting. For example, Lotus Corp. created what it calls its "thirty-five rules of thumb" to manage each phase of an alliance, from formation to termination. Hewlett-Packard developed sixty different tools and templates, included in a three-hundred-page manual for guiding decision making in specific alliance situations. The manual included such tools as a template for making the business case for an alliance, a partner evaluation form, a negotiations template

▼ The extent to which the alliance enabled each parent company to learn some critical skills from the alliance partner
▼ The level of harmony the partners involved in the alliance exhibited

Managers used a standard 1-7 (1 = low and 7 = high) survey scale. Alliances that received an above-average score on the four dimensions were rated "successes," and those that received scores below average were rated "failures." Assessments of alliance success and failure then were used to calculate an overall alliance success rate for each company. The alliance success rate is essentially a ratio of each company's "successful" alliances to all its alliances during the study period.

In recent years academics have begun using a market-based measure of alliance value creation and success based on abnormal stock-market gains. To estimate incremental value creation for each company, we built a model to predict stock price based on daily firm stock prices for 180 days before an alliance announcement. The model also includes daily market returns on the value-weighted S&P 500. Abnormal stock-market gains reflect the daily unanticipated movements in the stock price for each firm after an alliance announcement.

outlining the roles and responsibilities of different departments, a list of ways to measure alliance performance, and an alliance termination checklist.

Other companies, too, have found that creating tools, templates, and processes is valuable. For example, using the Spatial Paradigm for Information Retrieval and Exploration, or SPIRE, database (www.pnl.gov/infoviz/spire/spire.html), Dow Chemical developed a process for identifying potential alliance partners. The company was able to create a topographical map pinpointing the overlap between its patent domains and the patent domains of possible alliance partners. With this tool, the company discovered the

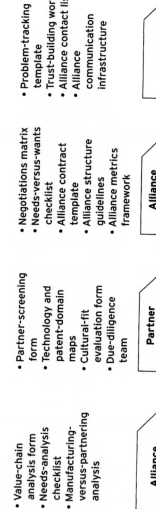

Alliance Business Case
- Value-chain analysis form
- Needs-analysis checklist
- Manufacturing-versus-partnering analysis

Partner Assessment and Selection
- Partner-screening form
- Technology and patent-domain maps
- Cultural-fit evaluation form
- Due-diligence team

Alliance Negotiation and Governance
- Negotiations matrix
- Needs-versus-wants checklist
- Alliance contract template
- Alliance structure guidelines
- Alliance metrics framework

Alliance Management
- Problem-tracking template
- Trust-building worksheet
- Alliance contact list
- Alliance communication infrastructure

Assessment and Termination
- Relationship evaluation form
- Yearly status report
- Termination checklist
- Termination-planning worksheet

Figure 8.3. Tools to Use Across the Alliance Life Cycle.

potential for an alliance with Lucent Technologies in the area of optical communications. The companies subsequently formed a broad-based alliance between three Dow businesses and three Lucent businesses that had complementary technologies.

After identifying potential partners, companies need to assess whether or not they will be able to work together effectively. Lilly developed a process of sending a due-diligence team to the potential alliance partner to evaluate the partner's resources and capabilities and to assess its culture. The team looks at such things as the partner's financial condition, information technology, research capabilities, and health and safety record. Of particular importance is the evaluation of the partner's culture. In Lilly's experience, culture clashes are one of the main reasons alliances fail. During the cultural assessment, the team examines the potential partner's corporate values and expectations, organization structure, reward systems and incentives, leadership styles, decision-making processes, patterns of human interaction, work practices, history of partnerships, and human resource practices. Nelson M. Sims, Lilly's executive director of alliance management, states that the evaluation is used both as a screening mechanism and as a tool to assist Lilly in organizing, staffing, and governing the alliance.

Dedicated alliance functions also facilitate the sharing of tacit knowledge through training programs and internal networks of alliance managers. For example, Hewlett-Packard (HP) developed a two-day course on alliance management that it offered three times a year. The company also provided short three-hour courses on alliance management and made its alliance materials available on the internal HP alliance Web site. HP also created opportunities for internal networking among managers through internal training programs, companywide alliance summits, and "virtual meetings" with executives involved in managing alliances. And the company regularly sent its alliance managers to alliance management programs at business schools to help its managers develop external networks of contacts.

Formal training programs are one route; informal programs are another. Many companies with alliance functions have created roundtables with opportunities for alliance managers to get together and informally share their alliance experience. To that end, Nortel initiated a three-day workshop and networking initiative for alliance managers. BellSouth and Motorola have conducted similar two-day workshops for people to meet and learn from one another.

Increasing External Visibility

A dedicated alliance function can play an important role in keeping the market apprised of both new alliances and successful events in ongoing alliances. Such external visibility can enhance the reputation of the company in the marketplace and support the perception that alliances are adding value. The creation of a dedicated alliance function sends a signal to the marketplace and to potential partners that the company is committed both to its alliances and to managing them effectively. And when a potential partner wants to contact a company about establishing an alliance, a dedicated function offers an easy, highly visible point of contact. In essence, it provides a place to screen potential partners and bring in the appropriate internal parties if a partnership looks attractive.

For instance, Oracle put the partnering process on the Web with Alliance Online (now Oracle Partners Program) and offered terms and conditions of different "tiers" of partnership (http://alliance.oracle.com/join/2join_pr2_1.htm). Potential partners could choose the level that fit them best. At the tier 1 level (mostly resellers, integrators, and application developers), companies could sign up for a specific type of agreement on-line and not have to talk with someone in Oracle's strategic-alliance function. Oracle also used its Web site to gather information on its partners' products and services, thereby developing detailed partner profiles. Accessing those profiles, customers easily matched the products and services they desired with those provided by Oracle partners. The Web site allowed the company to enhance its external visibility, and it emerged as the primary means of recruiting and developing partnerships with more than seven thousand tier 1 partners. It also allowed Oracle's strategic-alliance function to focus the majority of its human resources on its higher-profile, more strategically important partners.

Providing Internal Coordination

One reason that alliances fail is the inability of one partner or another to mobilize internal resources to support the initiative. Visionary alliance leaders may lack the organizational authority to access key resources necessary to ensure alliance success. An alliance executive at a company without such a function observed: "We have a difficult time supporting our alliance initiatives, because many times the various resources and skills needed to support a particular alliance are located in different functions around the company. Unless it is a very high-profile alliance, no one person has the power to make sure the company's full resources are utilized to help the alliance succeed. You have to go begging to each unit and hope that they will support you. But that's time consuming, and we don't always get the support we should."

A dedicated alliance function helps solve that problem in two ways. First, it has the organizational legitimacy to reach across divisions and functions and request the resources necessary to support the company's alliance initiatives. When particular functions are not responsive, it can quickly elevate the issue through the organization's hierarchy and ask the appropriate executives to make a decision on whether a particular function or division should support an alliance initiative. Second, over time, individuals within the alliance function develop networks of contacts throughout the organization. They come to know where to find useful resources within the organization. Such networks also help develop trust between alliance managers and employees throughout the organization—and thereby lead to reciprocal exchanges.

A dedicated alliance function also can provide internal coordination for the organization's strategic priorities. Some studies suggest that one of the main reasons alliances fail is that the partnership's objectives no longer match one or both partners' strategic priorities.[3] As one alliance executive complained, "We will sometimes get far along in an alliance, only to find that another company initiative is in conflict with the alliance. For example, in one case, an internal group started to develop a similar technology that our partner already had developed. Should they have developed it? I don't know. But we needed some process for communicating internally the strategic priorities of our alliances and how they fit with our overall strategy."

Companies need to have a mechanism for communicating which alliance initiatives are most important to achieving the overall strategy—as well as which alliance partners are the most important. The alliance function ensures that such issues are constantly addressed in the company's strategy-making sessions and then are communicated throughout the organization.

Facilitating Intervention and Accountability

A 1999 survey by Andersen Consulting (now Accenture) found that only 51 percent of companies that form alliances had any kind of formal metrics in place to assess alliance performance.[4] Of those, only about 20 percent believed that the metrics they had in place were really the appropriate ones to use. In our research we found that 76 percent of companies with a dedicated alliance function had implemented formal alliance metrics. In contrast, only 30 percent of the companies without a dedicated function had done so.

Many executives we interviewed indicated that an important benefit of creating an alliance function was that it compelled the company to develop alliance metrics and to evaluate the performance of its alliances systematically. Moreover, doing so compelled senior managers to intervene when an alliance was struggling. Lilly established a yearly "health check" process for each of its key alliances, using surveys of both Lilly employees and the partner's alliance managers. After the survey an alliance manager from the dedicated function could sit down with the leader of a particular alliance to discuss the results and offer recommendations. In some cases, Lilly's dedicated strategic-alliance group found that it needed to replace the leader of a particular Lilly alliance.

When serious conflicts arise, the alliance function can help resolve them. One executive commented, "Sometimes an alliance has lived beyond its useful life. You need someone to step in and either pull the plug or push it in new directions." Alliance failure is the culmination of a chain of events. Not surprisingly, signs of distress are often visible early on, and with monitoring, the alliance function can step in and intervene appropriately.

HOW TO ORGANIZE AN EFFECTIVE STRATEGIC-ALLIANCE FUNCTION

One of the major challenges of creating an alliance function is knowing how to organize it. It is possible to organize the function around key partners, industries, business units, geographical areas, or a combination of all four. How an alliance function is organized influences its strategy and effectiveness. For instance, if the alliance function is organized by business unit, then the function will reflect the idiosyncrasies of each business unit and the industry in which it operates. If the alliance function is organized geographically, then knowledge about partners and coordination mechanisms, for example, will be accumulated primarily with a geographical focus.

Identify Key Strategic Parameters and Organize Around Them

Organizing around key strategic parameters enhances the probability of alliance success. For example, a company with a large number of alliances and a few central players may identify partner-specific knowledge and partner-specific strategic priorities as critical. As a result, it may decide to organize the dedicated alliance function around central alliance partners.

HP is a good example of a company that created processes to share knowledge on how to work with a specific alliance partner (see Figure 8.4). It identified a few key strategic partners with which it had numerous alliances, such as Microsoft, Cisco, Oracle, and America Online and Netscape (now part of AOL Time Warner), among others. HP created a partner-level alliance manager position to oversee all its alliances with each partner. The strategic-partner-level alliance managers had the responsibility of working with the managers and teams of the individual alliances to ensure that each of the partner's alliances would be as successful as possible. Because HP had numerous marketing and technical alliances with partners such as Microsoft, it also assigned some marketing and technical program managers to the alliance function. The managers supported the individual alliance managers and teams on specific marketing and technical issues relevant to their respective alliances. Thus HP became good at sharing partner-specific experiences and developing partner-specific priorities.

Citicorp developed a different approach. Rather than organize around key partners, the company organized its alliance function around business units and geographical areas. In some divisions the company also used an alliance board—similar to a board of directors—to oversee many alliances. The corporate alliance function was assigned an R&D and coordinating role for the alliance functions that resided in each division. For instance, the e-business solutions division engaged in alliances that were typically different from those of the retail banking division; therefore, the alliance function needed to create alliance management knowledge relevant to that specific division. Furthermore, to respond to differences among geographical regions, each of Citicorp's divisions created an alliance function within each region. For example, the e-business solutions alliance group in Latin America would oversee

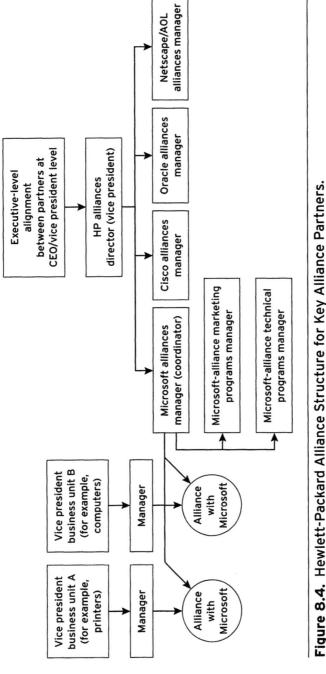

Figure 8.4. Hewlett-Packard Alliance Structure for Key Alliance Partners.

all Citicorp's Latin American alliances in the e-business sector. The e-business division's Latin American alliance board would review potential Latin American alliances—and approve or reject them.

Organize to Facilitate the Exchange of Knowledge on Specific Topics

The strategic-alliance function should be organized to make it easy for individuals throughout the organization to locate codified or tacit knowledge on a particular issue, type of alliance, or phase of the alliance life cycle. In other words, in addition to developing partner-specific, business-specific, or geography-specific knowledge, companies should charge certain individuals with responsibility for developing *topic-specific* knowledge.

For example, when people within the organization want to know the best way to negotiate a strategic-alliance agreement, what contractual provisions and governance arrangements are most appropriate, which metrics should be used, or the most effective way to resolve disagreements with partners, they should be able to access that information easily through the strategic-alliance function. In most cases, someone within the alliance function acts as the internal expert and is assigned the responsibility of developing and acquiring knowledge on a particular element of the alliance life cycle. For some companies it may be important to develop expertise on specific types of alliances—for example, those tied to R&D, marketing and cobranding, manufacturing, standard setting, consolidation joint ventures, or new joint ventures. The issues involved in setting up such alliances can be very different. For example, whenever the success of an alliance depends on the exchange of knowledge—as is the case in R&D alliances—equity-sharing governance arrangements are preferable because they give both parties the incentives necessary for them to bring all relevant knowledge to the table. But when each party brings to the alliance an "easy to value" resource—as with most marketing and cobranding alliances—contractual governance arrangements tend to be more suitable.

Locate the Function at an Appropriate Level of the Organization

When done properly, dedicated alliance functions offer internal legitimacy to alliances, assist in setting strategic priorities, and draw on resources across the company. That is why the function cannot be buried within a particular division or be relegated to low-level support within business development. It is critical that the director or vice president of the strategic-alliance function report to the COO or president of the company. Because alliances play an increasingly important role in overall corporate strategy, the person in charge of alliances should participate in the strategy-making processes at the highest level of the company. Moreover, if the alliance function's director reports to the company president or COO, the function will have the visibility and reach to cut across boundaries and draw on the company's resources in support of its alliance initiatives.

A CRITICAL COMPETENCE

Companies with a dedicated alliance function have been more successful than their counterparts at finding ways to solve problems regarding knowledge management, external visibility, internal coordination, and accountability—the underpinnings of an alliance management capability.

But although a dedicated alliance function can create value, success does not come without challenges. First, setting up such a function requires a serious investment of the company's resources and its people's time. Businesses must be large enough or enter into enough alliances to cover that investment. Second, deciding where to locate the function in the organization—and how to get line managers to appreciate the role of such a function and recognize its value—can be difficult. Finally, establishing codified and consistent procedures may mean inappropriately emphasizing process over speed in decision making.

Such challenges exist. But the company that surmounts them and builds a successful dedicated strategic-alliance function will reap substantial rewards. Companies with a well-developed alliance function generate greater stock market wealth through their alliances and better long-term strategic-alliance success rates. Over time, investment in an alliance management capability enhances the reputation of a company as a preferred partner. Hence an alliance management capability can be thought of as a competence in itself, one that can reap rich rewards for the organization that knows its worth.

Acknowledgments

This research greatly benefited from the support of the Wharton Emerging Technologies Management Research Program, Mack Center for Managing Technological Innovation.

ADDITIONAL RESOURCES

A helpful resource is John Harbison and Peter Pekar's *Smart Alliances: A Practical Guide to Repeatable Success*, published in 1998 by Jossey-Bass.

For a more scholarly development of ideas in this chapter, we recommend Y. Doz and G. Hamel's 1998 book from Harvard Business School Press, *The Alliance Advantage: The Art of Creating Value Through Partnering;* J. Dyer and H. Singh's 1998 "The Relational View" in *Academy of Management Review;* R. Gulati's "Alliances and Networks," which appeared in *Strategic Management Journal* in 1998; and "Building Alliance Capability: A Knowledge-Based Approach" from the 1999 *Academy of Management Best Paper Proceedings* and "Alliance Capability, Stock Market Response and Long-Term Alliance Success" from the 2000 *Academy of Management Proceedings*, both by P. Kale and H. Singh.

Also of interest are J. Koh and N. Venkatraman's "Joint Venture Formations and Stock Market Reactions," which appeared in 1991 in *Academy of Management Journal;* M. Lyle's "Learning Among Joint-Venture

Sophisticated Companies" in a 1998 *Management International Review* special issue; and Bernard Simonin's 1997 article "The Importance of Collaborative Know-How" in *Academy of Management Journal.*

NOTES

1. B. Anand and T. Khanna, "Do Companies Learn to Create Value?" *Strategic Management Journal,* March 2000, *21,* 295–316.
2. P. Kale, J. Dyer, and H. Singh, "Alliance Capability, Stock Market Response and Long-Term Alliance Success," in *Academy of Management Proceedings,* Academy of Management, Pace University (Briarcliff Manor, New York: Academy of Management, Pace University, 2000).
3. J. Bleeke and D. Ernst, *Collaborating to Compete* (New York: Wiley, 1993); and "The Way to Win in Cross-Border Alliances," *Alliance Analyst,* March 15, 1998, pp. 1–4.
4. "Dispelling the Myths of Alliances," *Outlook,* 1999, p. 28.

CHAPTER NINE

Innovation: Location Matters

MICHAEL E. PORTER
SCOTT STERN

The defining challenge for competitiveness has shifted, especially in advanced nations and regions. The challenges of a decade ago were to restructure, lower cost, and raise quality. Today, continued operational improvement is a given, and many companies are able to acquire and deploy the best current technology. In advanced nations, producing standard products using standard methods will not sustain competitive advantage. Companies must be able to innovate at the global frontier. They must create and commercialize a stream of new products and processes that shift the technology frontier, progressing as fast as their rivals catch up.

What are the drivers of innovation? Traditional thinking about the management of innovation focuses almost exclusively on *internal* factors—the capabilities and processes within companies for creating and commercializing technology. Although the importance of these factors is undeniable, the *external* environment for innovation is at least as important. For example, the striking innovative output

---

First published in the Summer 2001 issue of *MIT Sloan Management Review*.

of Israeli firms is due not simply to more effective technology management, but also to Israel's favorable environment for innovation, including strong university-industry linkages and a large pool of highly trained scientists and engineers. The most fertile location for innovation also varies markedly across fields. The United States was an especially attractive environment for innovation in pharmaceuticals in the 1990s, while Sweden and Finland saw extraordinary rates of innovation in wireless technology.

Our research has documented the patterns of innovation across the Organization for Economic Cooperation and Development (OECD) as well as in emerging nations over the past quarter century in order to understand how national circumstances explain differences in innovative output. We find that a relatively small number of characteristics of a nation's business environment explains a striking proportion of the large differences in innovative output across countries. Our findings reveal the striking degree to which the local environment matters for success in innovative activity and show the sharp differences in the relative progress of OECD and emerging countries in innovative vitality.

Location matters for innovation, and companies must broaden their approaches to the management of innovation accordingly: by developing and commercializing innovation in the most attractive location, taking active steps to access locational strengths, and proactively enhancing the environment for innovation and commercialization in locations where they operate.

THE ROLE OF
NATIONAL INNOVATIVE CAPACITY

The vitality of innovation in a location is shaped by *national innovative capacity*. National innovative capacity is a country's potential—as both a political and economic entity—to produce a stream of commercially relevant innovations. It is not simply the realized level of innovation but also reflects the fundamental conditions, investments, and policy choices that create the environment for innovation in a particular location.

We have developed a framework to identify the sources of innovative capacity that enable a nation to innovate at the global frontier.[1] Although the framework was created for application at the national level, managers can also use it to evaluate innovative capacity at the regional or local level.[2] The framework includes three broad elements (see Figure 9.1). Together they capture how location shapes a company's ability to innovate at the global frontier.

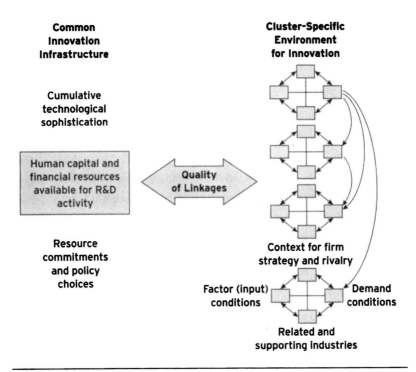

Figure 9.1. Elements of the National Innovative Capacity Framework.

The Common Innovation Infrastructure

This is the set of crosscutting factors that support innovation throughout an entire economy. They include the overall human and financial resources a country devotes to scientific and technological advances, the public policies bearing on innovative activity, and the economy's level of technological sophistication. Important policy choices include the protection of intellectual property, the extent of tax-based incentives for innovation, the degree to which antitrust enforcement encourages innovation-based competition, and the openness of the economy to trade and investment. A strong common innovation infrastructure requires national investments and policy choices stretching over decades.

The Cluster-Specific Environment for Innovation

While the common innovation infrastructure sets the basic conditions for innovation, it is ultimately companies that introduce and commercialize innovations. Innovation and the commercialization of new technologies take place disproportionately in clusters—geographical concentrations of interconnected companies and institutions in a particular field. The cluster-specific innovation environment is captured in the "diamond" framework introduced in 1990.[3] Four attributes of a location's microeconomic environment affect overall competitiveness as well as innovation—the presence of high-quality and specialized inputs; a context that encourages investment together with intense local rivalry; pressure and insight gleaned from sophisticated local demand; and the local presence of related and supporting industries (see Figure 9.2).

Clusters offer potential advantages in perceiving both the need and the opportunity for innovation. Equally important, however, are the flexibility and capacity that clusters can provide to act rapidly to turn new ideas into reality. A company within a cluster can often more rapidly source the new components, services, machinery, and other elements necessary to implement innovations. Local suppliers and partners can and do get involved in the innovation process; the

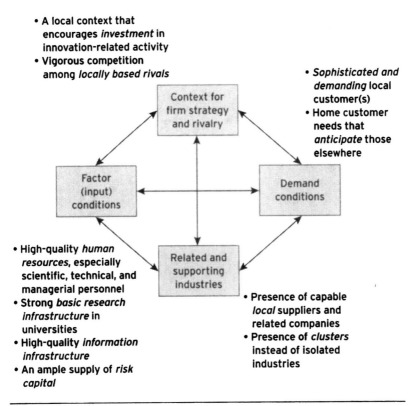

- A local context that encourages *investment* in innovation-related activity
- Vigorous competition among *locally based rivals*

- *Sophisticated and demanding* local customer(s)
- Home customer needs that *anticipate* those elsewhere

- High-quality *human resources*, especially scientific, technical, and managerial personnel
- Strong *basic research infrastructure* in universities
- High-quality *information infrastructure*
- An ample supply of *risk capital*

- Presence of capable *local* suppliers and related companies
- Presence of *clusters* instead of isolated industries

Figure 9.2. What Drives Innovation in an Industrial Cluster?

complementary relationships involved in innovating are more easily achieved among participants that are nearby. Reinforcing these advantages for innovation is the sheer pressure—competitive pressure, peer pressure, customer pressure, and constant comparison—that is inherent within a cluster. We focus on clusters (for example, information technology) rather than individual industries (for example, printers), then, because of powerful spillovers and externalities across discrete industries that are vital to the rate of innovation.

The competitiveness of a cluster and its innovativeness depend on the quality of the diamond in a country. For example, the Finnish pulp-and-paper cluster benefits from the twin advantages of pressures from demanding domestic consumers and intense local rivalry, and Finnish process equipment manufacturers are world leaders, with companies such as Kamyr and Sunds leading the world in the commercialization of innovative bleaching equipment. And this is only one example. A strong innovation environment within national clusters is the foundation for global competitive advantage in many fields, from pharmaceuticals in the United States to semiconductor fabrication in Taiwan.

The Quality of Linkages

The relationship between the common innovation infrastructure and a nation's industrial clusters is reciprocal: strong clusters feed the common infrastructure and also benefit from it. A variety of formal and informal organizations and networks—which we call "institutions for collaboration"—can link the two areas. A particularly important example is a nation's university system, which provides a bridge between technology and companies. Without strong linkages, upstream scientific and technical advances may diffuse to other countries more quickly than they can be exploited at home. For example, although early elements of VCR technology were developed in the United States, it was three companies in the Japanese consumer electronics cluster that successfully commercialized this innovation on a global scale in the late 1970s. Of course, taking advantage of the national environment for innovation is far from automatic, and companies based in the same location will differ markedly in their success at innovation. Nevertheless, sharp differences in innovative output in different locations suggest that location exerts a strong influence.

EXPLAINING NATIONAL INNOVATIVE OUTPUT

To understand how location affects innovation, we set out to explain the differences in innovative output across countries using measures drawn from the national innovative capacity framework. Our measure of innovation output is the number of international patents granted by the U.S. Patent and Trademark Office to inventors from a country, expressed on a per capita basis to control for the size of the country. We compiled data on international patenting in seventeen OECD countries over the past twenty-five years, as well as in a group of emerging economies. We then related patenting output to measures of the common innovation infrastructure, the quality of the clusters' innovation environment, and the strength of the linkages between these two elements (see box, How We Measured National Innovative Capacity).

Offering insights into the important influences on national innovative capacity and the relative weight of different factors, this approach makes it easier to compare innovative capacity across countries and over time. To measure each country's innovative capacity in a given year, we used its *expected* per capita international patenting rate as determined by the country's policies and the resources it was devoting to innovation during that period.

Our findings are striking. The measures we used explain *more than 99 percent* of the variation in international patenting across countries during this time. Overall, the propensity of companies within a given nation to innovate is strongly related to the features of the national innovation environment. Our results show that national innovative output is most significantly affected by the number of scientists and technologists in the workforce, the aggregate level of R&D spending, the effectiveness of intellectual property protection, openness to international competition, and the intensity of spending on higher education. Patenting productivity is also significantly affected by the extent to which R&D is *financed* by industry, *performed* by universities, and *specialized* within a range of technologies.

Moreover, no single national attribute is dominant in explaining innovative output. Favorable national innovative capacity results from strength along multiple dimensions rather than from superiority in one or two particular areas. Also, the

▼

How We Measured National Innovative Capacity

To understand how location matters for innovation, we undertook a series of quantitative studies to examine the relationship between national innovative output and measures of national innovative capacity.[1] These studies offer insight into the most important influences on national innovative capacity and how to weight the relative impact of each. They also allow a comparison of innovative capacity across countries and over time.

Because our focus was on innovation at the technology frontier and on comparing innovation across nations, we measured national innovative output using the number of patents the U.S. Patent and Trademark Office (USPTO) granted to foreign and U.S. inventors from the late 1970s through the mid-1990s.[2] Over this time the rate of international patenting at the USPTO increased dramatically—from fewer than twenty-five thousand per year in the late 1970s to more than seventy-five thousand by the late 1990s.

We used USPTO patents as an indication of innovative intensity for several reasons. When a foreign inventor files a U.S. patent, it is a sign of the innovation's potential economic value because of the costs involved. Also, the use of U.S. patents ensures a commitment to a standard of technological excellence that is at or near the global technology frontier.

Of course, no single measure of innovation is ideal. We therefore also explored several alternative measures of innovation success, such as the pattern of exports in international high-technology markets. Overall, however, international patents constitute the best available measure of innovation that is consistent across time and location.

Using data from seventeen OECD countries over the past quarter century, we examined the linkage between international patenting productivity and

---

[1] For a more detailed discussion of our empirical methodology, see S. Stern, M. E. Porter, and J. L. Furman, "The Determinants of National Innovative Capacity," working paper 7876 (Cambridge, Massachusetts: National Bureau of Economic Research, 2000).

[2] For a useful introduction to the application of patent statistics for evaluating innovation, see Z. Griliches, "Patent Statistics as Economic Indicators: A Survey," *Journal of Economic Literature,* 1990, *28*(4), 1661-1701; and J. Eaton and S. Kortum, "International Technology Diffusion: Theory and Measurement," *International Economic Review,* 1999, *40*(3), 537-570.

various measures of national innovative capacity. Although these measures cannot capture the full subtlety of national innovative capacity, our results suggest that this set of measures of the nation's innovation environment can explain the overwhelming share of the variation in international patenting rates across countries and time.

Common Innovation Infrastructure

Measures that indicate the strength of a nation's common innovation infrastructure are relatively available. We used the number of employed scientists and engineers, the overall level of R&D expenditures, the share of GDP devoted to expenditures on higher education, a measure of the effectiveness of intellectual property protection, and a measure of the economy's openness to international trade. We used GDP per capita as a control for the economy's aggregate technical sophistication. Each of these measures varies substantially across countries and time. For example, though their living standards are similar, the percentage of the workforce who are scientists and engineers is three times higher in Japan than in Italy or Spain.

Cluster-Specific Innovation Environment

Measuring cluster-specific conditions is more difficult, and we used proxies that were less direct. We used the share of national R&D expenditures funded by the private sector to reflect the overall private R&D environment. The robustness of an industrial cluster is also reflected in a second indirect measure, the degree of technological specialization, which we determined by looking at the relative concentration of patenting activity across technological fields. If a country's innovation resources are more focused, other things being equal, R&D productivity should be higher.

Quality of Linkages

Measures here are also necessarily indirect and include the share of national R&D expenditures *performed* in the university sector. Universities are perhaps the single most important institutions linking a nation's clusters and the common innovation infrastructure. Linkages also take place through channels that are more difficult to measure, such as venture-capital networks, the Blue List Institutes in Germany, and other informal company networks.

locational determinants of innovation have been remarkably stable over time.

Innovation in OECD Countries

From our statistical findings, we constructed an index of national innovative capacity for the OECD nations (see Figure 9.3). The index reveals how the innovation environment has been changing.

The innovative capacity of OECD countries has converged substantially over the last quarter century. Although the United States and Switzerland maintain their top-tier positions across three decades, the *relative advantage* of these leaders has declined. Countries such as Japan and Germany, as well as a group of Scandinavian nations, have invested in the conditions underpinning national innovative capacity and improved their relative standing as innovators.

Improvements by countries in national innovative capacity are the result of concerted improvements along several dimensions. Denmark and Finland have made major gains in innovative capacity since the mid-1980s, for example, by substantially increasing their R&D workforce, raising R&D investment (particularly in the private sector), and emphasizing policies that support open international competition and strong intellectual property protection. They join Sweden in establishing a region of world-class innovation. However, had Denmark and Finland simply raised R&D expenditures without addressing other areas, they would have had a much more limited impact.

National innovative capacity is not the same thing as short-term competitiveness. Japan, for example, continues to improve its environment for innovation, as it has since the early 1970s, despite continued economic stagnation and difficulties in reforming other aspects of its economy. Conversely, several Western European countries, including the United Kingdom, France, and Italy, have at best maintained innovative capacity, despite some success in current competitiveness. Although each nation possesses strengths

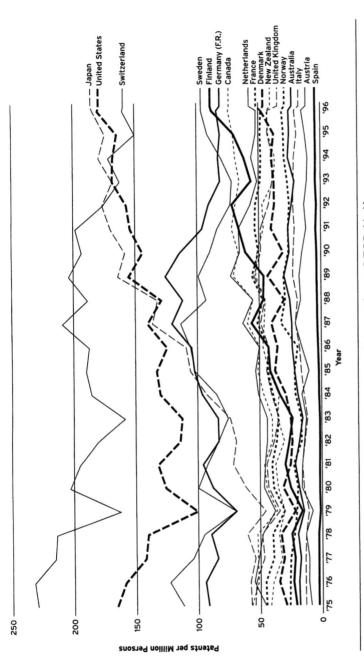

Figure 9.3. Tracking the Innovative Capacity of Seventeen OECD Nations.

The annual innovative capacity of each country is equal to its *expected* international patenting productivity as determined by the national environment for innovation.

Source: M. E. Porter and S. Stern, *The New Challenge to America's Prosperity: Findings from the Innovation Index* (Washington, D.C.: Council on Competitiveness, 1999), p. 34.

that support innovation in some parts of its economy, the commitment to innovation has been mixed. Italy boasts a vibrant textile cluster, for example, and the United Kingdom supports an outstanding scientific research system, yet neither has increased its overall commitment to innovation commensurate with the leading innovator countries. The consequences for long-term national living standards are beginning to be felt.

Innovation in Emerging Nations

Our study also shows that new centers of innovative activity are emerging outside the OECD. Singapore, Taiwan, South Korea, and Israel have made substantial investments in upgrading their innovative capacities over the past decade and achieved large increases in patenting rates. Ireland has also established the infrastructure and industrial clusters consistent with strong innovative activity.

Conversely, several countries that have drawn much attention as potential economic powers—India, China, and Malaysia—are not yet generating meaningful levels of world-class innovative output on an absolute or relative basis. These countries have developed neither a base for innovation nor clusters with a large innovative capacity.

We also used the national innovative capacity framework to rationalize the weak overall innovation performance of Latin American economies and the recent positive trends in countries such as Costa Rica[4] (see box, Assessing National Innovative Capacity: Latin America).

Regional Differences

Although our focus is on national differences in innovative capacity, sharp differences also occur between states and regions within nations (see Figure 9.4, p. 254). These regional differences reflect the same considerations we have described at the national level. The quality of common innovation infrastructure often varies by region, and clusters are often concentrated geographically.

Assessing National Innovative Capacity: Latin America

Although Latin American companies have greatly improved their competitiveness in international markets in recent decades, they continue to produce very little new-to-the-world technology. For example, several countries in Latin America are awarded fewer than ten U.S. patents per year. In 1997, for example, many Latin American countries registered per capita rates of international patenting that were less than *one-fiftieth* the rates in most Western European countries, though per capita incomes were greater than one-fifth of those of Western Europe. In other words, Latin American firms were fifty times less likely to patent a world-class innovation than their Western European counterparts. What is behind this low rate of innovation performance, and how does Latin America differ from other emerging areas that *are* producing world-class technological innovation?[1]

The Latin American innovation shortfall is the result of several factors. For example, in leading innovator economies the university system provides training and also undertakes basic research. Throughout the Spanish-speaking world, however, universities have historically played a limited role in the innovation process. Latin American higher education has often remained isolated from industry and only loosely involved in national science and technology policy. Similarly, even though openness to international competition encourages innovation by fostering knowledge spillovers and competitive pressures, Latin American economies have a history of being largely closed, which has lowered their rates of innovation.

During the late 1970s several Latin American countries actually realized a higher level of international patenting than a comparison group of emerging Asian economies; in sharp contrast, by the second half of the 1990s, patenting in the Asian economies dwarfed the Latin American output. (See "Latin American Innovative Performance Relative to Emerging Asian Economies" in this box.) This difference in performance reflects, at least in

(continued)

[1] M. E. Porter, J. L. Furman, and S. Stern, "Los factores impulsores de la capacidad innovadora nacional: Implicaciones para España y America Latina" in *Claves de la economia mundial* (Madrid: ICEX, 2000), pp. 78-88. For an English-language version, see M. E. Porter, J. L. Furman, and S. Stern, "The Drivers of National Innovative Capacity: Implications for Spain and Latin America," working paper 01-004 (Boston: Harvard Business School, 2000).

▼

Assessing National Innovative Capacity: Latin America (cont.)

Latin American Innovative Performance Relative to Emerging Asian Economies

Country	1976-1980	1995-1999	Growth Rate
Emerging Latin American economies			
Argentina	115	228	0.98
Brazil	136	494	2.62
Chile	12	60	4.00
Costa Rica	22	48	1.18
Mexico	124	431	2.48
Emerging Asian economies			
China	3	557	191.33
Hong Kong	176	1,694	8.63
Singapore	17	725	41.65
South Korea	23	12,062	523.43
Taiwan	135	15,871	116.56

Note: The first two columns are the total number of U.S. patents in each country during each five-year period.

part, the Asian economies' high rate of investments in national innovative capacity relative to those of Latin American nations.

Within Latin America national innovative capacities differ substantially. (See "Some Determinants of National Innovative Capacity in Six Latin American Countries in 1998" in this box.) Argentina employed the greatest number of scientists and engineers per capita. Argentina, Chile, and Brazil maintain high per capita R&D expenditures and engage in intellectual property and competitiveness policies that support innovative activity relevant to Colombia, Costa Rica, and Mexico.

Some Determinants of National Innovative Capacities in Six Latin American Countries in 1998

Country	Full-Time-Equivalent R&D Workers per Million Population	R&D Expenditure ($ Million) per Million Population	Strength of Intellectual Property Protection[a]	Openness to International Competition and Trade[b]
Argentina	1,212.2	32.8	4.7	8.5
Brazil	433.7	35.3	3.3	5.4
Chile	639.2	32.0	6.1	8.8
Colombia	–	9.0	5.0	5.0
Costa Rica	557.0	32.2	6.0	6.0
Mexico	365.3	15.2	6.1	7.9

Note: Calculations are based on data from the Ibero American Network of Science and Technology Indicators (the RICYT), 2000, and the *World Competitiveness Yearbook* (Lausanne, Switzerland: IMD, 1998).
[a]Ranking is based on a 1–10 scale, where 1 = "weakest" and 10 = "strongest."
[b]Ranking is based on a 1–10 scale, where 1 = "least open" and 10 = "most open."

Despite rapid economic growth in much of Latin America over the last decade, the region still faces substantial challenges in developing innovative capacity at a level commensurate with those of leading OECD countries. Some Latin American countries seem to be moving to address this challenge. The Costa Rican government is encouraging the development of an information technology cluster; these policies are, in turn, helping to upgrade each element of Costa Rica's national innovative capacity.[2] Maintaining a consistent record of investments and policy choices to enhance the innovation environment will be essential to determining whether Latin America is able to sustain and enhance its competitiveness over the next generation.

[2] See M. E. Porter and N. Kettelhohn, "Building a Cluster: Electronic and Information Technology in Costa Rica," draft (Boston: Harvard Business School, 2000).

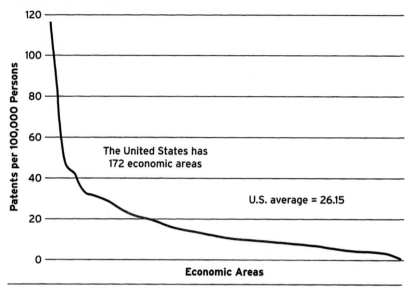

Figure 9.4. Patenting Per Capita Across the United States in 1997.

Source: Cluster Mapping Project, Institute for Strategy and Competitiveness, Harvard Business School.

IMPLICATIONS FOR INNOVATION MANAGEMENT

Innovation is strongly affected by location: the *external* environment for innovation. This insight holds critical implications for companies and creates a new, broader agenda for management. Choosing R&D locations and managing relationships with outside organizations should not be driven by input costs, taxes, subsidies, or even the wage rates for scientists and engineers (as they often are). Instead, R&D investments should flow preferentially to the most fertile locations for innovation (see box, Mapping Innovative Capacity: A Tool for Managers). Harnessing and extending locational advantages takes an equal weight to R&D process management. Locational advantages—rooted in proprietary information flows, special relationships, and special access to institutions—are competitive advantages that are difficult for outsiders to overcome. They help explain an apparent paradox of globalization: ideas and technologies that can be accessed from a distance cannot serve as a foundation for competitive advantage because they are widely available. In a global economy this makes harnessing local advantages crucial.

Locate R&D investments and commercialize new technologies in environments with strong innovative capacity. Though innovation is often serendipitous and internal project management has an important impact on success, opportunities for effectively developing new products, processes, and services arise by locating in countries (and regions within countries) with a favorable common innovation infrastructure and strong clusters in their field.

A location may be favorable for other reasons (such as offering low manufacturing costs or access to key markets) but unfavorable for innovation. Managers must make R&D locational choices strategically, recognizing that there tend to be only a few true innovation centers in each industry and that even modest improvements in the innovation environment can hold dramatic consequences for competitive advantage. For example, though biomedical research takes place throughout the world, more than three-fourths of all biotechnology pharmaceutical patents have their origin in a handful of regional clusters in the United States.

R&D locational choices are particularly important for companies that aspire to global strategies. It is important to establish a presence in countries whose innovation environments are the most favorable. When dispersing R&D, however, it is important that one location remains the home base for each product line or business unit. Otherwise, disparate locations can create problems that slow down innovation and commercialization rather than enhance it.

Locations with strong intracluster knowledge spillovers can make it harder to protect ideas from local competitors. However, most companies within a cluster are usually not direct competitors but sources of complementary ideas, products, or services. Strong

▼

Mapping Innovative Capacity: A Tool for Managers

The national innovative capacity framework provides a means to access the locational influences of innovation. A good starting point for using this framework is to compile data on the national or regional track record of innovation: domestic patents, international patents, trademark applications, and counts of new products. Evaluating a region's innovation performance requires collecting and analyzing measures in the context of the framework's three elements.

Common Innovation Infrastructure

Comparisons across countries can include the size and composition of the science and engineering workforce, the country's overall level of educational attainment, and the funding for R&D over time. To evaluate national innovation policies, the *Global Competitiveness Report* offers nuanced measures, including the strength of intellectual property protection, the effectiveness of antitrust enforcement, the availability of risk capital, and the economy's openness to international product market competition.[1]

Cluster-Specific Innovation Environment

Defining clusters and drawing cluster boundaries is a creative process informed by understanding the most important complementary relationships across industries and institutions to competition. Cluster boundaries should encompass all firms, industries, and institutions with strong linkages, whether vertical or horizontal. Clusters normally consist of a combination of end-product, machinery, materials, and service industries, usually classified in separate categories. They often involve (or potentially involve) both traditional and high-tech industries. Clusters vary in their state of development, and cluster boundaries evolve as new companies and industries

[1] The *Global Competitiveness Report* is published annually by Oxford University Press.

emerge, established industries shrink or decline, and local institutions develop and change. Technological and market developments spawn new industries, create new linkages, or alter served markets. Regulatory changes also contribute to shifting boundaries. After clusters are defined, the task is to assess the state of the cluster diamond.[2]

Linkages

Managers must also assess the quality and the depth of the institutions in a nation or region to link together firms and institutions, particularly the local university system. A competitive university system combines teaching and research with a history of responsiveness to industrial innovation opportunities. This combination provides a powerful mechanism for connecting the common innovative infrastructure to the needs of clusters. In countries such as England, however, the presence of universities with a strong scientific orientation has not historically translated into an engaged player in the coordination and management of innovation.

Another important linking mechanism is risk-capital providers. In the United States, venture capitalists play this role. In other countries, provision of risk capital takes place in various ways, from banking institutions to public-private financing entities.

Defining the Relevant Geographical Region

While the nation is an appropriate focus for many fields, innovative capacity often varies *within* countries. In these cases, national policy differences may be less important than evaluating the local innovation infrastructures and understanding the dynamics of local clusters.

[2] M. E. Porter, *On Competition* (Boston: Harvard Business School Press, 1998), pp. 197-287.

innovation clusters, then, can progress much faster than other locations even though some firms and subsidiaries within the cluster have trouble staying ahead.

Proactively access the local strengths. Capturing locational advantages in innovation involves more than sending delegations or establishing R&D listening posts. Companies must proactively invest to tap into the strengths of their local environment. This involves such things as active participation in industry associations, investing to build deep relationships with local universities, cultivating and assisting programs that train skilled personnel, and paying particular attention to the most sophisticated local customers.

Companies in the same locational cluster may differ in how they leverage the local cluster's capacity for innovation. For example, most high-technology companies in the Route 128 corridor around Boston, Massachusetts, take advantage of the ready supply of engineers and the spillovers among firms within the local information technology and life sciences clusters. Yet only a subset of these companies have directed resources toward interactions with local academic researchers and membership in partnership programs with MIT research centers.

Enhance local innovative capacity. In most cases, the question is not just where to locate internationally but how to shape the local environment to make it more conducive to innovation. Companies have an important stake in regional innovative capacity. This means that, even individually, they should encourage public investment and policies that enhance the national innovation infrastructure and improve the clusters. The most effective role for government is not to simply subsidize R&D (a policy which is likely to increase R&D wages without commensurate increases in the level of innovation) but to improve the innovation environment. Industry associations can offer a unified voice in encouraging appropriate government policies. However, collective private sector organizations also have an important independent role in such areas as establishing training programs, creating new research centers, and supporting standards organizations. Here private investments create "public goods" that can be of immense competitive value.

A BROADER AGENDA

Building a foundation for competitive advantage requires a clear understanding of the role location plays in both innovation and competitiveness. Reduced communication costs and more open borders actually enhance the importance of location as traditional sources of advantages are "competed away." Managers can no longer simply manage the innovation process within their companies; they must also manage the process of how their companies enhance and take advantage of opportunities in the local environment. Indeed, long-term competitive advantage relies on being able to avoid imitation by competitors. Ironically, then, location-based advantages in innovation may prove more sustainable than simply implementing corporate best practices.

Acknowledgments

The authors would like to acknowledge the contributions and insights of Jeff Furman, with whom they have conducted much of the research that this chapter builds on. They also would like to thank the Council on Competitiveness for its contributions.

NOTES

1. A full exposition of the National Innovative Capacity Framework as well as a full reference list of our prior research in this area is included in S. Stern, M. E. Porter, and J. L. Furman, "The Determinants of National Innovative Capacity," working paper 7876

(Cambridge, Massachusetts: National Bureau of Economic Research, 2000). This framework synthesizes and extends three areas of prior theory: ideas-driven endogenous growth, described in P. Romer, "Endogenous Technological Change," *Journal of Political Economy, 98,* S71–S102; cluster-based national industrial competitive advantage, described in M. Porter, *The Competitive Advantage of Nations* (New York: Free Press, 1990); and national innovation systems, described in R. R. Nelson, ed., *National Innovation Systems: A Comparative Analysis* (New York: Oxford University Press, 1993).

2. The Cluster Mapping Project, based at the Institute for Strategy and Competitiveness at Harvard Business School, has charted striking differences in the patterns of innovation across the United States' economic areas.

3. The "diamond" framework, introduced in Porter, *The Competitive Advantage of Nations,* has been used extensively to understand the foundations of global competitive advantage. The national innovative capacity framework emphasizes the linkage between industrial clusters and innovation.

4. M. E. Porter, J. L. Furman, and S. Stern, "Los factores impulsores de la capacidad innovadora nacional: Implicaciones para España y America Latina" in *Claves de la economia mundial* (Madrid: ICEX, 2000), pp. 78–88. For an English-language version, see M. E. Porter, J. L. Furman, and S. Stern, "The Drivers of National Innovative Capacity: Implications for Spain and Latin America," working paper 01-004 (Boston: Harvard Business School, 2000).

PART THREE

New Dimensions for Innovation

CHAPTER TEN

Software-Based Innovation

JAMES BRIAN QUINN
JORDAN J. BARUCH
KAREN ANNE ZIEN

A revolution is now under way. Most innovation occurs first in software.[1] And software is the primary element in all aspects of innovation from basic research through product introduction:

▼ Software provides the critical mechanism through which managers can lower the costs, compress the time cycles, and increase the value of innovations. It is also the heart of the learning and knowledge processes that give innovations their highest payoffs.

▼ In many cases, software is the core element in process innovations or in creating the functionalities that make products valuable to customers. In others, software is the "product" or "service" the customer actually receives.

▼ Software provides the central vehicle enabling the inventor-user interactions, rapid distribution of products, and market feedback that add most value to innovations. Consequently, customers—and

---

First published in the Summer 1996 issue of *MIT Sloan Management Review.*

the software itself—make many inventions that the company's technologists, acting alone, could not conceive.

All this demands a basic shift in the way managers approach innovation, from strategic to detailed operational levels. Some portions of the innovation process may still require traditional physical manipulation, but leading companies have already shifted many steps to software. And those who do not will suffer. Managers can shorten innovation cycles through other means, but through properly developed software, they can change their entire innovation process, completely integrating, merging, or eliminating many formerly discrete innovation steps.[2] In the process, they can dramatically lower innovation costs, decrease risks, shorten design and introduction cycle times, and increase the value of their innovations to customers.

SOFTWARE DOMINATES
ALL INNOVATION STEPS

Innovation consists of the technological, managerial, and social processes through which a new idea or concept is first reduced to practice in a culture. *Discovery* is the initial observation of a new phenomenon. *Invention* provides the first verification that a real problem can be solved in a particular way. *Diffusion* spreads proved innovations broadly within an enterprise or society. All are necessary to create new value. Software dominates all aspects of the cycle from discovery to diffusion.

▼ *Basic research.* Most literature searches, database inquiries, exchanges with other researchers, experimental designs, laboratory experiments, analyses of correlations and variances, hypothesis testing, modeling of complex phenomena, review of experimental results, first publication of results, enhancements to existing databases, and so on are performed through software. To a large extent software search tools determine what data researchers see and what questions they ask. In many frontier fields—like astronomy, semiconductors, or biotechnology—researchers may be able to observe, measure, or precisely envision phenomena only through electronic measures or electronic modeling (software).

For example, in 1991 a group at IBM's Watson Research Center completed calculations from a full year's continuous run on its high-powered GF 11 computer. Based on known physical evidence, the group had established the masses of seven basic particles, including hadrons, important in quark research. By 1995 two further years of calculations had established both the mass and the decay rate of an elusive subfamily of hadrons, called "glueballs," which had gone unrecognized in preceding laboratory experiments. These massive computations had both discovered a new particle and provided an important confirmation of quantum chromodynamics, the theory governing the behavior of quarks.[3]

▼ *Applied research.* Most of the preceding activities are common to applied research as well. However, at this stage, practical data about market, economic, or performance phenomena become important. Most major innovations are preceded by a defined need.[4] In many fields data about the marketplace, user patterns, environmental trends, or specific constraints to application now come directly from software. Examples include market shifts sensed through electronic point-of-sale (EPOS) data, epidemiological measurements of medical problems or outcomes, satellite scanning of environmental changes, and real-time performance data about financial transactions, communication systems, or marketing distribution programs' effectiveness.[5] New object-oriented software, like that developed by Trilogy Corp., is rapidly extending these capabilities across a wide spectrum of industries.[6]

▼ *Development.* At the developmental level virtually all design of physical systems, subsystems, components, and parts now occurs first in software. Most things—from buildings to ships, aircraft, automobiles, circuits, bridges, tunnels, machines, molecules, textiles, advertising, packaging, biological systems, dams, weapons systems, or spacecraft—are first designed in software. Specialists try to design into their models all the known science-technical relationships, physical dimensioning, system constraints, flow rates, and dynamic response patterns understood from earlier technical work, experiments, tests, or operations. CAE/CAD/CAM systems interconnect whatever knowledge exists about these physical science systems and their potential manipulability in manufacturing. Other software systems test CAD representations of potential designs against anticipated variations in use or operating environments—without building physical models. Simulations often allow much less expensive and more effective test information than the experimenter could possibly afford to achieve through physical models. This is especially true for very large-scale, extreme-environment, submicroscopic, complex dynamic-flow, or potentially dangerous systems, where physical experimentation might be impossible.

▼ *Manufacturing engineering.* Software now provides the same kinds of data-gathering, analytical, and test capabilities for complex process design and manufacturing engineering as we described for product designs. In process design, software allows inexpensive experimentation, yield prediction, workstation design, process layout, alternative testing, three-dimensional analysis, network manipulation, quality control, and interface-timing capabilities that would otherwise be impossibly expensive. Software is especially helpful in allowing workers, technologists, and managers to visualize solutions and work together on complex systems. Further, knowledge-based systems now allow the design coordination, manufacturing monitoring, and logistics control needed to find and source innovative solutions worldwide.[7]

▼ *Interactive customer design.* Software models and shared screens allow multidisciplinary (marketing-manufacturing-development) teams to interact continuously with customers, capturing their responses through video, audio, physical sensing, and computer network systems. Through software, customers already participate directly in the design of new or customized fabrics, furnishings, entertainment services, auto and aircraft parts, homes and commercial buildings, and insurance, legal, or accounting products.[8] Such customer participation is a crucial element in both lowering risks and enhancing the customer value of designs. More important, by designing "hooks" on their software (to allow others to innovate further on their own), companies can leverage their internal capabilities enormously by tapping into their customers' and sophisticated suppliers' creative ideas.

▼ *Postintroduction monitoring.* After new products are in the marketplace, software can upgrade their effectiveness in use (aircraft), oversee their proper maintenance (elevators), and add value by introducing new knowledge-based features directly into the customer's system (computers, financial services, or accounting systems). Manufacturers have placed sensing and maintenance software into various products—from health care devices to automobiles, power generation systems, and home appliances—that can anticipate and even automatically correct potentially dangerous or disruptive failures. Service companies—like utilities, telecoms, retailers, airlines, banks, hospitals, or wholesalers—use in-line sensing to (1) ensure intended response times, signal levels, accuracy of information, and performance reliability and (2) search out their customers' changing utilization patterns to improve products further.

▼ *Diffusion and organizational learning.* After new concepts are successfully tested in the marketplace, software helps implement introductions rapidly across wider geographical areas with higher accuracy, consistency, and performance reliability than would be possible otherwise. The practice is widespread in service enterprises, such as fast foods, maintenance, accounting, reservations, or financial-services companies. But it is equally essential to firms like Asea-Brown-Boveri, Ford, and Boeing in transferring physical product designs or manufacturing know-how from one location to another. Further, software is becoming the critical element in facilitating the organizational learning that continual rapid innovation requires, whether in services or manufacturing. It enables both experienced and less-skilled people to perform at much higher levels by incorporating important knowledge components into the equipment that personnel use and the data banks that contact people have at the customer interface. Brokerage houses, accounting firms, banks, insurance companies, and product distributors all depend on software to enable their people to "jump the learning curve" for rapid product and process introductions.

▼ *New value-added systems.* Software is often the strategic element in unlocking higher value-added opportunities and indeed in restructuring entire companies and industries.[9] For example, in the late 1980s Intel was concerned about the commoditization of integrated circuits. Intel's chips were being copied, and its patents were running out. In early 1991 Intel CEO Andy Grove asked his executives to create the basis for a new personal computer with much higher performance, lower costs, and video communications capabilities. This required contributions from many other companies, including entertainment, telecommunications, software, and systems groups. The core of the challenge was in software. Grove commissioned a team to learn about all aspects of personal computing, including software, that Intel had not earlier considered its charter. Ultimately, these initiatives became a comprehensive strategy to move Intel from a narrow role as a "semiconductor supplier" to that of a system supplier. These efforts grew into the Intel Architecture Labs, anticipating new uses and applications for personal computers, entertainment, and computing. Through its software interconnections and alliances, Intel has become a center for changing the entire value-added concept of its industry.[10]

SOFTWARE FOR FAST CYCLE INNOVATION

There are many aspects to improving the cycle time of innovation.[11] But none is more crucial—and has received less attention—than software. As the following examples demonstrate, software can entirely eliminate many traditional steps in the innovation process. It can consolidate others into a simultaneous process. And it can provide the communication mechanisms and disciplined framework for the detailed interactions that multidisciplinary teams need to advance complex innovations most rapidly.

For example, Boeing went directly from software into production of its $170 million 777 aircraft, cutting out many sequential steps formerly in the design cycle. It installed seventeen hundred workstations to link some 2,800 engineering locations worldwide. Using rules developed from earlier scientific models, wind tunnel tests, field experience, and supplier-customer models supporting its systems, Boeing's 250 different multifunctional "design/build" teams could pretest and optimize the structural elements, operating systems, and consumer convenience aspects of each major component in the aircraft's four-million-part configuration. Boeing's three-dimensional, digital CAD/CAM software eliminated many previous blueprint, specification, tool- and die-making, and physical prototyping steps.

Instead, software provided each department or external fabricator with the capacity to produce its tools, parts, or subassemblies directly from digital electronic instructions. It also allowed Boeing to cut or mold whatever physical models were needed for its own wind tunnel, systems, or stress tests. Because all the specifications for interacting suppliers could be coordinated directly from the software to ensure precise fits, assembly tolerances, surfacing, and materials compatibilities, there was a reduction of 60 to 90 percent in prototype errors and rework costs.[12]

The software compressed or eliminated many of the "build and bust" tests that were previously necessary and made needed "first off" tests of physical components and systems much more reliable. At all phases software systems allowed many groups—within and outside the company—to operate in parallel without losing interface coordination. The system's 1.8 trillion bytes of production data coordinated all downstream production and sourcing decisions. All this substantially decreased design cycle times, costs, and potential errors. But the real test was that software produced a better quality, more flyable aircraft at lower cost.[13]

In chemistry and biotechnology, companies generally attempt to design and assess new molecules as much as possible in software before building actual chemical structures. Using well-researched rules about how different components will combine, biotechnology researchers can pretest the most likely and effective combinations for a new biotech structure. They can assess which receptors are most likely to respond in a certain fashion, how to relocate or reshape a molecule's receptor or bonding structures, and what transport mechanisms can best deliver "bonding" or "killer" agents. Researchers can often observe actual interaction processes using electron or scanning-tunneling microscopes that can extend observation capabilities by orders of magnitude beyond ordinary optical limits.[14] Such equipment is itself largely software driven by electronic sensing and amplification. Electronic models, based on the best-known laboratory data about biochemical processes, shorten cycle times for process development and allow detailed process monitoring to ensure quality during experimental and early scale-up phases.

SOFTWARE ENHANCES INNOVATION RESULTS

Although important, decreasing individual experimentation, modeling, and scale-up times is not always the crucial issue. Frequently, the optimizing calculations for designs or operations are so complex that they could not be done at all without computer capabilities. In other cases, lacking computer models, scientists would have to rely much more on hunches and limited experimentation, decreasing both the variety and quality of experiments and the capture of knowledge from these experiments. Human inaccuracies would quickly throw off calculations, leave out critical variables, cause inaccurate experiments, and lead to wrong results. Without software, innovators often could neither adequately measure nor interrelate the details of large-scale scientific experiments, the physical reactions within a system, or the interaction patterns between the system and important external forces. Examples include gene sequencing, weather and environmental system analyses, large-scale integrated circuit designs, atomic orbit calculations, multiphase gas flow analyses, or space flight trajectories.

Further, from an organizational viewpoint, in analyzing or developing such systems, it would be essentially impossible for the required number of different knowledge specialists to personally work together effectively. They could not achieve results within reasonable time frames or with needed precision without software tools and software-based communications devices. The organizational software support for large-scale systems designs—like those for construction innovations, space shots, Ford's Taurus, or Boeing's 777—often becomes as important as the physical-design software.

Software Becomes Inventor

Software enables more sophisticated innovations than humans could achieve unaided. In many cases, software actually becomes the discoverer or inventor. Software designed as a learning system frequently generates answers beyond the imagination of its creators. It may identify and verify totally new patterns and problem solutions. It can even be preprogrammed to search for, capture, and flag the "fortuitous incidents" or "anomalies" that are often the essence of discovery. Properly designed software systems can actually create new hypotheses, test the hypotheses for critical characteristics, analyze potential system responses to exogenous variables, and predict counterintuitive outcomes from complex interactions. Software can learn from both positive and negative experiments and capture these experience effects in data files.

For example, the Cochrane Collaboration is a massive effort to collect and systematically review the entire published and unpublished literature on the roughly one million randomized control trials of medical treatments that have been conducted during the past fifty years. Because they are so difficult to access, most of those experiments' results have been ignored or otherwise lost to practitioners. The collaboration will collect, catalogue, and update these reviews to synthesize the latest state of knowledge about every available therapy or intervention and give its implications for practice and research. In the past, when such clinical data were systematically collected and analyzed, interesting new patterns were discovered that changed many practices, like mammographies, fetal monitoring, mastectomies, and prostatectomies.[15]

In large-scale systems "genetic" and related learning algorithms and software can often identify patterns, optimize research protocols, and define potential solutions by trial and error much more efficiently than can either direct physical experimentation or a preplanned sequence of hypothesis tests. Such programs can economically attack problems that were of unthinkable complexity a decade ago. In business applications self-learning programs can identify developing problems or opportunities in the competitive environment, suggest the most likely causes and alternative solutions available, eliminate those of least promise, and pretest or implement promising new options—as they commonly do in telecom switching, power distribution, vehicle routing, or ad campaign targeting and modification.

Leveraging Value Creation

A major contribution of well-designed software is that it allows the original innovator to tap into the creative potential of all the firm's customers and suppliers. Since more than 50 percent of all innovation occurs at these interfaces, this creates a substantial leveraging of the company's own capabilities. By designing "hooks" to allow customers to modify the product for their own use, the software can help generate further options and valuable uses that the original innovator could not possibly anticipate.[16]

For example, AT&T could never have forecast the full range of uses to which its institutional and home customers would ultimately apply the flexible software capabilities designed into cellular or digital telephone systems. Similarly, none of the personal computer's innovators could possibly have foreseen the enormous variety of uses to which such computers were put. By introducing flexible software that allowed users to program for their own special needs, microcomputers entered and created a variety of unexpected marketplaces—and generated many unanticipated options for new hardware and software. The Xerox Palo Alto Research Center produced the first icon-graphics interface, but even Xerox's sophisticated management did not appreciate its potentials. Only after Apple and Microsoft put an actual product into customers' hands did the innovation's value become evident. Early buyers quickly used the software to create greater value for their customers, who then used the results to add value for still other customers. Even now, no one can calculate the total value produced, but it is clearly thousands of times the value captured by Microsoft or Apple.

Because of the low-cost experimentation that software permits and the dominating importance of the value-in-use it creates for customers, increasing the "efficiency" of the program steps in software-based innovation is nowhere near as important as the potential value creation the software can create through the functionality it generates for customers and the multipliers of additional benefits further customers obtain from it. Too much attention is often placed on decreasing the cost of design steps and shortening internal process times in the innovation cycle rather than focusing on the critical internal learning and value creation processes that software facilitates.[17] Both are essential for effective innovation in today's hypercompetitive world.[18]

IDENTIFYING OPPORTUNITIES INTERACTIVELY

When managers think about software for innovation purposes, they tend to concentrate on CAD/CAM, EDI, process-monitoring, or imaging software. However, external software (database, strategic-monitoring, market-modeling, or customer interaction software) may be equally important. Software can identify subtle supplier, user, or environmental trends as potential problems or market opportunities long before personal observation might. Common examples are the "variance analysis trading" programs used in investing, the EPOS systems of retailing and fast foods, the customer monitoring programs of credit card or airline companies, or the "early warning systems" contained in strategic intelligence, environmental monitoring, or weather models. Given adequate models of external environments, experimenters—by monitoring experimental stores, focus panels, or sales counters—can test the impact of different design combinations and permutations in various use or "niche market" situations to see which design has the greatest potential value in any single use and across the system. Such software helps define what flexibilities are feasible and optimum to satisfy desired niches and future growth patterns. And it can avoid overselling of new ideas by technical staffs or their undervaluing by old-line managers.

Further, software representations of an innovation can become a sales tool, allowing individuals or customers to visualize a product or concept more easily, experiment with different features, and customize the product for their special needs. Software for this purpose is advancing rapidly. By pressing buttons in a distributor's office or on their home telephone or personal computer, customers can preview what features they want, see physical relationships, and actively design their own products. Software-supported interactive design is becoming common—both before and after a product's initial introduction—in many fields, including architectural, automobile, plumbing, services, financial, medical devices, boot and shoe, computer accessory, and integrated circuit markets. Unfortunately, very few companies have effectively integrated their market intelligence and product design systems. This is among the most exciting challenges and opportunities for innovation in most firms. By directly connecting users through software to their design processes, companies can virtually eliminate time delays, error costs, and product introduction risks in innovation.

User-Based Innovation and Virtual Shopping

The Internet and the World Wide Web have become prototypes for this new mode of user-based innovation. All innovation on the Internet is in software. Innovators reduce their concepts to practice in software form and present them electronically to customers on the Internet or Web. Customers can either utilize the innovation in its "offered form" or modify it for their particular uses. They can also ask the selling company to make the necessary modifications and transmit the results directly to them—by the Internet or other means. Institutions or individuals seeking new solutions can use the Internet as a virtual shop for potential answers, pretest those answers on their own systems, and purchase if desired. Conversely, they can post their needs onto the network to attract potential solutions. A manufacturer can solicit design proposals for new components, product features, or systems anywhere in the world. Or a farmer in the Philippines can query a worldwide network of agricultural and livestock knowledge to find out how best to eliminate an obnoxious weed or "buffalo proof" a fence.

Further, sophisticated users can scan the Web and use advanced visually oriented programs like Visual Basic or Power Object to modify the Web's offerings for their own or further customers' use. With high-level languages, desktop computer users can simply create electronic products or programs that the computer priesthoods of the past would have found intransigent, if not impossible. They can immediately test their solutions in terms of their specific needs. In essence, the innovation process has been inverted. The customer has become the innovator, and all intervening steps in the innovation process have disappeared.

New methods for introducing product concepts, transacting, and paying over the system are constantly appearing. As these infrastructures come into place, they are changing the entire nature of innovation worldwide. Anyone with access to the Internet and Web can present innovations instantly to a worldwide marketplace, obtain interactive market responses, and readapt the innovation for specific user purposes. All innovators in the world thus become potential competitors. And all customers and suppliers become potential sources of leverage for internal innovation.

MANAGING SOFTWARE INNOVATION PROCESSES

How can executives best manage this software-based, interactive innovation in their companies? The answer lies not in hiring more programmers but in effectively managing innovation processes through software and by learning to develop and manage software itself more effectively. The rest of this chapter will outline how successful companies do this.

Three Critical Systems

Software systems have long been used to plan and monitor "hard" innovation processes. The program evaluation and review technique (PERT) and the critical path method (CPM) were among the early techniques touted to improve these processes. However, these are *not* the focus for innovation today. Rarely have PERT-CPM implementations exploited the capabilities that open software systems, self-learning programs, and other interactive software processes now present. To provide such interactive and learning capabilities—while supporting the depth of detailed expertise that each important subsystem demands—current software structures generally revolve around three relatively independent but interacting modules connected by a common language and set of interface rules:

1. The database and model access system—linked to external scientific or technical sources
2. The processing engine—focused on internal operating parameters
3. The environmental and user interface system—linked to market and environmental sources

The database system embodies both the current raw data and the state-of-the-art external models a manager needs to manipulate that data effectively. If properly set up, the system is constantly updated to include the latest available references, user practices, experiments, transactions, operating data, and models. Structuring the database for constant refreshment—and maintaining an open and precise classification system to access its information—are among the most difficult of all software system problems. Yet they are most important to continual innovation.

New experimental data and tested models provide constant clues as to needed or possible changes in the rate processes or interaction weightings that can improve a technical system's performance. New conceptual models from research worldwide may redefine both new data needs and the relevancy of old solutions. Clearly, those who continue to use old paradigms after they are subverted get wrong answers, as do those who use last year's information or solutions for today's problems. Since even the most precise models and operating systems are only as useful as their databases, many successful firms—like American Express, Intel, Reader's Digest, or American Airlines—treat their databases as their most valuable assets. Unfortunately, they often do not link them effectively to other critical modules for innovation purposes.

Software engines, containing the primary processing, manipulation, and operating systems logic, tend to receive more attention. This area has traditionally been the glamorous portion of software development, where new or unique algorithms can create fame for their programmers. This is where proprietary intellectual property seems to be created, rather than in improving the flexibility and quality of the data inputs or the manipulability of outputs. Engine design is extremely important to innovation in terms of allowing flexible experiments, increasing operating efficiencies, and ensuring output quality. Nevertheless, many of the highest innovation payoffs have come from expanded database availability and easier-to-use software interfaces—such as those first provided by the Mac operating system or Windows and later by Mosaic, Java, or HTML— rather than through increased sophistication in manipulating the data. For efficiency, however, each of these innovations also required a new engine—just as next-generation speeds and power demands will probably require new engine architectures, like massively parallel processors.

Interfaces are crucial in making the three systems work together and in enabling various users' access to important databases for their special purposes. Compatible—preferably seamless—interfaces are critical to leveraging innovation internally and with external customers and suppliers. Software like HTTP/HTML and SQL has been a major step in this regard. Navigator, Yahoo, and other search and agent software systems have made the Internet and Web much more accessible. But their originators say that intranets within companies will ultimately be their largest users. The best interfaces are as unobtrusive as possible. They are usually a result of interactive development with users throughout all phases of both the design and implementation processes.[19] Well-designed interfaces also incorporate future "hooks" that allow external customers and internal users to create or explore many unanticipated innovative possibilities over time. Conversely, converting internal systems into tools that can readily access details about changing customer interactions and rapidly advancing scientific-technical environments makes them into invaluable cornerstones for fast, flexible innovation.

The highest potentials for value-added innovation lie in direct and integrated connection among user interfaces, self-learning operations engines, and thoroughly compatible external and internal databases. But few companies have successfully achieved this continuity. More have done so in services than in manufacturing. What can be learned from the experiences of those who have been successful?

Interacting Subsystems, Not Megasystems

First, end-to-end integration through a single "megasystem" is extremely difficult to accomplish.[20] Those who have been most successful have concentrated individually on the three critical subsystems—databases, engines, and user interfaces—and used carefully predefined interface standards to link them effectively. This leaves each subsystem free to contribute as quickly as possible, allows incremental implementation and interactive learning, and avoids the long and costly development times for which megasystems are so notorious.

Second, the most successful companies concentrate on developing system software that, like the World Wide Web, insulates users from having to understand the complex rules and sophisticated methodologies of its internal operations. Through user-friendly prompts and menus, these intranets enable connecting parties to query and customize the system's central knowledge for their own purposes. Thus they encourage maximum innovation around each user's specialized needs. Rather than hoarding or controlling all information, effective architectures help decentralized users and customers capture much of each innovation's value for themselves. Properly programmed, the systems can learn from their decentralized users' experiences and make this learning available instantly to others on the network. Financial-services systems provide a classic example that is being widely emulated in other service systems, like fast foods, retailing, or airlines.

A brokerage or insurance company's central engine manipulates all transactions data from the marketplace, embodies the most updated financial methodologies and tax, accounting, or regulatory rules for doing business, and provides the access and data that decentralized agents or brokers need for adapting the firm's services to specific customers. At headquarters cadres of mathematically sophisticated analysts both constantly upgrade the system's capabilities and design new products for all the parties it serves. Centralized software commands much of the firm's own internal investment portfolio, based on preprogrammed rules and changing regulations, tax structures, and economic or market trends.

As the center creates new products in response to these changes, they are instantly diffused to broker or agent offices for adaptation to individual customer needs. Other software monitors individual customers' transactions and past investment patterns. It helps brokers detect significant changes and signals local brokers when to adjust their clients' portfolios. It warns customers if unusual patterns indicate possible fraud or misuse of their assets and provides up-to-date account data on demand. For effectiveness the central system's interfaces must match those of both upstream information providers (like government or market data sources) and downstream users (providing the simplest and most transparent interconnections possible).

Similarly, the system architectures of leading product companies (like Ford, Hewlett-Packard, Nike, Sun, or Boeing) allow researchers, designers, manufacturing engineers, or marketers to call in virtually unlimited modules of capability from databases, on-line operations, or contracted sources anywhere in the world. These companies' capacity to find solutions, mix-and-match options, and test outcomes is paced primarily by their internal system's modeling software and capability to interface upstream and downstream knowledge bases. Their systems allow them to tap into worldwide sources of innovation and to connect these in new ways to their customers. Their suppliers can inform them precisely about new options, process capabilities, or problem solutions through software. In conjunction with on-line customer systems, advanced companies and their suppliers can design and pretest a wide variety of innovations in electronics. These include soft-goods designs (interactively on electronic pallets with buyer-customers), aircraft performance or customer comfort designs (through mathematical or graphics simulations), architectural designs (in three-dimensional software models that customers can "walk through"), alternate designs for shoreline control strategies (through large interactive models with the actual stakeholders participating), or advanced molecular designs (in simulated life systems or flow process environments).

INTEGRATING INNOVATION SUBSYSTEMS

Many companies have partially integrated their software systems, from their marketplaces through production processes. Such systems now allow electric power systems to respond instantaneously to changing demand loads. Oil companies routinely plan their drilling, shipping, pipeline, and refining activities through such models. An entire shipping fleet (like Exxon's) can be redirected within a few minutes in response to changing market price, supply, refining, shipping, tax, or tariff situations. Within a few days' time, companies like Ford can reassign an entire automobile line's sourcing based on changes in exchange rates or other critical market characteristics.

However, few companies have interlinked their marketing and operations systems with their scientific databases and design processes. Such integration can substantially enhance the responsiveness, degree of advance, and customer impact of innovations.

It can also significantly lower innovation risks, investments, and cycle times.

For example, Fluent, Inc., a division of Aavid Thermal Technologies, develops computational fluid dynamics software to analyze fluid-flow phenomena in industrial processes. Based on equations describing the physical effects of fluid flows under various circumstances, Fluent's software models can handle the entire innovation process from geometry definition to computation, design evaluation, and process control. The model for each specific application is constantly updated to reflect both new research and experimental findings, as well as real-world effects in actual customer-use situations. Fluent's software "learns" from these inputs and captures the latest findings in its analyses and design recommendations.

For example, design and selection of proper mixing equipment is critical in the scale-up of chemical processes. Fluent gathers information on the performance of various mixing devices from tests performed by mixing equipment manufacturers, such as Lightnin and Chemineer, and models the performance characteristics of these devices in its software. Process engineers at companies like Dow and Du Pont then use these computer models to simulate the performance of the mixing devices for the specific fluids, flow conditions, and constraints of their processes. They can test a variety of mixing configurations in software—allowing process engineers to select the "best" design reliably and inexpensively, bypassing a number of costly scale-up tests. Extensions of Fluent's capabilities can enable an automobile company to pretest the aerodynamic characteristics of various car designs in software, aircraft companies to pretest wing or fuselage designs, or chemical producers to pretest various multiphase flow designs for processes without building costly prototypes and facilities.

Virtual Skunk Works

Such software systems not only decrease the time and manpower cost of development, they also create a virtual skunk works that substantially lowers the investments needed for lab tests, pilot plants, and scale-up and increases the knowledge output of the innovation process. Under old mechanical or chemical engineering design paradigms—because interaction parameters were poorly understood and very complex—a company would proceed through a complicated series of ever larger physical-test, pilot, scale-up, and plant shakedown trials that were very costly in terms of both time and dollars. Even though such empiricism might eventually be successful in practice, the company never knew why key interactions worked. By combining process science, physical constraints, and user environments in a single electronic model, experimenters can obtain a level of process insights they never had before. Most important, they can visualize and understand why things do (or do not) work. The model provides a reliable discipline for recalibrating people's intuitions. And its visual and printed outputs help educate users to adopt the innovation faster and with better results.

Going beyond such internal virtual skunk works, designers can also use software representations about the best available *external* suppliers' capabilities to determine an optimum means of manufacture. By constantly surveying external best practices, they can determine the implicit costs of producing internally versus outsourcing. Their models can extend into virtual storerooms that optimize specification, sourcing, and logistics for future parts as models and features change.

By tapping into the best worldwide scientific and consumer knowledge bases, these systems substantially leverage the company's other investments in its development teams' skills and specialized facilities. The simulations and their updated databases become major contributors to the company's learning capabilities. They continually capture, codify, and make available all accessible internal and external knowledge about a problem. The software's capabilities are important assets in attracting key technical people and enabling them to attack challenges at the frontiers of their fields. Properly designed software systems allow smaller, more flexible teams to perform at greater levels of sophistication than larger teams can without them. Innovation costs decrease, and output values increase exponentially.

However, managers should be aware that software can also impose its own limitations on innovation. Unless they are cautious, the structure of the software will limit the databases investigated, options considered, manipulations available, and user data evaluated. They must keep all three (database, engine, and market) critical systems as updated, open, and flexible as possible. Any modularity (except in the ultimate modularity of a single datum) will introduce some constraints. The capacity of an enterprise to move from one technology's S curve (or technical performance limits) to another's may well depend on whether it has developed adequate transitional software to consider the next S curve's characteristics and needs in its analyses. This often depends on the software's capacity to handle sufficiently refined details about customers, internal systems, and external technical data.

The Smallest Replicable Units

To avoid such limitations—and to maintain needed flexibilities—successful innovation and software managers find it useful to break units of activity and information down to the "minimum replicable level" of detail for the tasks or data to be analyzed. In earlier years the smallest replicable measuring unit for organizations and data might have been an individual part, subassembly, office, supplier, or customer class. As volumes increased and computer capabilities became greater, it often became feasible for the corporation to manage and measure critical performance variables at much more detailed, feature, activity, customer characteristic, or technical levels.

In some service industries—like banking, publishing, communications, structural design, entertainment, or medical research—it soon became possible to disaggregate the critical units of service activity into digitized sequences, electronic packets, data blocks, or bytes of information that could be endlessly combined or manipulated for new effects or to satisfy individual customer and operating needs. In manufacturing, the capacity to measure and control to ever more refined levels led to mass customization.[21] In all industries, seeking out such microunits enables the highest possible degree of segmentation, strategic fine-tuning, value-added definition, and cost control to help connect and target new innovations in the marketplace. Interestingly, the larger the organization is, the more refined these replicability units can be, and the greater their leverage for creating added value.

Important to the success of American Airlines' Sabre system, Motorola's pagers, AT&T's cellular telephones, the Human Genome Project, and the Internet have been (1) their early definition of data breakdowns into the smallest repeatable units and (2) the creation of database rules and interfaces that allowed endless variations of user combinations, types of experimentation, and production options. As object-oriented software becomes more widely available, the capture and use of such detailed information is becoming easier—as are the corresponding opportunities for innovating in software. Object orientation promises to accelerate and facilitate the kinds of end-to-end compatibility that the Internet now provides in the public-access realm.

User Becomes Innovator

The Internet's TCP/IP communications standards have made it possible for tens of millions of computers and their users to "talk" together and to innovate together. Using similar software, the number of people connected through intranets within companies is now growing even more rapidly than the Internet. Web-compatible software languages (Mosaic, Java, and HTML) that run well on many different personal computer architectures now provide a huge virtual disk drive of sources and uses for innovation. A *BusinessWeek* article forecast, "These will cause a basic shift in the software business no less seismic than the fall of the Berlin Wall. . . .

[They] will enable the deconstruction and the construction of a new economic model for the software industry."[22] They provide a potent new model for interactive worldwide innovation, based on the combinative powers of the Internet's millions of access points.

Using minimum replicable unit concepts, various network softwares (like Navigator, Java, and Yahoo) have become the mediating structures through which *users* can innovate their own solutions from a wide variety of alternatives. More powerful yet may be the instant diffusion that they allow for known technologies once posted on the Internet or the Web. Java creates a sixty-four-kilobyte software virtual computer, which can be placed inside most interconnecting devices, including telephones, and can make almost any personal computer into a multimedia machine. This should expand both innovation and diffusion possibilities for various new concepts, especially if Microsoft includes Java in its Windows offerings. If such capabilities become widely used, they will achieve the ultimate in decreasing innovation cycles, costs, risks, and diffusion times. The customer will become the innovator. Under these circumstances adoption and adaptation times and risks for producers drop to zero. The software "applets" of a Java-like system will become the minimum replicable elements of effective distributed computing, while the network becomes both the computer itself and an instantaneous distribution system.

New business methodologies—like paying single-use fees for applet software or individual databases—seem likely to further revolutionize many businesses in such industries as software, distribution, publication, education, banking, communications, entertainment, and professional services. The lines between application, content, and support services may quickly disappear in many markets. The sheer variety of object-oriented, network-capable systems (like Visual Basic, OLE, Collabra, Taligent, and Java) seems likely to accelerate interactive innovation opportunities in most fields.

For example, in manufacturing, clothing designers no longer need to design their line in advance on a make-or-break basis.

Instead, they can offer a series of suggested samples that salespeople show to potential buyers physically and electronically. Then, by working on an electronic palette, the salesperson and the buyer jointly sketch precisely what modifications the buyer wants. The palette can be connected directly to the design unit at the clothing manufacturer's plant where professionals interact electronically with the retail buyer to detail and price the buyer's exact desires. Virtually any product—from insurance policies and travel tours to pagers, bathroom fixtures, houses, automobiles, or yachts—can be interactively custom-designed to meet the specific and varying needs of niche markets or individuals throughout the world.

MANAGING SOFTWARE-BASED INNOVATION

To take proper advantage of such revolutionary opportunities, many companies will have to dramatically improve their own internal software management capabilities. The alternative may be oblivion. The ultimate goal is to develop and integrate the company's three major subsystems—databases, engines, and market-environmental interfaces—to a high standard. On their way to achieving this, however, the company can garner very large payoffs by breaking its software processes down into four different groupings and managing each with tested techniques appropriate to that problem category.

Although software development is notoriously difficult to manage, the most innovative companies—whether in products or services—seem to converge on several approaches, each useful for a different strategic purpose.[23] What characteristics do these approaches share? One commonality is that all simultaneously enable independent and interdependent innovation. And all involve interactive customer participation. New software, like most innovations, is first created in the mind of a highly skilled, motivated, and individualistic person, hence independent. But to be useful the software (or device it supports) usually must connect to other software (or hardware) systems and meet specific user needs, hence interdependent. Interesting innovation problems are generally so complex that they require high expertise from many "nonprogrammer" technical people and users for solution.[24] How do successful companies achieve the needed balance between deep professional knowledge, creative individualism, coordinated integration, and customer participation?

Individual Inventor-Innovators

As in the physical sciences, knowledgeable independent inventors and small groups create the largest number of software innovations, particularly at the applications level. In essence, a few highly motivated individuals perceive an opportunity or need, assemble software resources from existing databases and systems, choose an interlinking language and architecture on which to work, and interactively design the program and subsystem steps to satisfy the need as they perceive it. Those who want to sell the software externally first find some real-life application or customer, consciously debug the software for that purpose, and then modify and upgrade it until it works in many users' hands for various purposes.

Many important software innovations, from VisiCalc to Mosaic, started this way. Virtually all video game programs come into being in this fashion, as do new customized programs to solve local enterprises' problems. Millions of inventor-innovators use largely trial-and-error methods to design new software for themselves, improve old systems, or create totally new effects. Like other small-company innovators, there is no evidence that the process is either efficient or consistent in form. Vision, expertise, and persistence are the most usual determinants of success.[25] The sheer number of people trying to solve specific problems means that a large number of innovations prove useful in the marketplace, although a much greater number undoubtedly die along the way.

Larger companies have learned to harness individual software inventors' capabilities in interesting ways. For example, as a corporate strategy, MCI has long encouraged individual inventor-entrepreneurs to come up with new software applications (fitting its system's interfaces) to provide new services over its main communication lines. AT&T Bell Labs created Unix to assist computer science research. AT&T later gave Unix to universities and, eventually, to others, slowly realizing that as individuals created programs to provide local solutions or to interface with others, they would require more communications interconnections. Unix was consciously designed to encourage individuals to interact broadly and to share their useful solutions with others. The "hooks" it provided later allowed AT&T to sell many more services than it could have possibly forecast or innovated internally.

Small Interactive Teams

In many of the larger "applications houses"—like Microsoft, Oracle, and Netscape—small, informal, interactive teams are the core of the innovative process. The complexity of these firms' programs is too great for a single individual to develop them alone. In most cases, the target concept is new, discrete, and relatively limited in scope. Relying heavily on individual talents and personal interactions, these firms typically make little use of computer-aided software engineering (CASE) tools or formalized "monitor programs" to manage development. They operate in a classic skunk works style, disciplined by the very software they are developing.

For example, Microsoft tries to develop its applications programs utilizing very small teams. Major programs typically begin when Bill Gates or a few of his designers agree to the performance parameters and the broad systems structures needed to ensure interfaces with other Microsoft programs or customer positioning. Overall program goals are broken down into a series of targets for smaller subsystems, each capable of being produced by a two- to five-person team that operates quite independently. Interfaces are controlled at several levels: "programmatic specifications" to make operating systems perform compatibly, "application interfaces" to interconnect component systems (like memory or file management), and "customer interfaces" to maintain user compatibility. Other than these, the original target functionalities, and time constraints, there are few rigidities. Detailed targets get changed constantly as teams find out what they can and can't accomplish for one purpose and how that affects other subsystems.

Microsoft's key coordinating mechanism is "build-test-drive." At least every week—but more often two to three times per week—each group compiles its subsystem so the entire program can be run with all new code, functions, and features in place. In the "builds," test suites created by independent "test designers" and the software itself become the disciplining agents. If teams do not correct errors at this point, interactions between components quickly become so vast that it is impossible to fit all program pieces together, even though each subsystem might work well alone. As soon as possible, the program team proposes a version for a specific (though limited) purpose, gives it to a customer to test, and monitors its use in detail. Once it works for that purpose, the program goes to other customers for beta tests in other uses. This approach both decreases developmental risks and takes advantage of customers' suggestions and innovations.[26]

Monitor Programs

Such "informal" approaches serve particularly well for smaller free-standing or applications programs, although Microsoft has used them for larger operating systems. In most cases, designers of larger "operations" or "systems" software find some form of "monitor program" useful. These monitors establish the frameworks, checkpoints, and coordinating mechanisms to make sure all critical program elements are present, compatible, cross-checked, and properly sequenced. They allow larger enterprises to decentralize the actual writing of code among different divisions or locations while ensuring that all functions and components work properly together. No element is forgotten or left to chance, and interface standards are clearly enforced. Weapon systems, AT&T "long lines," and Arthur Andersen have used this programming method successfully. Many firms have found that such formal monitors both lower the cost and increase the reliability of large-scale systems designs.

For example, Andersen Consulting (now Accenture) usually must provide under contract both a unique solution for each customer's problem and a thoroughly tested, fault-free systems product. For years Andersen has combined a highly decentralized process for writing each section of the code with a rigorous centralized system for program coordination and control. Two tools, called "METHOD/1" and "DESIGN/1," have been at the center of its process. METHOD/1 is a carefully designed, step-by-step methodology for modularizing and controlling all the steps needed to design any major systems program. At the highest level are roughly ten "phases," each broken into approximately five "segments." Below this are a similar number of "tasks" for each job and several "steps" for each task. METHOD/1 defines the exact elements the programmer needs to go through at that particular stage of the process and coordinates software design activities, estimated times, and costs for each step.

DESIGN/1 is a very elaborate CASE tool. DESIGN/1 keeps track of all programming details as they develop and disciplines the programmer to define each element carefully. It governs relationships among all steps in the METHOD/1 flowchart to avoid losing data, entering infinite loops, using illegal data, and so on. In addition to ensuring that each step in METHOD/1 is carefully executed, it allows customers to enter "pseudo-data" or code so they can periodically test the "look and feel" of screen displays and to check data entry formats for reasonableness and utility during development. The integrated METHOD/1 and DESIGN/1 environment is extremely complex, taking up some fifty megabytes on high-density diskettes. A dedicated team of specialists continually maintains and enhances these programs.[27]

Design to Requirements

The most common approach to developing operations software is neither as informal as Microsoft's nor as formal as Andersen's. The process tends to follow a general sequence:

1. Establish goals and requirements (what functionalities, benefits, and performance standards are sought).
2. Define the scope, boundaries, and exclusions from the system (the limits of the system).
3. Establish priorities among key elements and performance requirements (what is needed, highly desired, wanted, acceptable in background, and dispensable if necessary).
4. Define interrelationships (what data sets, field sizes, flow volumes, and cross-relationships are essential or desirable).
5. Establish what constraints must be met (in terms of platforms, network typologies, costs, timing, and so on) in designing the system.
6. Break the total problem down into smaller, relatively independent subsystems.
7. For each subsystem, set and monitor specific performance targets, interface standards, and timing-cost limits, using agreed-on software test regimes and monitoring programs. Often the design software itself provides the ultimate documentation and discipline for all groups.

Because quite dissimilar skills may be needed for each step, different ad hoc teams typically work on the database system, the engine (or platform) system, and external interface systems. A separate interfunctional group (perhaps under a program manager) usually coordinates activities across divisions or subsystems. Using a combination of software and personalized performance scheduling and evaluation techniques, this group, along with independent test designers, ensures maintenance of task functionalities, component and subsystem performance, time frames, dependencies among tasks, output, quality, and priorities. If the software under design has to support existing processes, successful cross-functional teams typically reengineer the processes first, then design the software prototypes while interactively engaging users throughout the full design and implementation process. Higher-level managers need to see that all these processes are in place and operate effectively.

MULTIPLE INTERACTIVE SYSTEMS

Each design approach has been very useful for its specific innovative purposes. However, self-learning, multiple interactive (database, engine, and customer interface) systems are rapidly changing the entire nature of the discovery-innovation-diffusion process.

In many cases, software now learns from its own experiences and reprograms itself to find new optima. Using built-in decision criteria, the software constantly updates itself based on inputs from exogenous environments. Its learning systems may teach it to take actions directly—as learning-based chess, automated paper production, or stock-trading programs do. Or they may constantly monitor environments and signal humans or other systems to take needed actions when parameters approach learned limits—as in aircraft and nuclear plant emergency programs or in banking credit card fraud prevention systems.

In operational applications self-learning software has proved useful in many flow process, micromanufacturing (semiconductor), health-monitoring, and logistics system designs. It is used daily in retail, financial, communications, chemical-processing, and utility service monitoring systems and provides some of the most important problem and opportunity identification capabilities driving innovation in these fields. In both manufacturing and services the key to responsive customer-based innovation is to break both operations and markets down into such compatible detail that managers can discern, by properly cross-matrixing their data, how a slight change in one arena can affect some critical aspect of performance in another. The ability to micromanage, target, and customize operations using the knowledge bases that size permits is fast becoming the critical scale economy and opportunity for value creation.

For example, General Mills Restaurants' (GMR's) sophisticated use of technology has helped it innovate a friendlier, more responsive atmosphere and lower competitive prices in its unique dinner house chains—Red Lobster, Olive Garden, and Bennigan's. At the strategic level, it taps into the most extensive disaggregated databases in the industry and uses conceptual mapping technologies to define precise unserved needs in the restaurant market. Using these inputs, a creative internal and external team of restaurateurs, chefs, and culinary institutes arrives at a few concept test designs. Using other models derived from its databases, GMR can pretest and project the nationwide impact of selected concepts and even define the specific neighborhoods most likely to support that concept. Other technologies combine to designate optimal restaurant siting and create the architectural designs most likely to be successful.

On an operations level, by mixing and matching in great detail the continuously collected performance data from its own operations and laboratory analyses, GMR can specify or select the best individual pieces and combinations of kitchen equipment for each location. It can optimize each facility's layout to minimize personnel, walking distances, cleanup times, breakdowns, operations, and overhead costs. Once a restaurant is functioning, GMR has an integrated EPOS and operations management system directly connected to headquarters computers for monitoring and analyzing daily operations and customer trends. An inventory, sales-tracking, personnel, and logistics forecasting program automatically adjusts plans, measures performance, and controls staffing levels and products for holidays, times, seasonality, weather, special offers, and promotions. All of these lower innovation investments, cycle times, and risks.

At the logistics level, using one of the industry's most sophisticated satellite, earth-sensing, and database systems, GMR can forecast and track fisheries (and other food sources) worldwide. It can predict long- and short-term seafood yields, species availability, and prices, and can plan its menus, promotions, and purchases accordingly. It knows its processing needs in such detail that it teaches suppliers exactly how to size, cut, and pack fish for maximum market value and minimum handling costs to GMR, while achieving minimum waste and shipping costs for the supplier. Its software systems have allowed GMR to innovate in ways that others could not.

CONCLUSION

Software is and will be at the core of most innovation during the next several decades. The World Wide Web has already stirred up imaginative possibilities for a plethora of new markets, products, services, arts, and information potentials—all software based. These will grow exponentially as more and more minds interconnect to utilize them. But startling as these prospects are, they provide only glimpses of the many opportunities that software innovation presents. When combined with software's capacity to learn on its own, create new solutions, deal with inordinate complexities, shorten cycle times, lower costs, diminish risks, and uniquely enhance customer value, effective software management has now become the key to effective innovation for any company or institution. Innovators who recognize this fact will have a genuine competitive advantage. Managers who ignore this caveat do so at their companies' peril.

NOTES

1. Software is a set of instructions designed to modify the behavior of another entity or system. Although one can code molecules to modify pharmaceutical or chemical systems in a predictable fashion, it is primarily information technology software that is changing innovation processes. We will direct our discussion to the latter.

2. For the best single source of the traditional analytics for doing this, see P. Smith and R. Reinertsen, *Developing Products in Half the Time* (New York: Van Nostrand Reinhold, 1992).

3. D. Weingarter, "Quarks by Computer," *Scientific American*, February 1996, *274*, 116–120.

4. For classic studies of the process, see J. Jewkes, D. Sawers, and R. Stillerman, *The Sources of Invention* (New York: St. Martin's Press, 1958); Battelle Memorial Laboratories, "Science, Technology, and Innovation," report to the National Science Foundation (Columbus, Ohio: Battelle Memorial Laboratories, 1973); and J. Diebold, *The Innovators: The Discoveries, Inventions, and Breakthroughs of Our Times* (New York: Dutton, 1990).

5. For many thoroughly explained examples, see T. Steiner and D. Teixeria, *Technology in Banking* (Burr Ridge, Illinois: Irwin, 1990); and National Research Council, *Information Technology in the Service Society: A Twenty-First Century Lever* (Washington, D.C.: National Academy Press, 1994).

6. For examples and details, see "IBM Attacks Backlog," *Computerworld,* October 11, 1993, pp. 1, 7; J. McHugh, "Trilogy Development Group," *Forbes,* June 3, 1996, pp. 122–128; "Boeing Overhaul Taking Flight," *Information Week,* September 26, 1994, p. 18; and P. Anderson, "Conquest," Tuck School of Business case (Hanover, New Hampshire: Tuck School of Business, Dartmouth College, 1996).

7. J. B. Quinn and F. G. Hilmer, "Strategic Outsourcing," *Sloan Management Review,* Summer 1994, *35*, 43–55.

8. Details on numerous examples appear in J. B. Quinn, *Intelligent Enterprise: A Knowledge and Service Based Paradigm for Industry* (New York: Free Press, 1992).

9. Many innovative new organization forms depend heavily on software

for their implementation. See J. B. Quinn, P. Anderson, and S. Finkelstein, "Managing Professional Intellect: Getting the Most out of the Best," *Harvard Business Review,* March-April 1996, 74, 71–80.

10. J. Moore, "The Death of Competition," *Fortune,* April 15, 1996, pp. 142–144.

11. P. A. Roussel, K. N. Saad, and T. J. Erickson, *Third Generation R&D: Managing the Link to Corporate Strategy* (Boston: Harvard Business School Press, 1991).

12. K. Sabbagh, *The Twenty-First Century Jet* (New York: Scribner, 1996).

13. J. Main, "Betting on the Twenty-First Century Jet," *Fortune,* April 20, 1992, pp. 102–104, 108, 112, 116–117.

14. For a description of the electronic processes and interactions with other fields that molecular designs in biotechnology require, see B. Werth, *The Billion-Dollar Molecule* (New York: Touchstone Books, 1995).

15. "Looking for the Evidence in Medicine," *Science,* April 5, 1996, pp. 22–24.

16. E. von Hippel, *Sources of Innovation* (New York: Oxford University Press, 1988).

17. P. Senge, *The Fifth Discipline: The Art and Practice of the Learning Organization* (New York: Doubleday, 1994).

18. R. D'Aveni, *Hypercompetition* (New York: Free Press, 1994).

19. J. B. Quinn and M. Baily, "Information Technology: Increasing Productivity in Services," *Academy of Management Executive,* August 1994, 8, 28–51.

20. The National Research Council found attempts to build such megasystems among the most costly errors that large users had made in installing information technology. See National Research Council, *Information Technology.*

21. J. Pine, *Mass Customization: The New Frontier in Business* (Boston: Harvard Business School Press, 1993).

22. For an excellent overview of the generally available network software in early 1996, see "The Software Revolution," *BusinessWeek,* December 4, 1995, p. 78.

23. F. Brooks, *The Mythical Man-Month* (Reading, Massachusetts: Addison-Wesley, 1975).

24. R. Moss Kanter, *The Change Masters* (New York: Simon & Schuster, 1983); and J. Utterback, *Mastering the Dynamics of Innovation* (Boston: Harvard Business School Press, 1994).

25. J. Kotter and J. Heskett, *Corporate Culture and Performance* (New York: Free Press, 1992).

26. For a more detailed view of this process, see "Microsoft (B)," in H. Mintzberg and J. B. Quinn, *The Strategy Process: Concepts, Contexts, Cases,* 3rd ed. (Upper Saddle River, New Jersey: Prentice Hall, 1996).

27. For further details on this process, see "Andersen Consulting (Europe)," in Mintzberg and Quinn, *Strategy Process.*

CHAPTER ELEVEN

Innovation by User Communities: Learning from Open-Source Software

ERIC A. VON HIPPEL

I magine product development without manufacturers. Today's user innovation communities are making that idea increasingly real. Open-source software projects, among others, have led to innovation, development, and consumption communities run completely by and for users. Such communities have a great advantage over the manufacturer-centered development systems that have been the mainstay of commerce for hundreds of years. Each using entity, whether an individual or a corporation, is able to create exactly what it wants without requiring a manufacturer to act as its agent. Individual users in a user innovation community do not have to develop everything they need on their own but can benefit from others' freely shared innovations.

First published in the Summer 2001 issue of *MIT Sloan Management Review.*

EXAMPLES OF
USER INNOVATION COMMUNITIES

User innovation communities existed long before the advent of open-source software and extend far beyond it. They are not limited to information products such as software code. Some develop physical products. Consider and compare two examples of early-stage user innovation communities—one in software, the other in sports.

Apache Open-Source Software

Apache open-source software is used on Web server computers that host Web pages and provide appropriate content as requested by Internet browsers. Such computers are the backbone of the World Wide Web.

The server software that evolved into Apache was developed by Rob McCool (at that time a University of Illinois student) for, and while working at, the National Center for Supercomputing Applications (NCSA). The source code as developed and periodically modified by McCool was posted on the Web so that users at other sites could download, use, and further modify and develop it.

When McCool departed NCSA in mid-1994, a small group of Web masters who had adopted his server software for their own sites decided to continue developing it. Eight users gathered all the documentation and bug fixes and issued a consolidated patch. This "patchy" server software evolved over time into Apache. Extensive user feedback and modification yielded Apache 1.0, released on December 1, 1995.

After four years and many modifications and improvements contributed by many users, Apache became the most popular Web server software on the Internet, garnering many industry awards for excellence. Despite strong competition from commercial software developers such as Microsoft and Netscape, it is currently used by approximately 60 percent of the millions of Web sites worldwide.

High-Performance Windsurfing

High-performance windsurfing, the evolution of which was documented by MIT doctoral candidate Sonali Shah in a March 2000 MIT Sloan working paper (http://opensource.mit.edu), requires gear suitable for midair jumps and turns. Previously, windsurfers used their boards essentially as small, agile sailboats, and the boards' specifications reflected that.

The fundamentals of high-performance windsurfing were developed in 1978 in Hawaii by users. Larry Stanley, a pioneer in the sport, explained to Shah how a major innovation in technique and equipment came about:

> In 1978, Jurgen Honscheid came over from West Germany for the first Hawaiian World Cup and discovered jumping, which was new to him, although Mike Horgan and I were jumping in 1974 and 1975. There was a new enthusiasm for jumping, and we were all trying to outdo each other by jumping higher and higher. The problem was that . . . the riders flew off in midair because there was no way to keep the board with you—and as a result, you hurt your feet, your legs and the board.
>
> Then I remembered the "Chip," a small, experimental board we had built with foot straps, and thought, "It's dumb not to use this for jumping." That's when I first started jumping with foot straps and discovering controlled flight. I could go so much faster than I ever thought and when you hit a wave it was like a motorcycle rider hitting a ramp; you just flew into the air. All of a sudden not only could you fly into the air, but you could land the thing and not only that, but you could change direction in the air!
>
> The whole sport of high-performance windsurfing really started from that. As soon as I did it, there were about 10 of us who sailed all the time together, and within one or two days there were various boards out there that had foot straps of various kinds on them and we were all going fast and jumping waves.

By 1998 more than a million people were engaged in windsurfing, and a large fraction of the boards sold incorporated the user-developed innovations for the high-performance sport.

Both of the user innovation communities just described have evolved and become more complex. Although they look different on the surface, they are similar in fundamental ways. Both grew to include many thousands of volunteer participants. Participants in open-source software projects interact primarily via the Internet, using various specialized Web sites set up by other volunteer users (see box, Free and Open-Source Software). Participants in innovating sports communities tend to interact by traveling to favorite sites and contests for their sport. Most users of open-source software simply use the source code, relying on interested volunteers to write new code, debug existing code, answer requests for help posted on Internet help sites, and help coordinate the project. Similarly, as Shah and Nikolaus Franke show in an April 2001 MIT Sloan working paper, most participants in an evolving sport simply play the game, relying on those so inclined to develop new techniques and equipment, try out and improve on innovations, voluntarily provide coaching, and help coordinate group activities such as meets.

Often commercial enterprises attach to or complement user innovation communities. Red Hat and VA Linux Systems are well-known examples of commercial involvement in the open-source software context; professional sports leagues and commercial producers of sports equipment are examples in the case of sports communities.

USER INNOVATION COMMUNITIES SHOULDN'T EXIST, BUT THEY DO

Manufacturers, not users, traditionally have been considered the most logical developers of innovative products for two reasons. First, the financial incentives to innovate have seemed higher for manufacturers than for users. After all, a manufacturer has the opportunity to sell to all users what it develops. Individual user-innovators, on the other hand, typically can expect to benefit finan-

▼

Free and Open-Source Software

When people say that software is "free" or "open source," they mean that a user may obtain a copy at no cost and then legally study its source code, modify it, and distribute it to others—also for free. A software author uses his or her own copyright to guarantee those rights to all users by affixing to the code a standard licensing notice, such as the General Public License, commonly referred to as "copyleft" (a play on the word *copyright*). Well-known examples of open-source software are the GNU/Linux computer operating system, Perl programming language, and Internet e-mail engine Sendmail.

The practice of granting extensive rights to users through licensing dates back to the free-software movement that Richard Stallman launched in the early 1980s. Stallman founded the Free Software Foundation to counter the trend toward proprietary development of software packages and release of software without source code. Then, in 1998, several prominent computer hackers, including Bruce Perens and Eric Raymond, launched the Open Source Initiative. The founders had some political differences with the free-software movement but agreed in general with its licensing practices. They also advanced new ideas about how to spread the practices more broadly.

Many thousands of free and open-source software projects exist today, and the number is growing. SourceForge, a repository of open-source projects (http://sourceforge.net), lists more than ten thousand projects and more than one hundred thousand registered users. It is becoming easier to undertake new projects as effective project design becomes better understood and as prepackaged infrastructural support for projects, such as SourceForge provides, becomes available on the Web.

cially only from their own use of their innovations. In order to benefit from diffusion of an innovation to the other users in a marketplace, innovating users would have to obtain intellectual property protection and set up licensing arrangements—costly endeavors with uncertain outcomes.

Second, manufacturers, through their production, distribution, and field support capability, appear to have an edge in getting widespread diffusion of an innovation. Such tasks involve large economies of scale for physical products. How could users accomplish them as cost-effectively as manufacturers? One might imagine users uniting in a fit of passion—such as the indignation many computer hackers feel toward Microsoft. But as a stable part of an ordinary economic landscape? Never!

Yet, impossible or not, user communities clearly do innovate. Moreover, when products they develop compete head to head against products developed by manufacturers—Apache against Microsoft's and Netscape's server software, for example—the former seem capable of beating the latter handily in the marketplace. Not only do the communities exist; they even triumph. As Galileo is said to have murmured after officially recanting his statement that the earth moves around the sun, "And yet it moves!" What is going on?

Conditions That Favor User Innovation Communities

User communities engaged in innovation, development, and consumption are most likely to flourish when three conditions are met: at least some users have sufficient incentive to innovate; at least some users have an incentive to voluntarily reveal their innovations and the means to do so; and user-led diffusion of innovations can compete with commercial production and distribution. When only the first two conditions hold, a pattern of user innovation and trial will occur, followed by commercial manufacture and distribution of any innovations proven to be of general interest.

Incentives for Users to Innovate. Users have sufficient incentive to innovate when they expect the benefits of innovating to exceed their costs. Clearly, users engaged in the development of open-source software and novel sports equipment consider that condition to be met. The costs incurred by innovating users, many of whom report enjoying as well as benefiting from their efforts, can be extremely low or even negative.

Empirical research documents that user innovation exists in many fields and is concentrated in the most advanced and motivated lead-user segment of the user community. My 1988 book *The Sources of Innovation* showed that such was the case for industrial products and processes, and recently it has been shown to be true for consumer products as well. As Christian Luthje reported in a 2000 University of Munich working paper, 10 percent of German lead users of outdoor consumer sports equipment actually improved their equipment or created entirely new equipment. With hundreds of thousands of such users in Germany, there is a tremendous amount of user innovation in that category alone.

Consider the saying "If you want something done right, do it yourself." In the case of product and service development, the adage holds true for users in part because a manufacturer cannot know what users want as well as they themselves do—and in part because, even knowing exactly what users want, the manufacturer lacks the incentive to match their wishes in every detail.

New-product developers must have accurate information on users' needs and the context of use if they are to create products that will meet those needs precisely. Such information is generated at user sites, but it is typically "sticky": costly to transfer from users' sites to outside developers. (For example, the conditions that cause software— or jumping windsurfers—to crash are available for free at the site of a user with the problem but can be difficult to reproduce elsewhere.) Also, because users' needs and habits constantly change, the necessary information cannot be transferred to manufacturer-based developers all at once. Rather, it evolves at the user site as the user experiments with prototype innovations. Recall that the windsurfers discovered that they could control the direction of a board when it was in the air only *after* they began experimenting with their prototype foot straps.

Manufacturers are the agents of users with respect to new products and services. It is their job to develop and build what users want and need; they do not want the products for themselves. If manufacturers' incentives don't match those of users, users end up paying an "agency cost" when they delegate design to manufacturers. That agency cost often takes the form of products not being the best possible fit with users' needs. Manufacturers want to spread their development costs over as many users as possible and hence design products that are a close enough fit to induce purchase from many users. One can see that incentive at work in the users' groups manufacturers set up to get advice on desired product improvements. At group meetings, manufacturer representatives seek specifications for new products that many user-members would find acceptable and commonly urge them to make "really difficult compromises."

Manufacturers explain that they cannot afford to design and build a product unless many users will buy it: a view that is reasonable but likely to retard innovation. As research shows, innovations that only a few leaders use today may be in general demand tomorrow—particularly if lead users have a chance to innovate, to learn by doing, and to develop the general utility of their innovations.

Incentives for Users to Reveal Innovations Freely. Progress and success in user innovation communities is contingent on at least some users freely sharing their innovations with others. Without that, each user would have to develop the innovation anew, which would create a huge system-level cost, or else innovators would have to protect and license their innovations and collect revenues, burdening user communities with high overhead.

Research has shown that users in a number of fields do freely reveal details of their innovations to other users and even to manufacturers. Users in open-source software communities post improvements and code on project Web sites, where anyone can view and download them for free. Free revealing is also present in the sports innovation example: innovating users gather on the beach, inspect one another's creations, and imitate or develop additional modifications that they, in turn, freely reveal.

How are we to understand free revealing? It does not make conventional economic sense. In theory, innovating users should attempt to keep their innovations secret. After all, innovating users spend money and time to create their innovations, and revealing them without compensation to noninnovating users, either directly or via a manufacturer, should represent a loss.

Users will reveal innovations when their benefits outweigh their costs. In the case of user innovation communities, the costs of revealing are generally low. In a July 2000 MIT Sloan working paper, Dietmar Harhoff and colleagues identified two kinds of costs associated with revealing an innovation: the cost associated with the loss of proprietary intellectual property and the cost of diffusion. Innovating users generally will expect intellectual property losses to be low if their rivalry with potential adopters is low. (Thus town libraries share information freely because they serve different populations, do not seek to gain market share from one another, and have little rivalry.) Even rivals who would prefer not to reveal an innovation will do so if they expect that others will reveal it if they do not, as K. Lakhani and I demonstrated in a May 2000 MIT Sloan working paper. That belief is held by many open-source software project participants. Also, users that cannot hide their innovations, such as high-performance windsurfers experimenting on the open beach, must reveal them.

When the costs of freely revealing an innovation are low, even a low level of benefit can be adequate reward. Various researchers, including Josh Lerner and Jean Tirole (in a March 2000 working paper for the National Bureau of Economic Research) and Georg von Krogh (in a spring 1998 *California Management Review* article), have observed that adequate rewards may include improved reputations, expected reciprocity, and helping to build a community.

Innovation Diffusion by Users. Full-function communities in which users actually produce their innovations, bypassing manufacturers, can exist only when user manufacture and distribution can compete with commercial production and distribution. In the case of open-source software, innovations can be produced and distributed essentially for free on the Web because software is information rather than a physical product. In the case of the sports innovation example, however, innovations in equipment are embodied in a physical product that requires physical production and distribution and involves economies of scale. The result for physical products generally is that innovation can be carried out by users and within user innovation communities, but production and diffusion of products incorporating those innovations is usually handled by manufacturing companies (see Figure 11.1).

For information products, general distribution within and beyond the user community is carried out by the community itself—no manufacturer required.

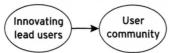

For physical products, general distribution typically requires manufacturers.

Figure 11.1. Methods of Distributing User Innovations.

ONGOING EXPLORATION OF
USER INNOVATION COMMUNITIES

The advent of the World Wide Web and the consequent proliferation of open-source software development projects has led to a growing academic focus on the phenomenon of user innovation communities in general and open-source software in particular. Thousands of open-source software projects provide natural laboratories for studying the phenomenon. Areas of interest include the conditions under which open-source software projects are likely to succeed, how they can be managed most successfully, and what attracts volunteers. Our understanding of such issues is expanding daily.

However, the phenomenon is changing even as we study it. The rationale for user innovation, followed by manufacturer production in the case of physical products, is compelling, and joint user-manufacturer innovation models are evolving rapidly. An example I explored in the summer 2001 *Journal of Product and Innovation Management* comes from the field of custom integrated circuits. Customers are provided with tool kits that allow them to make innovations. Each year, thousands of customers use such tool kits to design billions of dollars' worth of custom circuits that are both precisely suited to their needs and easily producible in manufacturers' facilities.

But what is most exciting is that innovation communities composed of users and for users, communities that according to traditional economic views shouldn't exist, work well enough to create and sustain complex innovations without *any* manufacturer involvement. This means that in at least some, and probably in many, fields users can build, consume, and support innovations on their own. As we learn to understand such communities better, we will be in a position to improve them and systematically extend their reach and attendant advantages throughout the economy.

CHAPTER TWELVE

Weird Ideas That Spark Innovation

ROBERT I. SUTTON

E very manager knows that innovation requires drastically different practices from those required for routine work, yet many
companies still struggle to switch gears when shifting from the routine to the innovative. Even when managers say they want more
innovation, their organizations often undermine it. A big part of the
problem is that managers instinctively recoil when they see what
innovation actually requires: the right practices seem strange, even
wrongheaded. In particular, many managers can't bring themselves
to lose money right now to test ideas that may never make money,
in hopes that a tiny percentage of those ideas will make money later.

A few years ago I met with an executive about sparking innovation in her multibillion-dollar corporation. Profits were falling,
and stock analysts were complaining that the company wasn't innovative. The manager complained that her CEO hated taking risks
and that he would reject any program that might reduce quarterly
profits, even if it had long-term benefits. He believed the company

---

First published in the Winter 2002 issue of *MIT Sloan Management Review.*

could innovate without deviating from the practices that were making money right now.

The CEO was dreaming the impossible dream, but he is not alone. There are managers in every industry who keep saying they want innovation but keep doing things to stifle it. Fortunately, there are some weird but proven ways to avoid this common syndrome.

ORGANIZING FOR ROUTINE VERSUS INNOVATIVE WORK

Stanford University's James March expresses the difference between routine and innovative work as *exploiting* old ideas versus *exploring* new possibilities. Exploiting means relying on past history, well-developed procedures, and proven technologies to make money now. McDonald's Corp., for example, knows that customers expect every Big Mac to look and taste the same, so the company uses old knowledge to make the next Big Mac just like the last one.

But in the long run companies cannot survive by relying only on tried-and-true actions. They must keep exploring new procedures and technologies to satisfy customer demand, to gain advantage over competitors, or just to keep pace. McDonald's uses some of the cash from all those hamburgers to explore new possibilities. For example, the company is experimenting with a technology for cooking its fries in 65 seconds rather than the current 210 seconds. Both exploration and exploitation are necessary for moving forward, even though the principles behind them differ by 180 degrees. No wonder the practices that are so right for one are so wrong for the other.

The basic organizing principles for exploration are enhancing variance, seeing old things in new ways, and breaking from the past.

Enhance Variance

Innovation requires increasing the diversity of ideas in a company. As Thomas Edison said about inventing, "You need a good imagination and a pile of junk." Promising ideas can come from what appears to be varied sorts of junk. That is true not only for inventing new technologies, products, and compounds but also for improving established processes. So even when Toyota Motor Corp. or Intel want to *reduce* variance in manufacturing processes, they use brainstorming, constructive confrontation, and experiments to *increase* variance in the pool of solutions considered.

See Old Things in New Ways

Sailing champion Jeff Miller has said that great sailors have *vu ja de,* a play on the phrase *déjà vu. Vu ja de* lets sailors (who race in the same places again and again) see things in a new light each time so that they can keep learning from every race. Innovative people have the same ability. Consider statistician Abraham Wald and his discovery of the best places to strengthen U.S. warplanes during World War II.

Military leaders were concerned because so many planes were being shot down. They thought more armor could help but didn't know where to put it. Wald marked bullet holes in the airplanes that returned from battle. He found that two sections of the fuselage— between the wings and between the horizontal stabilizers on the tail—had far fewer holes than other parts of the plane. He suggested putting more armor there, rather than where there were many holes. Why? The planes he analyzed had not been shot down. So it was the holes Wald *wasn't* seeing—in the planes that weren't returning— that needed extra protection.

Break from the Past

There is a lot of hype, much of it justified, about the dangers of clinging to the past. Yet all the excitement can make us forget that most new ideas are bad and most old ideas are good. The failure rate for new products and companies is dramatically higher than for old ones. Dozens of new breakfast cereals fail every year, but Cheerios and Wheaties persist. If there were truth in advertising, the slogan "innovate or die" would be replaced with "innovate and die." Tried and true wins out over new and improved most of the time.

But not all the time. The world does change, new technologies and products are developed, and consumer preferences do shift. So although the failure rate may be high, every company needs to keep trying to break from the past.

Consider the tea bag. Tea bags had been square since being introduced to British consumers in 1951. No company tried to change the shape until 1986, when Tetley began studying consumer reactions to round bags. After the round-bag rollout in January 1990, Tetley's share of the English tea market rose from 15 to 20 percent, slightly behind Brooke Bond's PG Tips. Not to be outdone, PG Tips introduced in 1996 the Pyramid tea bag, with a three-dimensional shape—and was soon reporting that sales were eclipsing Tetley's round bags in many regions.

EIGHT GEAR-SWITCHING TECHNIQUES

I offer eight weird techniques to get teams and companies to stop doing work by rote and start innovating. Each technique either provokes emotions (generally unpleasant) that interrupt mindless action, busts up the cognitive frame, makes you identify and reject your dearest beliefs, or explodes the composition of organizations and teams. Perhaps not all the practices will work for every company, but each is inspired by sound research and actually is used in innovative companies.

Incite Discomfort and Dissatisfaction
Being uncomfortable or unhappy may not be fun, but it helps people break free of ingrained and mindless actions.

Provoke Unpleasant Emotions in Others. Colleagues and others may react to the unfamiliar with feelings such as irritation, anxiety,

and disapproval. But if everyone always likes your ideas, it probably means they aren't new.

The belief that new ideas provoke discomfort is helping Her-
man Miller develop Resolve, a furniture system that "re-solves" the
dull uniformity of the traditional cubicle environment. "Instead of
muted-gray walls and severe right angles, it features lightweight,
translucent screens and generous 120-degree angles," lead designer
Jim Long told *Fast Company* for their April 2000 issue. "My
metaphor is a screen door. . . . It offers openness, but not complete
openness, not total visibility." When Long showed a Resolve prototype to two hundred managers, designers, and facility managers and
received complaints and criticisms, he was pleased; if the reaction
had been more positive, it "would have meant that the ideas were
too ordinary."

Make Yourself Uncomfortable. Innovation requires inventors to
work on ideas that make them squirm too. After all, discomfort is a
sign that the project is unfamiliar or risky. That is why at Intel, Mary
Murphy-Hoye exhorts researchers on her team, "Scare yourself; otherwise you aren't doing anything new."

Smash the Cognitive Frame

To change rigid mindsets it is helpful to treat everything as temporary and to ignore the experts.

Treat Everything Like a Temporary Condition. The principles
for routine work reflect the assumption that everything is a permanent condition. The principles for innovative work reflect the
reverse assumption. Both are useful fictions. Exploiting old knowledge makes sense only if what worked will keep on working. Breaking from the past makes sense only when old ways are obsolete or
about to be. Leaders of innovative companies constantly warn that
just because things are working well now doesn't mean that they
will work later. In June 2000 *Dow Jones Online News* quoted Jorma

Ollila, CEO of Finnish telephone giant Nokia: "We are not as quick as we were six years ago. . . . You start to believe that what you created three years ago is so good because it was good two years ago and 18 months ago and you continue to make money. And then there's someone in Israel and Silicon Valley just loving to kill you with a totally new technology."

Sustaining innovation requires treating everything, including teams, organizations, procedures, and product lines, as temporary. When CEO Bob Galvin was considering how to market Motorola's color televisions in 1967, for example, he used the name Quasar to keep the product distinct from the Motorola brand. He treated the line as temporary, so that if Motorola ever wanted to sell the Quasar business, the company wouldn't have to disentangle it from the Motorola brand. In time, televisions became commodities with slim profit margins, and in 1974 Motorola was able to sell Quasar to Matsushita Electrical Industrial Co.

Ignore the Experts. In the creative process—especially in the early stages—ignorance is bliss. People who don't know how things are supposed to be aren't blinded by existing beliefs. They can see things that so-called experts have rejected or never thought about. The virtues of ignorance and detachment are evident in Nobel Prize–winning work, including James Watson and Francis Crick's discovery of DNA structure, Kary Mullis's invention of the polymerase chain reaction, and Richard Feynman's contributions to physics. In *Genius* Feynman's biographer, James Gleick, describes how Feynman refused to read the academic literature. Feynman "chided graduate students who would begin their work in the normal way, by checking what had already been done. That way, he told them, they would give up the chances of finding something original."

Jane Goodall's groundbreaking research on chimpanzees also illustrates the virtues of naïveté. Anthropologist Louis Leakey wanted to hire Goodall to do two years of intensive chimpanzee observation. Because she lacked scientific training, Goodall hesitated to take the job, but as she describes it in her memoir, *In the Shadow of Man,* Leakey convinced her that he wanted someone "with a mind uncluttered and unbiased by theory, who would make the study for no other reason than a real desire for knowledge." Later Goodall and Leakey concluded that if she had not been ignorant of existing theories, she never would have been able to observe and explain so many new chimp behaviors.

When Daniel Ng in his innocence opened the first McDonald's in Hong Kong 1975, experienced competitors snorted, "Selling hamburgers to the Cantonese? You must be joking!" In the May-June 2000 issue of *Foreign Affairs* magazine, Ng reflected that his initial success was probably due to his lack of management training. He now operates more than 150 McDonald's restaurants in Hong Kong.

Identify and Reject Your Dearest Beliefs

Everyone has preconceptions about what makes sense, but sometimes it's useful to forget them and pursue the absurd and unacceptable. This can help teams and companies to recognize when routine practices have become sanctified and to start questioning their dearest beliefs.

Think of Something Ridiculous and Plan to Do It. Thinking up dumb things to do helps bring to the surface what people believe but have a hard time articulating. Unlike talking about only "smart" ideas, it creates a broad palette of options, which promotes both *vu ja de* and constructive variance.

Justin Kitch, currently CEO of Web site builder Homestead, once worked at Microsoft developing educational products for children. One day he led a brainstorming session on the worst product the company could possibly build. He thought that if the team came up with something really bad and did the opposite, a strong, original product could result. With great hilarity, the team decided that a computer-controlled talking Barney doll for teaching numbers would be the product with the least possible educational value. (Contemporary educational-media theorists believed that designing software for rote learning was a laughable waste of the medium's power.) Kitch reports, "I still have the drawing. I made it as a total joke, and I gave it to my boss. . . . I couldn't believe it: They built exactly what we brainstormed would be the worst possible product." Kitch refuses to accept any credit—or blame—for Microsoft's ActiMates Interactive Barney even though it won numerous awards for its educational value when it was sold a few years later. I still think he was onto something that more companies ought to do to spark innovation.

Dumb ideas can lead to good ideas, or, as in the case just cited, they can turn out to be good ideas themselves. A useful technique is to have people list products, services, and business models that seem destructive and impractical—and then to imagine that the ideas are smart. This technique has two advantages. First, it forces people to expose and challenge assumptions that might be getting in the way of developing great ideas. Second, if a good idea arises that many people think is stupid, it's probably one competitors won't copy soon.

When the first Palm Pilot came out, for example, most observers thought it was doomed to failure. After all, Apple Computer, Microsoft, and many start-ups had lost hundreds of millions of dollars on handheld computers. When Palm sought funding, the typical venture capitalist said, "Please, no more pen-based computers. We have already lost enough of our investors' money on this failed concept." The experts' skepticism proved to be a huge advantage because competitors didn't respond until Palm's operating system had already become an industry standard.

Hold a "Sacred Cow" Workshop. Another way to question ingrained beliefs is to create special moments, meetings, and task forces in which people are charged with hunting down and eliminating "sacred cows." (Sacred cows are ineffective ways of thinking and acting that have outlived their usefulness but that people don't think about or are afraid to change.) In one innovative company, the CEO bought everyone Daisy the Black and White Cow, a Beanie Baby, and told people to throw the stuffed toys at colleagues defending sacred cows. A manager later confided that although the exercise seemed silly, the Beanie Babies helped the company eliminate some meaningless procedures.

Pillsbury, Madison, and Sutro (now Pillsbury Winthrop) used a more serious program to eliminate sacred cows. In 1999 the 125-year-old San Francisco–based law firm was still clinging to practices that the information revolution had rendered obsolete. The firm's chair, Mary Cranston, and managing partner Marina Park established a sacred cow task force to identify and eliminate habits that slowed change and wasted money. Task forces identified more than one hundred sacred cows, and specific attorneys and administrators were charged with eliminating them.

For example, each local office had its own method for billing clients and collecting late payments. Several senior partners insisted that such autonomy was crucial because clients would be offended by impersonal bills. The task force implemented a simpler, centralized system but allowed each bill to be sent with a personal letter from the responsible partner. The new system decreased the average time it took clients to pay bills from 4.5 months to 3.2 months, reduced related labor costs by 25 percent, and added several million dollars to the bottom line.

Explode the Composition of Organizations and Teams

Companies need to reenergize their organizations to pursue innovation effectively. Techniques include bringing in workers who march to a different drummer, as well as breaking up atrophied teams and building new ones.

Bring in Some Slow Learners. I am not advising you to hire stupid people; rather, I am advising you to hire people with a special kind of stupidity or stubbornness. To get variation, companies need people who are unable or unwilling to learn the organizational code. In the March-April 1991 issue of *Organization Science,* James March described this code as a company's "knowledge and faiths," its history, memories, and rules—those taken-for-granted and often unspoken assumptions about what is to be done and why. Most companies bring in newcomers who are similar to insiders, who learn the code quickly, and see things as insiders do. That makes sense if you want people to mimic tried-and-true ways. But innovation requires people who see things differently and aren't easily brainwashed.

March has shown that companies with large numbers of people who don't follow the code do better at exploration. Such people rely on their own knowledge to get work done, which produces more varied solutions. Companies that want innovation need to tolerate contrarians, heretics, and eccentrics even though many of their ideas lead to failure. Hiring only fast learners may be cost effective in the short term but undermines innovation over the long haul.

You might even hire some smart people who had bad grades in school. In his 1999 book *Origins of Genius,* creativity researcher Dean Keith Simonton points out, "To obtain high marks in school often requires a high degree of conformity to conventional ways of looking at the world and people." By contrast, smart people who get bad grades are listening to their inner voice, doing what they find interesting and right. Simonton writes, "Darwin disliked school and was quite content to be a mediocre student at the university; yet he was also deeply committed to self-education through extensive reading, scientific explorations of the English countryside, and conversations with established scientists."

Successful slow learners are often paired with fast learners who protect and insulate them—and translate and promote their ideas. As the book *Strawberry Fields Forever: John Lennon Remembered* recounts, the late John Lennon often disagreed "out of sheer whim and perversity" with those around him, especially Beatle Paul McCartney and manager Brian Epstein; he couldn't resist infuriating them with boasting and insults. Nevertheless, Lennon realized he needed them and admitted, "Paul and Epstein did have to cover up a lot for me. . . . Containing my personality from causing too much trouble." Lennon's talents might never have developed without their protection and compensating diplomacy.

Disband and Re-Form Teams. Teams can get trapped in the past. The longer groups are together, the more likely it is that they will become cliquish and ignore outsiders. A study of fifty teams by Ralph Katz, a professor of R&D management at Northeastern University, found that during R&D teams' first two years, the number of ideas is high but after about three or four years, the creative output peaks and declines. Katz believes that over time team members focus more strongly on the virtues of their own ideas and a not-invented-here attitude toward outsiders' ideas develops.

Katz proposes that one way to avoid a drop in creativity is to make sure teams die before they get old. That is what Lars Kolind did as CEO of Oticon, one of the world's leading makers of hearing aids. In late 1995 he noticed that product developers had spent a full year obsessed with a line of digital hearing aids. "The downside to this productive focus was a sense that long-standing project teams were hardening into something dangerously close to departments," he told *Fast Company* for their June 1996 issue. "I exploded the organization." All the teams were disbanded, and new teams were formed on the basis of time horizon rather than function. According to Kolind, "It was total chaos. . . . Within three hours, over a hundred people had moved. To keep the company alive, one of the jobs of top management is to keep it disorganized."

WEIRD AND WISE

The strange practices introduced here are grounded in research and used in innovative companies. But the exact methods a company uses to spark novel ideas and actions aren't as important as how people feel about what they do. Psychologists tell us that feelings—not cold cognitions—drive people to turn ideas into reality. Passion is part of what it takes. Joey Reiman is founder of BrightHouse, an "ideation" company that charges clients such as Coca-Cola Co. and Georgia-Pacific Corp. $500,000 to $1 million for a single idea. I can see Reiman in my mind's eye, roller-skating around a circular stage in Berlin, bellowing to an audience of advertising executives, "We do heartstorming, not brainstorming. Creativity is much more about what people feel than what they think." The passion is more subtle in other innovative companies, but you can always find it.

People in innovative companies also alternate between periods of unwavering belief and deep cynicism. This means that when you think about a weird management practice, convince yourself, for just a little while, that it will be extraordinarily effective. Ask yourself, How should my company be organized or managed differently? But the weird ideas presented here are not immutable truths. So a switch to cynicism is required to use them best. Treat them like toys that you might buy to mess around with: try to break them, take apart the pieces to see how they work, try to improve them, and mix them with your other toys. You will probably develop even better ideas along the way. Ultimately, anything that brings in new knowledge, helps people see old things in new ways, or helps a company break from the past will do the trick.

Jordan J. Baruch is a consultant to industry and government on the planning, management, and integration of strategy and technology. Since 1981 Baruch has been president of Jordan Baruch Associates of Washington, D.C. From 1977 to 1981, during the Carter administration, he served as assistant secretary of commerce for science and technology. From 1974 to 1977 he was a professor in the Tuck School of Business and Thayer School of Engineering at Dartmouth College. Baruch earned bachelor's and master's degrees in electrical engineering as well as a doctorate in electrical instrumentation from MIT.

Elected to the National Academy of Engineering in 1974, Baruch has been cited for his contributions in the transfer of technology to industry, in noise control systems, and in the application of computer technology. He is a member of the Institute of Electrical and Electronics Engineers and the American Association for the Advancement of Science.

John Seely Brown is chief scientist at Xerox Corporation, where he has been deeply involved in corporate strategy and in expanding the role of corporate research to include organizational learning, ethnographies of the workplace, complex adaptive systems, and techniques for unfreezing the corporate mind. His personal research interests include digital culture, ubiquitous computing, user-centered design, and organizational and individual learning. A major focus of his research has been human learning and the creation of knowledge ecologies for creating radical innovation.

Brown is a cofounder of the Institute for Research on Learning, a nonprofit institute for addressing the problems of lifelong learning. He is a member of the National Academy of Education and a fellow of the American Association for Artificial Intelligence. He also serves on numerous advisory boards and boards of directors. He has published more than ninety-five articles in scientific journals and was awarded the 1998 Industrial Research Institute Medal for outstanding accomplishments in technological innovation. Brown has published *Seeing Differently: Insights on Innovation* (1997) and *The Social Life of Information* (2000), cowritten with Paul Duguid. He holds a B.S. in mathematics and physics from Brown University and an M.S. in mathematics and a Ph.D. in computer and communication sciences from the University of Michigan.

Paul Duguid is a research specialist in the division of Social and Cultural Studies in Education at the University of California–Berkeley and a longtime consultant at the Xerox Palo Alto Research Center. He was formerly a member of the Institute for Research on Learning in Palo Alto. His commitment to multidisciplinary, collaborative work has led him to work with social scientists, computer scientists, economists, linguists, management theorists, and social psychologists. His writing has appeared in a broad array of scholarly fields, including anthropology, business and business history, cognitive science, computer science, design, education, economic history, human-computer interaction, management, organization theory, and wine history. Duguid has written essays and reviews for the *Times Literary Supplement*, the *Nation*, and the *Threepenny Review.*

Jeffrey H. Dyer is associate professor of organizational leadership and strategy at Brigham Young University and formerly taught at the Wharton School of the University of Pennsylvania. His research has won awards from McKinsey & Company, the Strategic Management Society, and the Institute of Management Sciences. Dyer's book *Collaborative Advantage: Winning Through Extended Enterprise Supplier Networks* (2000) details his eight-year study of the automotive industry. Focusing his research on Toyota Motor Corporation and DaimlerChrysler, Dyer interviewed more than two hundred executives and surveyed five hundred of their suppliers for the book. He has worked as a consultant for Motorola, Ford, Baxter International, Navistar, and Bang & Olufsen. He holds a Ph.D. in management, strategy, and organization from the University of California–Los Angeles.

Prashant Kale is assistant professor of corporate strategy and international business at the University of Michigan Business School. He has taught undergraduate and M.B.A. courses in business policy, corporate strategy, and strategic alliances. Before joining academia, Kale worked for several years in industry with leading multinational companies such as Johnson & Johnson, ICI, and Siemens, as well as for India's largest business group, the Tatas. His research focuses primarily on the role of strategic alliances and acquisitions in corporate strategy and on the way companies build alliance capability to create superior value. He is examining companies that operate in a variety of industries, including chemicals, pharmaceuticals, communications, and computer hardware and software. His other research interests include the role of technology and innovation in driving company growth and performance. Kale holds a doctorate from the Wharton School of the University of Pennsylvania, a master's degree from the Indian Institute of Management, Ahmedabad, and a bachelor's degree in engineering from the University of Pune, India.

Anil Khurana is the chief knowledge officer for TCG-Software, Inc., a fast-growing technology and management consulting firm. He is also adjunct professor at Boston University's College of Engineering, where he serves as program director for a National Science Foundation grant to study product development and innovation. Formerly a professor of technology and operations management at Boston University's School of Management, Khurana was a member of the founding team of the university's Bronner Hatchery, a business incubator.

Khurana has nearly twenty years' experience in management and consulting, with expertise in product development, technology and innovation, e-business, global strategy, and manufacturing effectiveness. He has published extensively in leading journals and has been recognized by the National Science Foundation, Decision Sciences Institute, and the Academy of Management. In addition to holding a Ph.D. and M.B.A. from the University of Michigan, Khurana earned undergraduate and graduate degrees in several engineering disciplines and in economics.

Wenyun Kathy Liu works in the Fixed Income Structured Products Group at Salomon Smith Barney, New York. She holds a bachelor's degree from the College of Foreign Affairs, Beijing, and master's degrees in operations research and political economy from MIT. She earned a doctorate from MIT in 2000. Her dissertation was titled "Essays in Management of Technology: Collaborative Strategies for the American Technology Industries."

Constantinos Markides is professor of strategic and international management, and chair of the strategic department, at the London Business School. He has researched and published on strategic innovation, corporate structuring, refocusing, and international acquisitions. He is the author of *Diversification, Refocusing, and Economic Performance* (1995), and *All the Right Moves: A Guide to Crafting Breakthrough Strategy* (1999). His work has also appeared in journals such as the *Harvard Business Review,* the *Sloan Management Review, Directors & Boards, Leader to Leader,* and the *Academy of Management Journal.*

Markides has taught many in-company programs and is on the academic advisory board of the Cyprus International Institute of Management. He is a member of the Academy of Management and the Strategic Management Society. He received his B.A. (with distinction) and M.A. in economics from Boston University, and his M.B.A. and D.B.A. from Harvard Business School. He has worked as an associate with the Cyprus Development Bank and as a research associate at Harvard Business School.

Marc H. Meyer is professor of management at Northeastern University, where his teaching and research focus on new product development and technological entrepreneurship. He is codirector of Northeastern's high-technology M.B.A. program. Meyer consults for corporations on next-generation products, systems, and services design. Meyer is presently studying services platforms with a number of financial-services companies and is a consulting researcher for IBM. He is also conducting joint research with Eindhoven University in the Netherlands on systems platforms, and he has received a grant from the National Science Foundation to study process-intensive platforms. Meyer has published in *Management Science, IEEE Transactions on Engineering Management, MIS Quarterly,* the *Journal of Product Innovation Management,* and the *Sloan Management Review.* He is coauthor (with Alvin P. Lehnerd) of *The Power of Product Platforms* (1997). Meyer did his undergraduate work at Harvard and earned master's and doctoral degrees from MIT.

Michael E. Porter is the Bishop William Lawrence University Professor at Harvard Business School (HBS). Porter is the fourth faculty member in HBS history to earn this distinction, the highest professional recognition given to Harvard faculty, and is one of about twenty current University Professors at Harvard. Porter is a leading authority on competitive strategy and international competitiveness. His ideas have now become the foundation for a required course at HBS. Porter teaches strategy, created and leads a workshop for newly appointed chief executive officers of billion-dollar corporations, and speaks widely on competitive strategy and international competitiveness to business and government audiences throughout the world.

Porter is the author of sixteen books and more than seventy-five articles. His book *Competitive Strategy: Techniques for Analyzing Industries and Competitors* (1980) is in its fifty-third printing and has been translated into seventeen languages. His second major strategy book, *Competitive Advantage: Creating and Sustaining Superior Performance* (1985), is in its thirty-second printing.

James Brian Quinn is the William and Josephine Buchanan Professor of Management Emeritus in the Tuck School of Business at Dartmouth College, where he was a faculty member from 1957 to 1993. His recent books have focused on technology and innovation in the services sector. In 1999 Quinn was one of two recipients of the first annual Outsourcing World Achievement Awards, cosponsored by PricewaterhouseCoopers and Michael F. Corbett & Associates. Quinn is well known in the Tuck community for the many traditions he began, including its TYCOON business simulation, entrepreneurship, and technology and management courses. He continues to teach in executive education programs worldwide.

Edward B. Roberts is the David Sarnoff Professor of the Management of Technology at the MIT Sloan School of Management. He focuses on technology strategy and management in newly emerging and major firms, including technology-based entrepreneurship, venture capital, corporate venturing, and new business development. His book *Entrepreneurs in High Technology: Lessons from MIT and Beyond*

(1991) won the Association of American Publishers award for outstanding books in business and management. Roberts is also interested in technological innovation in services, especially in the financial industry. He is the founder and chair of the MIT Entrepreneurship Center and cochair of the International Center for Research on the Management of Technology. He couples his MIT responsibilities with extensive activities as a cofounder, board member, and venture-capital investor in high-tech start-ups.

David Robertson has held a number of management positions in the software industry, including CEO of a procurement software company, vice president of marketing at an on-line credit and financing company, and vice president of product and industry marketing at Baan Company. Robertson also led the consulting services group at Art Technology Group and spent five years at McKinsey & Company. Robertson earned master's and doctoral degrees in management from the MIT Sloan School of Management and a bachelor's degree in computer engineering from the University of Illinois.

Stephen R. Rosenthal is professor of operations management and director of the Center for Enterprise Leadership at Boston University's School of Management. He teaches enterprise management and the design and development of new products and services. Rosenthal's research focuses on linking enterprise strategy with action, and on the managerial aspects of new product introduction. His most recent book is *Reaching for the Knowledge Edge: How the Knowing Corporation Seeks, Shares, and Uses Knowledge for Strategic Advantage* (2001).

Rosenthal has also held visiting faculty positions at numerous prominent universities in the United States and has consulted to a wide range of private and governmental organizations. He holds a doctorate in policy planning from the University of California–Berkeley; a master's degree in management from MIT; and a bachelor's degree in applied mathematics from Brown University.

Harbir Singh, the Edward H. Bowman Professor of Management at the Wharton School of the University of Pennsylvania, is the management department chair and codirector of the Mack Center for Technological Innovation. He serves on the editorial board of the *Strategic Management Journal* and the *Academy of Management Review*. His research areas include strategies for corporate acquisitions, corporate governance, joint ventures, management buyouts, and corporate restructuring.

Scott Stern is associate professor of management and strategy at the Kellogg School of Business, Northwestern University. Stern's primary fields of interest are the economics of technological change, industrial organization, the economics of organizations, and strategic management in high-technology industries. He holds a doctorate in economics from Stanford University.

Robert I. Sutton is professor of management science and engineering at Stanford Engineering School and codirector of Stanford University's Center for Work, Technology and Organization. His research interests include organizational creativity and innovation, the links between managerial knowledge and organizational action, the role of wisdom in organizational life, and group and organizational performance. Much of his research uses psychological or sociological theory to understand how organizations influence and are influenced by individuals and groups. His research emphasizes the development of theory and recommendations for practice based on direct observation of organizational life and interviews with managers, engineers, and other organization members. He is the author of *Weird Ideas That Work: 11½ Practices for Promoting, Managing and Sustaining Innovation* (2001).

Karl Ulrich is associate professor of operations and information management at the Wharton School of the University of Pennsylvania. Ulrich also serves as chair of Nova Cruz Products, a company he founded in 1999 to commercialize personal electric vehicles. Ulrich's research is focused on product design and development. His current projects study the management of product variety, with particular emphasis on the relationships among product architecture, market strategy, and production process design. His work has been published in *Management Science, Marketing Science,* the *Sloan Management Review,* and other journals. He is a coauthor of *Product Design and Development* (2000), the leading textbook on product design.

Ulrich was named one of the most popular business school professors in *BusinessWeek's* annual survey, and he is the winner of many teaching awards, including the Helen Kardon Moss Anvil Award. He has worked as an engineer or project manager in developing more than thirty new products and processes, including surgical instruments, tools, computer peripherals, and food-processing equipment, and has been granted seventeen patents. Ulrich serves on the boards of several technology-based ventures. He holds bachelor's, master's, and doctoral degrees in mechanical engineering from MIT.

James M. Utterback is professor of management and engineering, and chair of the Management of Technology Program, at the MIT Sloan School of Management. Utterback studies the emergence of dominant product designs and the development of products in keeping with a company's overall strategy. He also considers how to move concepts effectively to market. His book *Mastering the Dynamics of Innovation* (1994) focuses on the creative and destructive effects of technological change on the life of a company. His areas of expertise include product design, technological innovation, and manufacturing.

Eric A. von Hippel is a professor in the MIT Sloan School of Management. Focusing on the management of innovation, he discovers and explores patterns in the sources of innovation. His research aims to improve understanding of the causes of innovation and to create new innovation processes that identify better innovations more quickly. He has developed the lead-user method for systematic discovery of breakthrough products, services, and strategies, and a method that enables users to design their own mass-customized products and services. Von Hippel is the author of *The Sources of Innovation* (1995).

Karen Anne Zien is a leading innovation systems anthropologist and the principal of Apogee: Sustainable Innovation Systems. Apogee serves global companies and their strategic partners in Europe, Asia, and North America. Zien maintains the Creativity & Innovation Lab, providing resources and training for innovative business leaders. Zien's clients and research companies, in a variety of industries, are considered to be among the most innovative global enterprises. She is known as steadfast, insightful, and articulate through often ambiguous and chaotic environments of invention and innovation. She focuses on new strategies, businesses, processes, and products. Her consulting work stems from twenty years of internal business experience. She also spent fifteen years building partnerships and negotiating new ventures between American and Japanese organizations and, in recent years, has done the same in Europe.

With James Brian Quinn and Jordan J. Baruch, she coauthored *Innovation Explosion: Using Intellect and Software to Revolutionize Growth Strategies* (1997). Her recent articles include "The Spirituality of Innovation: Learning from Stories" and "Dreams to Market: Crafting a Culture of Innovation" (both with Sheldon Buckler), as well as "The Story of Innovation" and "Innovative Leaders Are Dream Spinners." Zien studied East Asian languages and civilizations at the University of Wisconsin and Harvard University. She holds an M.B.A. from the Graduate School of Management, Simmons College. She is an honorary citizen of Kyoto.

INDEX

CPSIA information can be obtained at www.ICGtesting.com
Printed in the USA
BVOW070713170812

298099BV00003B/10/P